The Strong and the Weak in Japanese Literature

This book uses texts from classical and modern Japanese literature to examine concepts of "respect for the strong", as a notion of an evolutionary society, and "sympathy for the weak", as a notion of a non-violent and changeless egalitarian society.

The term "strong" refers not only to those with strength and power; it also includes other ideal attributes such as beauty, youth and goodness. Similarly, the term "weak" implies not only the weak and the infirm but also the disadvantaged, the indecent, the unsophisticated and those generally shunned by society. The former are associated not only with the power of life, competition, evolution, progress, development, ability, effectiveness, efficiency, individuality, the future, hope and romance, but also with violence, fighting, bullying, discrimination and sacrifice. The latter, in contrast, evoke notions of peace, egalitarianism, anti-discrimination and welfare, as well as of stagnation, retreat, retrogression, degeneration and the decline of vital powers.

By using these two concepts, Murakami skilfully weaves a narrative that is part literary criticism, part social commentary. As such, the book will be of huge interest not only to scholars and students of Japanese literature but also to scholars and students of Japanese society and culture.

Fuminobu Murakami is Associate Professor in the Department of Japanese Studies, University of Hong Kong. He is author of *Postmodern, Feminist and Postcolonial Currents in Contemporary Japanese Culture* (Routledge, 2005) and co-editor of *Reading "The Tale of Genji"* (Global Oriental, 2009).

Routledge advances in Asia-Pacific Studies

1. Environment, Education and Society in the Asia-Pacific
Local traditions and global discourses
David Yencken, John Fien and Helen Sykes

2. Ageing in the Asia-Pacific Region
David R. Phillips

3. Caring for the Elderly in Japan and the US
Practices and policies
Susan Orpett Long

4. Human Rights and Gender Politics
Asia-Pacific perspectives
*Edited by Anne Marie Hilsdon, Martha Macintyre,
Vera Mackie and Maila Stivens*

5. Human Rights in Japan, South Korea and Taiwan
Ian Neary

6. Cultural Politics and Asian Values
The tepid war
Michael D. Barr

7. Social Policy in East and Southeast Asia
Education, health, housing and income maintenance
M. Ramesh

8. Sino-Japanese Relations
Facing the past, looking to the future?
Caroline Rose

9. Directors of Urban Change in Asia
Edited by Peter J. M. Nas

10. Education Reform and Education Policy in East Asia
Ka Ho Mok

11. The Strong and the Weak in Japanese Literature
Discrimination, egalitarianism, nationalism
Fuminobu Murakami

The Strong and the Weak in Japanese Literature
Discrimination, egalitarianism, nationalism

Fuminobu Murakami

LONDON AND NEW YORK

First published 2010
by Routledge
2 Park Square, Milton Park, Abingdon, Oxfordshire OX14 4RN

Simultaneously published in the USA and Canada
by Routledge
711 Third Avenue, New York, NY 10017, USA

First issued in paperback 2014

*Routledge is an imprint of the Taylor & Francis Group, an informa
business*

© 2010 Fuminobu Murakami

Typeset in 10/12pt Times NR MT by Graphicraft Limited, Hong Kong

All rights reserved. No part of this book may be reprinted or
reproduced or utilised in any form or by any electronic, mechanical,
or other means, now known or hereafter invented, including
photocopying and recording, or in any information storage or
retrieval system, without permission in writing from the publishers.

British Library Cataloguing in Publication Data
A catalogue record for this book is available from the British Library

Library of Congress Cataloging in Publication Data
Murakami, Fuminobu, 1951–
The strong and the weak in Japanese literature : discrimination,
egalitarianism, nationalism / Fuminobu Murakami.
    p. cm. – (Routledge advances in Asia-Pacific studies; 11)
    Includes bibliographical references and index.
    1. Japanese literature–History and criticism.   2. Literature and
society——Japan–History.   3. National characteristics, Japanese,
in literature.   4. Power (Social sciences) in literature.   I. Title.
    PL716.M78 2010
    895.6′09–dc22

                                                                    2009046178

    ISBN 13: 978-1-138-86289-0 (pbk)
    ISBN 13: 978-0-415-57386-3 (hbk)

In days of old, the Buddha was but a mortal; in the end, we ourselves will be Buddhas, too. How grievous that distinctions must separate those who are alike in sharing the Buddha-nature.

From *The Tale of the Heike*

Translated by Helen Craig McCullough

Contents

Preface   ix

1 Introduction   1

2 The strong and the weak in Japanese religious, philosophical and political writings   8

2.1 The strong and the weak 8

2.2 Respecting the strong and sympathising with the weak: Genshin's (941–1017) Essentials of Rebirth [into the Pure Land of Amida Buddha] (Ōjōyōshū) *(984–5) 10*

2.3 The triumph of the weak over the strong: Hōnen's (1133–1212) Passages on the Selection of the Nembutsu in the Original Vow (Senchaku hongan nembutsu shū) *(1198) 16*

2.4 Egalitarianism in a secluded class-based society: Itō Jinsai's (1627–1705) concept of Jin 23

2.5 Equality in battle and equality before God: Fukuzawa Yukichi (1835–1901) and Kitamura Tōkoku (1868–94) 30

3 Ugly ladies in *The Tale of Genji*   44

3.1 Two different views in The Tale of Genji *44*

3.2 The weak, low and fragile 46

3.3 Princess Safflower (Suetsumuhana) 51

3.4 Gen-no-naishi 57

3.5 Ōmi-no-kimi 63

4 Women, humble men and insulted people in *The Tale of the Heike*   69

4.1 Introduction 69

4.2 Women, humble men and insulted people 72

4.3 Polemical Engyō *and moderate* Kakuichi *81*

viii *Contents*

    4.4 The Engyō *text's love between men and women, husbands*
        and wives, and other family members, and the Kakuichi *text's*
        indifferent individualism 85
    4.5 Indecent Engyō *text and decent* Kakuichi *text 88*

5 Sacrifice and revenge, love and war, and a world without
    violence in *The Eight Dog Chronicles*   92

    5.1 The Confucian aspect of The Eight Dog Chronicles *92*
    5.2 The modernist aspect of The Eight Dog Chronicles *103*
    5.3 The postmodernist aspect of The Eight Dog Chronicles *111*

6 Dancing girl, geisha, mistress and wife in Kawabata
    Yasunari's stories: *The Dancing Girl of Izu*, *Snow Country*,
    Thousand Cranes* and *The Sound of the Mountain   119

    6.1 Femininity created by the male gaze 119
    6.2 Open/hidden discrimination against femininity: The Dancing
        Girl of Izu *129*
    6.3 Open/hidden discrimination against femininity: Snow Country *135*
    6.4 The perspective of ugly women: Thousand Cranes *and*
        The Sound of the Mountain *141*

7 Conclusion   150

  Notes   155
  Bibliography   169
  Index   190

Preface

This book was written in Hong Kong and Japan between 1999 and 2009 with financial support from the University of Hong Kong Committee on Research and Conference Grants as a publication project originally entitled "A Study of Weak People in Japanese Literature: From *Genji* to Kawabata". I thank the Committee for financially supporting this project.

Some chapters included here were previously presented at the International Symposium on Japanese Studies and Japanese Language Education, held once every two or three years in various universities in Hong Kong, and published in the proceedings of those symposiums. Sections of Chapter 2 are based on the paper "Words to Save the Weak" ("Jakusha kyūsai no kotoba"), presented at the 6th International Symposium on Japanese Studies and Japanese Language Education, held at City University of Hong Kong in November 2003, and later included in the proceedings published in March 2005 (Takahashi Rita et al. (eds) 2005, 1: 234–44). Chapter 3 is based on the paper "Ugly Ladies in *The Tale of Genji*" ("*Genji monogatari* no minikui himegimi"), presented at the 7th International Symposium on Japanese Studies and Japanese Language Education, held at Chinese University of Hong Kong in October 2006, and published in *Japanese Studies in the Asia-Pacific Region* (Mito, Ho and Miyazoe-Wong (eds) 2008: 69–78). Chapter 6 is based on "Woman in Kawabata Yasunari's Writing: *The Izu Dancer*" ("Kawabata Yasunari ga egaku josei: *Izu no odoriko*"), presented at the 4th International Symposium on Japanese Studies and Japanese Language Education, held at Hong Kong Polytechnic University in November 1999. This paper appeared in the proceedings published in March 2003 (Miyazoe-Wong (ed.) 2003: 348–55). I thank the organisers of the above symposiums for giving me the chance to present my papers and the participants at these conferences for their valuable comments.

I also sincerely thank Peter Cave and Barbara Hartley, who read the manuscript of this book and provided insightful comments and suggestions. I should also like to thank the anonymous reader at Routledge for his or her invaluable detailed comments and suggestions. Without this help, the book could not have been published. As with my previous book, I should like once again to thank the Institute of Human Performance (Sports Centre), The

x *Preface*

University of Hong Kong, and the Hong Kong Philharmonic Orchestra, for providing me with relaxation while I was working on this book. In addition, on this occasion, I should like to add the Hong Kong Amateur Athletic Association, organisers of the Standard Chartered Hong Kong Marathon, in which I have participated for the past five years, although without yet completing the full course.

I also express my thanks to my family, my wife Tomoko, our daughter Nanako, my wife's parents, my own parents, our siblings and their families, our friends, and my colleagues and students for supporting and encouraging me at various stages of writing this book. Last but not least, I thank Routledge editors Stephanie Rogers, Leanne Hinves, Ed Needle and Kathy Auger for their support and wonderful editorial work. Thank you very much.

Note: Almost all Japanese names appear in Japanese order with surname first – as in, for instance, Fukuzawa Yukichi, instead of Yukichi Fukuzawa. This rule is, however, reversed in the case of Japanese authors who publish material in English. The names of these writers are given in European order.

1 Introduction

This book follows on from a previous work, *Postmodern, Feminist and Postcolonial Currents in Contemporary Japanese Culture* (2005), in which I used the perspectives of postmodernism, feminism, queer studies and postcolonial studies to analyse material by four contemporary Japanese writers: Murakami Haruki, Yoshimoto Banana, Yoshimoto Takaaki and Karatani Kōjin. In that work, rather than defining modern/modernity/modernism as a spatiotemporal term, I regarded this idea mainly as an ideology that valued notions such as power, ideals, enlightenment, the future, development, progress, advancement and evolution. I also argued that, although this ideology had existed throughout history, it had become particularly entrenched in the present globalised world. This interpretation of modernity is generally maintained in the current book. Sometimes, however, I use the term in the spatiotemporal sense. There are also times when the ideological and spatiotemporal implications overlap.

As the basis of modernist ideology, I draw on the Hegelian rationalistic assumption that world history progresses from a state of wild savagery to a cultivated state in which the happiness of the collective, the wisdom of states and the virtue of individuals must be realised by the light of God and Law (Hegel 1900: 21). While this assumption appears to be "beautiful" and "right", it is imposed on individuals, irrespective of personal differences, from the outside. And, since it is regarded as ideal, all are compelled to move in the same direction. Thus, in opposition to positive interpretations of modernity, Zygmunt Bauman argues that the compelling force of progress in modernity is the major cause of the Holocaust (Bauman 1989: x, 5, 13–14, 76, 91). In order to overcome the modernist predicament, Deleuze and Guattari advocate schizophrenic infinitesimal lines of escape, instead of the paranoiac fascisising perspective of the large aggregates identified by Bauman (Deleuze and Guattari 1984: 276–80).

Not all commentators, however, are critical of the modernist project. Ulrich Beck, Anthony Giddens and Scott Lash, for instance, advocate "reflexive modernity". These theorists assert that, if orthodox modernisation means the disembedding and re-embedding of traditional social forms by industrial social forms, then reflexive modernisation means the disembedding and re-embedding

2 *Introduction*

of industrial social forms by another modernity. In this model, modernisation comes to understand its own excesses and the vicious spiral of destructive subjugation thus generated, and thereby begins to take itself as an object of reflection (Beck, Giddens and Lash 1994: 2, 112).[1] Nevertheless, the idea of progress appears also to underlie reflexive modernisation. Though opposed to the concept of direct *linear* progress, *reflexive* modernity ultimately implies a commitment to the incessant continuation of progress, reflex and new progress (Beck, Giddens and Lash 1994: 11–12; Giddens 1990: 36–45; Giddens 1991: 20–1).

My understanding is that this modernist ideology of progress based on power struggle gradually gained momentum throughout human history. Nevertheless, it was greatly accelerated by the triumph of rationalism in the Enlightenment project of the eighteenth century, finally reaching its zenith in the global capitalist systems of the present period. In contrast, I consider postmodernism to be the tendency to oppose modernism in various ways. On this understanding, in the previous book I critiqued the modernist division between individual differentiation leading to violent discrimination against outside others and coercive totalitarian identification with insiders.

Feminist theory and queer studies both present the potential to subvert this binarism in modern patriarchal capitalist society. Feminist scholar Gayle Rubin (Rubin 1975: 199) suggests that incestuous desire, that is, sexual desire based on kinship, has the possibility to reconfigure the existing binary opposition between erotic sexual desire towards strangers and the calm and tender emotions displayed towards the family. The first is almost inevitably related to violence and progress while the second is necessarily connected to stagnation and retreat. Following Rubin, feminists and queer studies scholars seek to complete the ideological paradigm-shift of deconstructing the modernist dualism based on male perspectives which includes reason/emotion, culture/nature, heterosexual/homosexual, man/woman, and so forth. Accordingly, they are now practically or politically attempting to realise the emancipation of women and homosexuals from dominant male/heterosexual discrimination (Judith Butler 1990: 72–8; Sedgwick 1991; Wittig 1992; Halperin 1995). Michel Foucault argues, and Gayle Rubin confirms, that, like gender, neither sexuality nor desire is a pre-existing, naturally given biological entity. Rather, they are forms of historically constructed social practice (Foucault 1978–86, 1: 105; Rubin 1984: 276). Since this practice gives power to some while marginalising others, the deconstruction of modernist hetero-sexuality is not only possible but also necessary. Accordingly, I argued in my previous book that contemporary Japanese society was characterised by both an erotically charged heterosexual/power-orientated desire to do violence to strangers (Oedipal triangle) and a gentle but incestuous/retrogressive emotion experienced in relation to the family (Amaterasu circle). I then suggested that this binary division could be deconstructed by changing desire. From this perspective, I discussed the opposition between the desire for eros and violence, and a conflicting desire for friendship and stagnation.

These elements appear in the current work in the form of "respect for the strong", as per the notion of evolution, and "sympathy for the weak", as this notion ideally appears in a non-violent and changeless egalitarian society. Drawing on this distinction, the current book will read a number of major works of Japanese literature and, in the process, raise a variety of questions about Japanese society.

There may be an argument that research which distinguishes so clearly between the strong and the weak in this way may itself be labelled discriminatory. However, although a case can be made that we should treat all people or all human beings equally, rather than respecting the strong and sympathising with the weak, this study examines the situation as it is rather than the ideal. In addition, as I shall argue later, treating all people equally in one society creates its own problem of discriminating against people in other societies.

The stark binary distinction between modernism and postmodernism seen in my previous book remains in many places in this book in the form of "respect for the strong" and "sympathy for the weak". In contrast to the former work, in which I attempted to deconstruct this binarism, the current book focuses more on identifying the various plural factors which interweave across and thereby link these two elements. Not only is it difficult to draw clearly a borderline between the strong and the weak; there are also many other factors, including aspects of culture, gender and sexuality, and the majority/minority and homeland residents/diaspora distinctions, that are critical to an understanding of the strong–weak relationship. As a starting-point, bearing these points in mind, I shall distinguish between "respect for the strong" and "sympathy with the weak", and also address related problems and questions arising from this distinction.

Although ostensibly conflicting, these two worldviews can, in fact, be mutually supportive. The Social Darwinist view may well regard the world as a space of evolutionary competition and struggle for survival in which the weaker are inevitably defeated and victimised by the stronger. However, this stance complements the egalitarian view of the world as a place of harmony and consonance in which the weak respect the strong, who then assist the former so that both may live in accord. The term "strong" in this book refers not only to those with strength and power; it also includes other ideal attributes such as beauty, youth and goodness. Similarly, the term "weak" implies not only the weak and the infirm, but also the disadvantaged, the indecent, the unsophisticated and those generally shunned by society. The former are associated not only with the power of life, competition, evolution, progress, development, ability, effectiveness, efficiency, individuality, the future, hope and romance, but also with violence, fighting, bullying, discrimination and sacrifice. The latter, in contrast, invoke notions of peace, egalitarianism, anti-discrimination and welfare, as well as stagnation, retreat, retrogression, degeneration and the decline of vital powers. A viewpoint orientated towards the strong supports those who can vigorously lead society, even if this

4   *Introduction*

results in the sacrifice of the weak. A viewpoint orientated towards the weak insists that those without power, such as the ill and the infirm, should be helped, consoled and saved, even if this strategy is to some extent hazardous to the future prosperity of human beings as a whole.

In spite of what might be regarded as a natural tendency towards respect for the strong and the beautiful and contempt for the weak and the ugly, there is often also a sense of sympathy for those without power. This sympathy is not solely the result of a moral imperative; it is also a recognition of an innate weakness within ourselves which corresponds to the weakness of others. It is likely that both views are necessary for the survival of human beings. When two opposing ideologies of this nature coexist, they often negotiate and compromise as much as conflict. In the current society, for example, we skilfully distinguish between the application of these two ideas, so that respect for the strong is apt to operate in our relations with heterogeneous others, while sympathy for the weak tends to appear in relations with the homogeneous family. I would argue that a feature of a good and impressive literary work which represents contemporary society in some distinct way is that it uniquely reflects the process of conflict, negotiation and compromise to which I have referred, and thus balances "admiration for the strong" and "compassion for the weak". In this book I shall investigate how selected fictional narrative discourse deals with the conflict, negotiation and compromise between these two seemingly contradictory ideologies.

Since previous studies have paid sufficient attention to the strong and the beautiful, the focus of this book will be the weak, the insulted and the victimised depicted in a number of major Japanese literary works. I shall examine the process by means of which weak, ugly, indecent and lowly ranked characters are despised and discriminated against, on the one hand, and how are they sympathised with, assisted, saved and placated, on the other.

My analysis in *Postmodern, Feminist and Postcolonial Currents in Contemporary Japanese Culture* focused on contemporary Japanese writers. This book, however, has a wider scope in that it examines material from the eleventh to the twentieth century. In order to analyse the weak and the strong depicted in a literary work, it is helpful to refer to the theoretical work of its contemporary period. However, the discussion of Japanese religious, philosophical and political material from the tenth to the twentieth century given here cannot be comprehensive, and it is certainly outside the scope of this book to conduct a deep hermeneutic study. Nevertheless, as a preface to the analysis that follows, Chapter 2 will provide a brief outline of the strong–weak issue as it appears in Buddhist, Confucian, Modernist and Christian thought in Japan.

The textual-analysis section of the book is arranged in historical order, beginning in Chapter 3 with my discussion of *The Tale of Genji*, the famous Heian period (794–c.1185) text written in the tenth and eleventh centuries. The focus of this chapter will be how the beautiful and sophisticated ladies and gentlemen of the Heian aristocracy are both admired and criticised from the perspective of women who are ugly, old and indecent. In adopting this perspective, the chapter will add a new viewpoint to the current trend of analysing power structures and narrative in *The Tale of Genji*. Building on previous studies by Mizuhara Hajime and Imanari Genshō (Motoaki), Chapter 4 considers the depiction of weak women, humble men and the insulted in *The Tale of the Heike*, a work compiled and revised during the thirteenth and fourteenth centuries. This chapter investigates the possibilities presented when critics read beyond the ostensibly despicable discrimination against the weak and the infirm featured in the text. Chapter 5 is a discussion of Kyokutei Bakin's *The Eight Dog Chronicles*, written in nineteenth-century late-Tokugawa Japan. Here, we examine the social forces at work by means of which assistance to the weak and the infirm can tighten social bonds and thereby contribute to the later formation of a belligerent nation-state sustained by aggression against surrounding communities. The chapter will also provide a useful introduction for Anglophone readers to a work rarely analysed in English. Finally, in Chapter 6, we shall consider how the relationship between weak women and strong men is omnipresent and significant in four stories from the twentieth-century modern era. These stories are Kawabata Yasunari's *The Dancing Girl of Izu* (1926), *Snow Country* (1935–47), *Thousand Cranes* (1949–51) and *The Sound of the Mountain* (1949–54). This study builds on and expands the present feminist approach to Kawabata's stories.

As the discussion proceeds, two points will become apparent regarding the strong–weak issue in Japan. The first is the fact that "respect for the strong" and "sympathy for the weak" often appear in the history of Japanese thought and literature simultaneously and contradictorily as both "respect for endeavour" (respect for the strong) in addition to "egalitarianism" (sympathy with the weak). In this regard, as depicted in the previous book, we shall note a binary division between the power-orientated desire to progress (respect for the strong/respect for endeavour) and a gentle but retrogressive emotion for friendship and stagnation (egalitarianism/sympathy with the weak). However, in this book I shall draw on the weak–strong binary to identify a distinction between philosophical, religious and political language, on the one hand, and fictional literary language, on the other. The former requires a monologic narrative which does not allow logical inconsistency, whereas the latter is related by means of a polyphonic narrative which allows the coexistence of contradictory notions.

The second point concerns the close relationship between egalitarianism and unity within the social group. European thinkers such as Thomas Hobbes, John Locke, Jean-Jacques Rousseau and Jeremy Bentham problematised the idea of egalitarianism as one of the major issues throughout the seventeenth to nineteenth centuries. This interest in and, in some cases, advocacy of egalitarianism accompanied the appearance in the modern industrial world of ideas such as nationality, nationalism, and the system of "nation-state".[2] The relationship between egalitarianism and nationalist tendencies was

6 *Introduction*

notably confirmed in the 1776 American Declaration of Independence and also in the 1789 "Declaration of the Rights of Man and of the Citizen of France". The concepts of egalitarianism and nationalism were thus in a sense born together from opposition to the previous despotic absolute monarchy and to the feudal privilege enjoyed by aristocratic and religious leaders. Together, these notions supported the liberation of the common people from the oppression of small numbers of socially high-status people privileged by birth within the territory of the nation. Egalitarianism specifically argued that, regardless of family background, one is by birth free from oppression and of equal worth to others. Although we must carefully distinguish the community of modern nationalism from the religious community of previous times, Benedict Anderson argues that nationalism can be aligned with large cultural systems, including both the *religious community* and the *dynastic realm*, in the sense that both function to unite people as a group (Anderson 2006: 11–12). For example, religious egalitarianism in Europe is evident in the writing of Thomas Aquinas (1225?–1274): "all men are equal as regards both nature and original sin; and inequality in them arises from the merits or demerits of their actions" (Aquinas 1911: 323; *Summa Theologica*, part 1, question 23, article 5). In Japan, too, egalitarianism was evident in the writing of the Heian-era religious thinker Saichō (767–822). Of interest here is the fact that, although writing over a thousand years ago, Saichō nevertheless advocated egalitarianism for the purpose of protecting the nation (Saichō 1975, 2: 680).

As we proceed through the chapters that follow, it will become apparent that the doubled-edged promise offered by egalitarianism as a system that can emphasise equality within the group while also working to distinguish violently one group from another is deeply embedded in the material to be analysed. To this extent, we might regard the simultaneous expression of these two sides of egalitarianism as an overarching characteristic of narrative produced in Japan, regardless of the historical time of a work's production. Paradoxically, it is by considering the viewpoint of the weak, the despised and the lowly in conjunction with that of the strong, the beautiful and the heroic in *The Tale of Genji*, *The Tale of the Heike*, *The Eight Dog Chronicles* and Kawabata Yasunari's stories that we shall most clearly see the emergence of a narrative discourse which supports the nationalist unity of the people of Japan.

Although some chapters have been published previously, this book is not a collection of papers. While key elements featured in the original papers have in large part been retained, the material has been extensively revised to ensure that all material resonates with the overarching theme of conflict between the weak and the strong, and the associated themes of egalitarianism and the unity of the people. In spite of the fact that each chapter began as an independent entity rather than as part of a unified concept, each individual study has been reconfigured into an integral part of a coherent whole.

With the exception of Kawabata's stories, the literary works dealt with in this book – *The Tale of Genji*, *The Tale of the Heike* and *The Eight Dog*

Chronicles – are written in the old form of Japanese and not easily accessed by the majority of modern-day readers. While the book is therefore inevitably specialised, every effort has been taken to ensure its suitability for a wide audience of general readers. Thus, the main text focuses on aspects of the discussion likely to be of interest to the general reader, while specialist readers are given detailed bibliographical information, original citation and further discussion in the endnotes. In this way, non-specialist readers can confine their reading to the main text, while researchers and scholars in the field have the option of consulting the accompanying endnote material.

2 The strong and the weak in Japanese religious, philosophical and political writings

2.1. The strong and the weak

In order to survey the contrast between helping the weak and respecting the strong as these notions appear in a selection of religious, philosophical and political writings from premodern and Meiji Japan, it will be useful to begin our discussion with an examination of Pure Land (Jōdo) Buddhism, the teachings of which advocate the salvation of the masses and the impoverished classes. In contrast to Christianity, which teaches that the Lord will save believers, Buddhist doctrine in general calls upon devotees to enlighten themselves through ascetic practice. However, Pure Land teaching differs from mainstream Buddhist doctrine in that believers are taught to rely fully upon Amida's power to grant them rebirth in the Pure Land.[1] This precept is based on an anecdote about Amida recounted in *The Larger Sutra on Amitāyus* (*Muryōjukyō*). According to this text, while still a disciple seeking enlightenment, the Bodhisattva Amida was given the name Dharmākara. He thereupon made forty-eight vows, promising that he would not accept enlightenment if he could not fulfil these vows. The eighteenth of these forty-eight vows, crucial for Pure Land teaching, says:

> When I attain buddhahood, if all sentient beings in the ten directions who aspire in all sincerity and faith to be born in my land *think of me even ten times* they shall be re-born in the Pure Land. If they are not, then may I not attain supreme enlightenment.
> (Nakamura, Hayashima and Kino (eds) 1963–4, 1: 157; my italics)[2]

Later, after enumerating Dharmākara's vows to the Lord Buddha, Ānanda, the devout follower and personal attendant to the Buddha, asked his master whether the Bodhisattva Dharmākara had yet attained Buddhahood and passed into Nirvāna. The Buddha replied that Dharmākara (Amida) had indeed attained Buddhahood and was dwelling in a western Buddha-land called "Peace and Bliss". Since he had become a Buddha, it was clear that each of the forty-eight vows of Amida as the Dharmākara Bodhisattva had been completely fulfilled (Nakamura, Hayashima and Kino (eds) 1963–4, 1:

169; Inagaki 2000: 253).[3] It is on the basis of this story that Pure Land Buddhism teaches that merely to think of Amida ten times guarantees rebirth in the Pure Land western paradise where the attainment of Buddhahood is also certain.

The exhortation in the eighteenth vow to think of Amida ten times is referred to in the original text as "*jūnen*" or "the ten nem(butsu)". In later developments of the Pure Land tradition, the nembutsu (the act of thinking of Amida Buddha) came to mean verbally reciting "Homage to Amida Buddha", or "Namu Amida butsu". However, in the early stages of Pure Land teaching, the nembutsu was roughly divided into four types – *shōmyō* or *kushyō* nembutsu (invoking Amida Buddha's name), *kannen* nembutsu (imaging Buddha's shape), *kansō* nembutsu (meditating Buddha's characters) and *jissō* nembutsu (contemplating the Buddha's genuine body or the Dharma-body of the Buddha) (Nakamura et al. (eds) 1989: 147, 650–1; Senchakushū English Translation Project (trans.) 1998: 189). Of these, the *shōmyō* or *kushyō* nembutsu (invocational nembutsu) was the least difficult to perform.

One of the representative works of Pure Land teaching in the Heian period was *The Essentials of Rebirth [into the Pure Land of Amida Buddha]* (*Ōjōyōshū*) (984–5) by the priest Genshin (941–1017), also known as Eshin Sōzu (bishop or abbot of the Eshin Cloister). Genshin's thought is often said to underlie *The Tale of Genji*, while the model of the bishop of Yokawa who appears in the "At Writing Practice" chapter of *Genji* is considered by some scholars to be a representation of Genshin.[4]

The Buddhist presence in *The Tale of the Heike* is exemplified by the presence of the historical figure of the priest Hōnen (1133–1212), one of the representatives of Kamakura Pure Land teaching. It is Hōnen who administers the Ten Commandments to Taira no Shigehira following the latter's assuming command of the Heike army when its troops set fire to various temples in Nara (McCullough (trans.) 1988: 333–5). It is surely no coincidence that each of the representative literary works presented here from the Heian and Kamakura periods features an important character associated with Pure Land Buddhism. This common presence suggests that the two works are likely to have areas of similarity. How, then, do Genshin's and Hōnen's religious works, on the one hand, and the *Genji* and the *Heike*, on the other, portray the weak and articulate the contrast between "respect for the strong" and "sympathy with the weak"? We shall expand upon this point in the chapters that follow.

With the advent of the Tokugawa period, Buddhism was replaced by Confucianism as the principal philosophical and social influence. While the former presents an ideal worldview, with Pure Land teaching especially being concerned with life after death, the latter addresses human relations in present society and the real world. Of the various Confucian scholars active in the Tokugawa period, we shall give close attention to the thought of Itō Jinsai (1627–1705). Since Confucianism advocates harmonious and reciprocal obligations between social superiors and inferiors, it presents as

10   *The strong and the weak in Japanese writings*

highly relevant to the issue of social relations between the weak and the strong. As we shall see later, Kyokutei Bakin, author of *The Eight Dog Chronicles*, the work examined in Chapter 5 and recognised as one of the representative romances of Tokugawa literature, was said to have admired Itō Jinsai.

Moving into the modern period covering the late nineteenth to the twentieth centuries, we shall first examine Fukuzawa Yukichi's (1835–1901) writing. Yukichi is commonly revered as the early-modern champion of notions of individual freedom, independence and egalitarianism in Japan. Although these assumptions are problematic, this writer is well worth examining in the context of the current discussion. In contrast to the utilitarian and pragmatic realism represented by Yukichi's thought, Christianity in the early-modern era was a belief system which sought human emancipation in an ideal world (Makibayashi 2001: 193–4). First introduced into Japan in the mid-sixteenth century, Christianity was proscribed by the Tokugawa government at the beginning of the seventeenth century and its adherents persecuted. However, following the Meiji Restoration in 1868, the ban on Christianity was lifted and the number of followers grew once more. Among various Christians of the time committed to helping those in need, Kitamura Tōkoku's (1868–94) thought stands out both for its strong advocacy of sympathy with the weak and the deep influence it had on later literature.[5] There is an interesting link between this thinker and the writer featured in Chapter 6, Kawabata Yasunari. Kawabata was at one time editor of a journal called *Literary World* (*Bungakukai*). This journal took its title from an earlier journal of the same title, one of whose editors was Tōkoku. As in the cases mentioned above, this connection suggests some common link between the work of these two identities (Kawabata 1980–4, 31: 153).

2.2. Respecting the strong and sympathising with the weak: Genshin's (941–1017) *Essentials of Rebirth [into the Pure Land of Amida Buddha]* (*Ōjōyōshū*) (984–5)

Buddhist thought in India, China and Japan has long been characterised by two conflicting doctrines. The first teaches that only a select elite can attain Buddhahood through long and arduous ascetic practice. The second maintains that all sentient beings, regardless of innate ability, have the potential to gain Buddhahood (Tokiwa 1944; Rhodes 1992: 1). In Japan, the Hossō School represents the former and the Tendai School the latter. The former originated as the Fa-hsiang School in China and was introduced to Japan in the seventh century by the priest Dōshō. Centred on the Gangōji and Kōfukuji temples in Nara, this doctrine flourished in Japan in the eighth century. The latter set of teachings, stemming from the Chinese T'ien-t'ai School, was introduced to Japan in the ninth century by the priest Saichō (767–822), and became the dominant religious power at the Enryakuji temple on Mount Hiei (Groner 1989: 53–4; Rhodes 1992: 2–9).

The strong and the weak in Japanese writings 11

The doctrinal conflict between these two schools is the focal point of a debate between Saichō and Tokuitsu, early-ninth-century representatives of the Tendai and Hossō schools respectively.[6] To summarise briefly, Tokuitsu (Hossō School) argues that the necessary seeds for attaining Buddhahood are hereditarily transmitted from parents to children. Those who have these seeds are called bodhisattva. However, he also argues that there is a different type of hereditary seed transmitted which leads people to become either an arhat (arakan), otherwise known as sravaka (shōmon), or a pratyekabuddha (engaku), both of whom are lower-class beings. Thus, three different teachings (vehicles) are required, corresponding to the three distinct types of seed. These different teachings lead to three different goals, enabling one to become (depending on the seed one has inherited) a bodhisattva, arhat/sravaka or a pratyekabuddha. Furthermore, there are two other classes of beings. The first is the unfortunate icchantika (issendai), which does not have Buddha-nature and can never attain Buddhahood. The second is an indeterminate category, the members of which can become either Buddha or arhat (sravaka) or pratyekabuddha. Thus, in total, there are five kinds of man. These include the four defined categories of (1) bodhisattva, (2) arhat or sravaka, (3) pratyekabuddha and (4) icchantika, in addition to the fifth indeterminate category. As a representative of the Hossō School, Tokuitsu considers that the decisive factor in attaining enlightenment is an innate ability genetically transmitted from parents to their children. Regardless of how diligently one practises Buddhist asceticism, if one lacks the inherent seeds of Buddhahood in the form of ability transmitted from one's ancestors, one can never attain enlightenment.

Against this view, Saichō of the Tendai School argues passionately in line with the *Lotus Sutra* that all sentient beings have the Buddha-nature and the innate ability to attain Buddhahood. Thus, all can reach Buddhist enlightenment through the sincere practice of devotion. He argues that the three different teachings are three different ways leading to the one goal, Buddhahood. There is, however, a difference in the way of teaching which must alter according to ability. Thus, weak people can be taught how to achieve enlightenment using an easy method, while a more difficult method can be used for stronger followers.[7] This debate is sometimes called the "Debate on 'Three Vehicles or One Vehicle; the Provisional or the Real'" (*San'ichi gonjitsu ronsō*).

As Uemura Shinchō comments, at the heart of the detailed Buddhist theological hermeneutics of this debate is the conflict between Tokuitsu's realistic position, which perceives the world as governed by Buddhist causal relations, and Saichō's idealistic position of egalitarianism, derived from Buddhist notions of self-denial (Uemura 1986: 213).[8] From the perspective of our discussion, Tokuitsu's position seems to respect the strong, or at least to distinguish between the strong and the weak, while Saichō seems to advocate helping all sentient beings including the weak and the inferior. I would like to pay attention here to two points in this debate, both of which are

12 *The strong and the weak in Japanese writings*

essential for our discussion. One is the relationship between egalitarianism and endeavour, while the other is the connection between egalitarianism and the unity of the people.

Let me first explore the relationship between egalitarianism and endeavour. Concerning this debate, Hakamaya Noriaki refers to the distinction between "one vehicle of unification", namely the three different kinds of teaching which are eventually united into one vehicle leading to Buddhahood, and "selection of the one vehicle", referring to Amida's selection of the invocational nembutsu as the easiest means to achieve Buddhahood. Hakamaya rejects the view that the debate is between Saichō's egalitarianism and Tokuitsu's discrimination. Rather he argues that both are discriminatory in the sense that Saichō's position is not on "selection of the one vehicle", but on "one vehicle of unification" (Hakamaya 1998: 181). Matsumoto Shirō explains the difference between "one vehicle of unification" and "selection of the one vehicle" by noting that, while the former proposes that different kinds of people should choose different means to be born into the Pure Land, the latter insists that only the easiest way, the (invocational) nembutsu, can lead all people to this paradise (Matsumoto 1990: 216–35). By distinguishing between those who are able to engage in formal Buddhist asceticism and those who lack this ability, the "one vehicle of unification" encourages all people to take their own proper means to be born in the Pure Land. For the former, this might involve long and difficult Buddhist practices; while, for the latter, it will mean simply chanting the nembutsu, that is, the name of Amida Buddha. In contrast, "selection of the one vehicle" asserts that only the easiest means, the invocational nembutsu, can lead all people to the Pure Land. Why should all people be required to seek enlightenment in this way? Because Amida's compassionate mind selected the simple means of chanting the nembutsu as the means to lead people to the Pure Land. "One vehicle of unification" is Saichō's position, whereas "selection of the one vehicle" is actually presented later by Hōnen in the twelfth to thirteenth century. Although Hakamaya regards the latter as unconditional egalitarianism, he considers Saichō's position, like Tokuitsu's, as discriminatory. We shall return to Hakamaya's criticism of Saichō when we introduce Hōnen's argument and address the relationship between egalitarianism and respect for endeavour.

The relationship between egalitarianism and the unity of the people can also be problematised in the Saichō–Tokuitsu debate. As Shioiri Ryōchū noticed and strongly declared from his own nationalistic position before the Second World War, and as briefly mentioned, Saichō insisted on egalitarianism for the purpose of protecting the nation (Shioiri 1937: 357–66; 1986: 187–8). This is apparent in the title of the book Saichō wrote during the debate – *Commentary on the Protection of the Nation* (*Shugo kokkai shō*). At the end of the book, Saichō concludes:

> I hope that from now on no one in the nation slanders Buddhist law (which advocates egalitarianism) and the population does not diminish;

when all families praise the Buddhist sutra (which teaches the one vehicle) we shall avoid the seven calamities. This is the true meaning of protecting the nation.

(Saichō 1975, 2: 680; my translation)

Ōtsu Yūichi and Murai Shōsuke argue that nationalism rose in Japan in the ninth century (Ōtsu 2005: 56–7; Murai Shōsuke 1995: 23–45). Certainly, this was an aristocratic nationalism rather than nationalism with sovereign power residing with the people in the modern sense of the word. However, it is very interesting to note that in the thought of Saichō the concept of egalitarianism appears together with the consciousness of nationalism. We shall discuss this point again when we consider Fukuzawa Yukichi's egalitarianism and nationalism, and also in Chapter 5 when we analyse *The Eight Dog Chronicles*. We might observe, however, that two of the issues featured in this book – the relationship between egalitarianism and endeavour, and that between egalitarianism and the unity of the people (nationalism) – can be found as early as Saichō's thought of the ninth century.

The focal point of the Saichō–Tokuitsu debate was discussed again by Ryōgen and Hōzō in the "Doctrinal Debate of the Ōwa Era", so called because it took place in the Ōwa Era (961–4). The debate was held in 963 for five days from 21 to 25 August, with two sessions held each day.[9] From the evening session of the second day to the morning session of the third day, Ryōgen and Hōzō addressed the previously mentioned topic of "Three Vehicles or One Vehicle; the Provisional or the Real". On this occasion, Hōzō conceded to Ryōgen. But the same topic arose again in discussion between the Hossō monk Chūzan (Chūsan) and the Tendai monk Juchō on the morning of the fifth day. This time the courtiers in attendance regarded Chūzan as the victor. Thus, the differing opinions on "Three Vehicles or One Vehicle; the Provisional or the Real" remained unresolved in both the Saichō–Tokuitsu and Ōwa debates.

Some time later, the Tendai monk Genshin (941–1017) discussed the same topic in his 1006 book, *Determining the Essentials of the One Vehicle* (*Ichijō yōketsu*). Here, Genshin supported the Tendai teaching of one vehicle.[10] Although Tokiwa Daijō dismisses *Determining the Essentials of the One Vehicle* as merely repeating the thought of Saichō, Yagi Kōe, Tamura Kōyū, Shimaji Taitō (Daitō) and Ōkubo Ryōjun consider that Genshin resolved the debate from the hermeneutic point of view. This latter position now seems to be dominant.[11] From the point of view of our discussion, interest in *Determining the Essentials of the One Vehicle* lies in the fact that the basic idea behind Genshin's detailed hermeneutic analysis of sutra texts is, as might be expected, not "selection of the one vehicle", but "one vehicle of unification".

I should like to follow on from this reference to "Three Vehicles or One Vehicle; the Provisional or the Real" by further discussing the relationship between egalitarianism and endeavour. Even if all sentient beings have the

14 *The strong and the weak in Japanese writings*

potential to gain Buddhahood, the question remains whether long and hard asceticism is necessary to attain Buddhahood or enlightenment, or whether this can be achieved merely by reciting the nembutsu, including the easiest invocative nembutsu. Genshin addresses this problem in *Essentials of Rebirth* (*Ōjōyōshū*), which he began writing in November 984 and completed the following April.[12] *Essentials of Rebirth*, like Dante's *The Divine Comedy*, features vivid pictorial depictions of hell and paradise (Pure Land of Amida). In order to avoid falling into hell, to escape from the cycle of reincarnation and to be reborn in the Pure Land, Genshin suggests the nembutsu practice (Genshin 1994, 1: 152–251; Marra 1988a: 45).

Genshin knows well that even practising the contemplative nembutsu, let alone following difficult and arduous Buddhist asceticism, is beyond the ability of ordinary people. In *Essentials of Rebirth* he therefore raises the question of ordinary human beings who lack the ability to undertake the ascetic practice required to make the vows necessary to attain enlightenment. How can ordinary humans practise the difficult kind of contemplative nembutsu; how they can keep their weak minds constantly concentrated on nembutsu practice; and how can dull and evil beings reach the Pure Land (Genshin 1994, 1: 170–7, 238–9, 307–8; 2: 148–52; Marra 1988a: 45–6; Andrews 1973: 55–6, 95–6)? In response to questions such as these, Genshin repeatedly asserts that, even if ordinary human beings are unable to attain Buddhahood through the difficult contemplative nembutsu or other arduous ascetic practices, they can be successful by sincerely concentrating on and practising the simple invocational nembutsu. This clearly shows Genshin's wish to help the weak and the poor. His position is absolutely emancipative for those unable to attain rebirth by undertaking hard ascetic practice or even the contemplative nembutsu.

Although Tendai School teachings maintain that all beings have the potential to attain Buddhahood, enlightenment is impossible without rigorous Buddhist practice in which only a small privileged elite can actually engage. In Tendai doctrine, the claim that everybody has the potential to attain Buddhahood is to some extent contradicted by the belief that without hard work nobody can achieve this state. Genshin's adherence to the Pure Land doctrine, in contrast, leads to the promise that even those who do nothing but wish to be born in the Pure Land will have this wish fulfilled merely by sincere and ardent recitation of the invocational nembutsu (Rhodes 1992: 76–7).

Genshin's insistence, however, leads to a more difficult and fundamental question: If the simple invocational nembutsu is enough for rebirth in the Pure Land, what role do the difficult contemplative nembutsu and other hard ascetic practices play in attaining enlightenment? Advocacy of the invocational nembutsu as the sole method to achieve rebirth in the Pure Land may be necessary to give the weak and the poor hope that they, too, can attain Buddhahood. However, if this is sufficient, how can the hard work of the strong and the industrious be fittingly rewarded? This is exactly the dilemma

The strong and the weak in Japanese writings 15

of the conflict between "sympathy for the weak and the poor" and "respect for the strong and the diligent". The former results in complete egalitarianism, while the latter eventually results in respecting the strong for making progress. From the secular point of view, the problem facing Genshin is the need to find evidence in the Buddhist sutras to support a compromise between sympathy with the weak and the infirm, and respect for the strong and the diligent. This fundamental question remains valid for us today. Should all be rewarded equally, regardless of ability, industriousness or achievement? Or should reward be based solely on criteria of this nature? While the former is the ideal of an egalitarian society, the latter is that of a society based on merit.

In order to answer this question, Genshin attempts to reconcile the two opposing ideas by suggesting that, although both paths can lead people to the Pure Land, the contemplative nembutsu is superior to the invocational form. He states: "if even those converted to Buddha's faith by only practising the invocational *nembutsu* are freed of the cravings and sins of the past ten-thousand kalpas, so much more rewarding must be practicing the contemplative *nembutsu* with a pure mind" (Genshin 1994, 2: 57; English translation is from Marra 1988a: 47; emphases are Marra's).[13]

But this attempt still does not solve the fundamental question: If the simple invocational nembutsu is sufficient for rebirth in the Pure Land, what is the purpose of the difficult contemplative nembutsu and other demanding ascetic practices? Concerning this dilemma, Genshin's thought is unclear and even contradictory. Elsewhere in *Essentials of Rebirth*, Genshin states that the nembutsu alone cannot guarantee rebirth in the Pure Land. He says: "It is impossible to catch a fowl using a net consisting of just one mesh. (Likewise, it is only by) employing myriad techniques to aid in the nembutsu contemplation that the great matter of rebirth is accomplished" (Genshin 1994, 1: 252; English translation is from Rhodes 1992: 73; see also Andrews 1973: 67). As Robert Franklin Rhodes comments, Genshin's position here is that the invocative nembutsu can be effective only when practised in conjunction with a number of preliminary and supportive practices (Rhodes 1992: 73).

Ishida Mizumaro points to a contradiction between the above section of *Essentials of Rebirth*, in which Genshin argues that the nembutsu can be effective only when practised in conjunction with a number of preliminary and supportive practices, and a text entitled *A Register of Deaths of Twenty-five Members of the Nembutsu-Samādhi Society Who Gathered at the Shuryōgon'in Temple and Prayed for Rebirth in Paradise* (*Shuryōgon'in nijūgo zammai kechien kakochō*) in which Genshin says that the invocative form of the nembutsu is sufficient for rebirth in the Pure Land. Ishida notes that this ambivalence or conflict in Genshin's position is a limitation only overcome later in the work of Hōnen (Ishida Mizumaro 1970: 447–9; 1987: 182–3).[14] As Allan A. Andrews also points out, Genshin draws on two criteria of excellence: one is a Tendai criterion which teaches the potential of the nembutsu for depth

16 *The strong and the weak in Japanese writings*

of insight, and thus for effecting enlightenment and bringing the practitioner to immediate Buddhahood; the other is a genuine Pure Land criterion concerning the ease and wide availability of the nembutsu. Ultimately, this conflict of priorities between two kinds of nembutsu and two notions of soteriology is never quite resolved in Genshin's thought (Andrews 1973: 56, 63, 89–90). Genshin's intention is to help all people be born in the Pure Land. But in the final analysis he cannot disregard the position of those who undertake hard effort to attain Buddhahood or enlightenment (Marra 1988a: 48).

What we do see in Genshin's *Essentials of Rebirth* is a clear, pictorial and distinctive contrast between the beautiful and blissful Pure Land and the horrible and hateful hell. Genshin's description of the fearful hell is remarkably effective, and emphasises the beauty and happiness of the Buddhist Pure Land. The distinction in Genshin's thought between beauty, truth and goodness, on the one hand, and ugliness, falsehood and evil, on the other, is obviously striking and poles apart. Likewise, Genshin cannot or will not compromise the two contradictory views of the need to help as many people as possible, which he juxtaposes against the idea that without endeavour one cannot attain enlightenment. Certainly these opposing views express a tendency towards polarisation. However, while Genshin's work has been critiqued as ambiguous and inconsistent, it is also true that his thought encompasses multiple perspectives. Although he may be susceptible to charges of failing to reconcile or resolve contradictory ideas, Genshin's work nevertheless accommodates various degrees of value judgement resulting in the ability both to sympathise with the weak and to respect the strong.

2.3. The triumph of the weak over the strong: Hōnen's (1133–1212) *Passages on the Selection of the Nembutsu in the Original Vow (Senchaku hongan nembutsu shū)* (1198)

Genshin's tradition of Pure Land teaching continued into the Kamakura period, at which time he was partly succeeded by Hōnen (1133–1212) (Andrews 1989: 20). Previous historical studies of Kamakura Buddhism argued that the Buddhist religion became popularised during this period. This view, whose advocates included Tsuji Zennosuke, Ienaga Saburō, Ishimoda Shō and Inoue Mitsusada, pervaded the academic world from the 1940s to 1970.[15] Soon after the Second World War, in the 1940s and the 1950s, for instance, Ienaga Saburō and Inoue Mitsusada argued that Kamakura Pure Land sect representatives, such as Hōnen and Shinran (1173–1262), theologically developed the Heian Pure Land teachings of Genshin and Yoshihige no Yasutane (?–1002) in a strong populist direction. In contrast, they declared, the previously dominant Buddhist powers, such as the Tendai and Shingon sects, declined during the Kamakura period as a result of their support for the power of the state.[16]

This view of the popularisation of new forms of Kamakura Buddhism is, however, later problematised. Richard K. Payne, for instance, cautions us to consider at least two points. One is that the eventual predominance of

The strong and the weak in Japanese writings   17

the new Buddhisms resulted from the ability to respond to popular concerns already given form in the Buddhist thought of earlier eras. The second is that the rising prosperity of the peasant class made it possible for the new Buddhisms to establish a productive connection with this group (Payne (ed.) 1998: 1–23). Payne points out the need to consider carefully and precisely the role played not only by the new Kamakura Buddhism but also by the old Heian Buddhism and its relation to the common people. As Payne notes, a similar view is held by Kuroda Toshio in Japan (Kuroda 1975). Kuroda disagrees with previous scholars who argued in favour of a drastic change in Buddhist thought from the old traditional Heian authoritarian Buddhism to the new popularised Kamakura Buddhism. He insists that the new sects were never the mainstream of Kamakura Buddhism but, rather, that they remained peripheral. Kuroda further argues that the dominant Kamakura schools, such as the Tendai and Shingon sects, were not thoroughly obedient to the civil authorities in power and that they also attempted to reform in order to accommodate the popularisation of Buddhism (Kuroda 1994: 60–1, 67, 124; English translation: 247–8, 254).[17]

Building on Kuroda's theory, Taira Masayuki re-evaluates Hōnen's thought. He argues that, while Tendai and Shingon Buddhism followed the Heian Pure Land doctrine and attempted to attract the common people during the Kamakura period, both Hōnen and Shinran negated these teachings. Taira considers that we should thus focus on the difference between Hōnen's Pure Land teaching and earlier Pure Land teachings which can be traced from Genshin to Pure Land teaching in the older Kamakura sects (Taira 1992: 51–2, 120; Sueki 1993: 248–9, 253–4). Bearing this in mind, let us first compare Hōnen's *Passages on the Selection of the Nembutsu in the Original Vow* (*Senchaku hongan nembutsu shū*) with Genshin's *Essentials of Rebirth*.[18]

In *Passages*, Hōnen begins by considering how to find the path to the Pure Land. Referring to such Chinese priests as Tao-ch'o (Dōshaku, 562–645), T'an-luan (Donran, 476?–542?) and Shan-tao (Zendō, 613–81), he concludes that the only method providing entry to the Pure Land is the nembutsu. To the question "Why did Amida elect to cast aside all other practices and take up the nembutsu alone as corresponding to his original vow of birth?", Hōnen offers two perspectives. First, he maintains that the nembutsu is superior while other ways are inferior. Second, he emphasises that, while reciting the nembutsu is easy, other means, such as making images of the Buddha and building stupas, having wisdom and intelligence, hearing and understanding many teachings, and observing the precepts and abiding by monastic rules, are difficult.

Hōnen begins his argument in a scholarly manner, referring mainly to his predecessors' achievements. However, as the discussion develops, it seems that his wish to save the weak and the poor strengthens beyond his control. Initially, there is a tentative tone to the argument, evident from the fact that Hōnen opens by posing a question: Was it not in order to bring all sentient beings without exception to birth in the Pure Land that Amida in his original

18   *The strong and the weak in Japanese writings*

vow cast aside difficult practice, selecting instead the easy one? As the discussion progresses, however, any suggestion of uncertainty dissipates, and Hōnen confidently affirms that Amida, being moved by impartial compassion and wishing to save all beings universally, *did not select* the manifold practices but *did select* the single practice of reciting the nembutsu. Rather than developing logically between the initial interrogation, rhetorical though it may be, and the final affirmation, Hōnen's argument merely unfolds as a well-known beautifully rhythmical repetition of narration as follows:

> If the original vow requires us to make images of the Buddha and to build stupas, the poor and destitute would surely have no hope of birth; if the original vow requires us to have wisdom and intelligence, the dull and foolish would surely have no hope of birth. . . .
> (*Senchakushū*, Iwanami bunko: 49–54; Kuroda Institute: 76–8)[19]

This lack of logic, however, is exactly the point that highlights Hōnen's wish to save the poor and the destitute, the foolish and the ignorant, those who lack experience, and those who are weak and infirm. So strong is his urge to save all humans, whom he considers equal, that his argument in support of this defies a logical framework. Hōnen considers all humans equal, whether they be strong or weak, good or evil. Thus, his priority is the salvation of all, which, he believes, must come before everything else. This is in spite of the fact that some are weak, poor and wicked, while others are strong, rich and good. Hōnen appears to have never considered this distinction. Or perhaps it is more accurate to say that he wanted to help all human beings, including the evil.

Previous Pure Land teachers, such as Genshin, also believed that the (invocational) nembutsu could bring people to the Pure Land. However, as Taira Masayuki has noted, the most crucial point in Hōnen's teaching was the insistence that the efficacy of the (invocational) nembutsu lies in the fact that this method was chosen by Amida himself. Taira sees in this insistence Hōnen's attempt to emancipate the common people from their groundless guilt and self-tortured consciousness (Taira 1992: 48, 55, 86, 170, 173–6, 190–1, 195, 197, 295–8, 303, 485–7).[20] Hōnen's thought liberated the weak from a sense of worthless inferiority engendered by a perceived lack of either strength or intelligence. Hakamaya Noriaki, following Taira, compares Hōnen's thought to that of Myōe, concluding that, while Hōnen is egalitarian in his advocacy of *tariki shugi* (to rely upon Amida's power), Myōe is discriminatory in his support of *jiriki shugi* (self-endeavour). Hakamaya further argues that, contrary to expectation, because the former negates the existence of ātman (ego) while the latter does not, Hōnen's thought is orthodox while Myōe's is heterodox (Hakamaya 1998: 80–5, 100, 201–6, 232, 245, 263, 266–7, 273, 323–4, 332–3; Sueki 1998: pts II and III).[21] Hakamaya asserts that one's own effort, or "*jiriki*" (self-endeavour), always contains a residual idea of ego, however minute or faint. This is in opposition to the basic teaching, featured in all forms of Buddhism, that in order to attain Nirvāna or Sambodhis (enlightenment) followers must be free from any thought of ego.[22]

Tokuitsu insists that hereditarily transmitted ability plays a crucial role in the attainment of Buddhahood. Thus, no matter how diligently one undertakes Buddhist practice, enlightenment is impossible if one's innate ability is unsuitable. Saichō and Ryōgen, however, emphasise the concept of endeavour. They insist that, regardless of the paucity of one's inherited ability, Buddhahood can be attained if one expends enough effort. Genshin continues the tradition of Saichō and Ryōgen by insisting that anyone can attain Buddhahood through sincere practice. But he is ambiguous concerning the degree of effort needed for rebirth in the Pure Land. On some occasions he claims that even those unable to do anything other than chant the nembutsu can enter the Pure Land. There are other occasions, however, when he argues that the invocational nembutsu can be effective only when practised in conjunction with a number of preliminary and supportive practices. This demonstrates a degree of ambiguity in both Genshin's admiration for the strong and the good and his sympathy with the weak and the evil. He, in fact, contradictorily supports both these ways. As we have seen, Genshin's thought has multiple viewpoints or different degrees of value judgement. Thus, while he may not have succeeded in compromising the conflict, he remains able to sympathise with the weak and to respect the strong. But, like Saichō and Ryōgen, Genshin follows the tradition of "one vehicle of unification" in the sense that he distinguishes between those who have the ability to do formal Buddhist practices and those who do not have such an ability. It is for this reason that he encourages the former to do long and hard Buddhist practice and the latter to take the easy way of chanting the nembutsu. Hōnen, however, not only claims that the invocational nembutsu is the only means to rebirth; he further insists that other means are *not* necessary, because the invocational nembutsu is Amida's selection ("selection of the one vehicle"). Here Hōnen clearly declares that he will attempt to help the weak and the infirm, even if they are evil or a hindrance to progress, and even if such assistance is unfair to the strong and the industrious. To the fundamental questions which Genshin could not answer of whether or not the simple invocational nembutsu is sufficient for rebirth in the Pure Land – and, if sufficient, what is the purpose of the difficult and hard contemplative nembutsu and other practices – Hōnen gave an unequivocal and resolute answer. He declared that the invocational nembutsu was not only a sufficient means; it was also the sole means to rebirth. All other means such as the contemplative nembutsu were *not* necessary because Amida, with his compassion for the weak and the infirm, chose only the invocational nembutsu. It was the duty of humans to follow the example set by this compassion.[23]

With his emphasis on inherited ability, Tokuitsu is, in a sense, an aristocrat who makes a point of hereditary social class distinction. On the other hand, Saichō and Ryōgen, who emphasise individual endeavour, are similar to those

20 *The strong and the weak in Japanese writings*

progressively orientated modernists who highly value ability, achievement and development. Hōnen is rather like Marx, who says at the beginning of *Capital* that the use-value, or usefulness, of an article is measured not by the quality of the individual worker's labour-power which is contained in the article, but by the quantity, that is by the labour-time involved. Marx cautions that, if the value of a commodity were determined by the quantity of labour expended during production, it would be more valuable the less skilled or lazy the worker who produced it. This is because a less skilled or lazy worker would need more time to complete the article. Concerning this point, Marx writes:

> However, the labour that forms the substance of value is equal human labour, the expenditure of identical human labour-power. The total labour-power of society, which is manifested in the values of the world of commodities, counts here as one homogeneous mass of human labour-power, although composed of innumerable individual units of labour-power.
>
> (Marx 1976, 1: 129)

Marx thus declares that he pays attention to a homogeneous mass of human labour-power rather than to the innumerable individual units of labour-power that constitute the homogenous mass. I believe that he writes this as an ideal rather than as a description of reality. While Marx measures use-value by calculating the value of an abstract average unit rather than an individual labourer's achievement, Hōnen tries to focus on the easiest way of chanting the nembutsu rather than on the individual person's hard practice. To a certain extent, both Marx and Hōnen disregard individual ability and achievement. However, while Marx uses the abstract social average as the standard, Hōnen focuses on people who have the least ability.

In Hōnen's thought, we see enormous sympathy for the weak and the poor and also a certain devaluation of the effort and exertion of the strong. A doctrine of complete egalitarianism such as this might even be labelled "unfair egalitarianism" in the sense that it seemingly disregards the important and meaningful distinction between the good and the bad, those who are serious and diligent, and those who are idle and lazy. Hōnen's thought might be partly related to the society of the time, which saw the collapse of the aristocratic establishment and the rise of a new samurai power accompanied by a dramatic change in value standards (Ōsumi 1968: 89–91). It is this change which permitted society to consider the possibility that those of low social status were not really all that low. However, mere consideration of the historical background is insufficient for our understanding of this issue.

We have seen when comparing Saichō's "one vehicle of unification" and Hōnen's "selection of the one vehicle" that Hakamaya Noriaki considers Saichō's position to be discriminatory. This is because Saichō distinguishes between those who have ability and those without ability, encouraging the

The strong and the weak in Japanese writings   21

former to do long and hard practice to achieve enlightenment and the latter to take the easy way of chanting the nembutsu. In contrast, Hakamaya regards Hōnen's "selection of the one vehicle" as unconditionally egalitarian, because it insists that, since Amida with his compassionate mind selected the nembutsu as the means to lead all people to the Pure Land, only this easiest of methods should be followed to achieve enlightenment. In fact, a method of distinguishing various abilities and allocating different persons with different abilities to their proper positions or roles is seen not only in the thought of Saichō and Genshin, but also in the Confucian Ogyū Sorai (1666–1728) and the modernist Fukuzawa Yukichi (1835–1901). The ideas of each of these thinkers are based on the notion of competition for survival whereby "proper" ability is allocated to a proper social position in order to win the power game. Sorai, for instance, points out that human beings have various abilities and thereby declares: "[T]he gentleman who develops his own virtue by studying the Way of the Ancient Kings must also be aware that this Way has numerous facets. Human nature is also highly plural" (Yoshikawa et al. (eds) 1973: 18; Najita 1998: 10–11). Sorai continues by pointing out that, through striving for personal development, each individual will be able to discover the special identification of his character with an aspect of the Way. It is in realising one's own virtue that one may be seen as a benevolent human capable of promoting peace and well-being. Fukuzawa Yukichi also maintains that different roles should be played by different talents, arguing that, while we may despise niggards, they are very useful if employed as servants. Similarly, we rely on hot-blooded youth in the case of fire or robbery, although they may present problems for families; the elderly are good at taking charge of the house while nobody is in; and women are best at entertaining guests. To consider each person's talent and ability, and to use a proper person for a proper purpose, is to utilise one's capacity well (Fukuzawa 1981b: 88–9).

This insistence, however, does not lead us to the fundamental solution of discrimination. For instance, it is easy to find a discriminatory attitude in Yukichi's claim that women should play the female role and men the male role, unless we regard the female and male roles as equal. That is, a hierarchical society structured according to high and low roles and positions, and in which people with different abilities are accordingly allocated different roles, is not emancipative. There is also a tendency in this structure for the strong – or certain members of this group at least – to force the weak to do difficult tasks for which the strong then take credit and appropriate the ensuing resources. However, if we regard all social roles as equal, whether heavy and difficult or light and easy, we are once again faced with the dilemma presented by choosing egalitarianism over endeavour. That is, if we say that the strong should undertake the difficult tasks, whereas the weak are allocated the easy tasks, but that both sets of tasks must be treated equally, then certainly the strong cannot appropriate the weak. But, in that case, there is very little incentive for the strong to take the difficult work. Thus, to insist

22 *The strong and the weak in Japanese writings*

on matching ability to position is one thing while emancipation from discrimination is another.

It is likely that, without the reformation of the current hierarchically constructed society, fundamental equality cannot be achieved. Furthermore, given that the current structure reflects an ideology grounded in human desire, equality cannot be achieved without a reformulation of ideology and desire – especially as these relate to individuality and totality or progress and stagnation. In this sense, while Hōnen's thought, like that of Marx, offers the possibility of social reformation which may lead to a reconfiguration of ideology and desire, Sorai's and Yukichi's thought rather confirms and follows current capitalist notions of competition as the basis of society. As suggested in the reading of his teachings given by Taira Masayuki and Hakamaya Noriaki, it would appear that Hōnen rejected social structures based on competition and would almost certainly have opposed the current progressive-orientated modernist and capitalist models.

In this regard, it is worth noting that, in his *Passages*, Hōnen asserts the importance of "cultivation with reverence" – to prostrate oneself with reverence before Buddha as well as before all holy beings – as one of the four modes of practice for attaining Buddhahood. Hōnen identifies five aspects of this "cultivation with reverence": first, to venerate holy beings; second, to venerate holy images and the scriptures; third, to venerate religious teachers; fourth, to respect those with whom one shares the same karmic relationship; and, fifth, to revere the three treasures (Buddha, the teachings of the Buddha, and the community of practising Buddhists) (*Senchakushū*, Iwanami bunko: 119–23; Kuroda Institute: 113–15). That is, as we shall discuss again later, while Sorai and Yukichi both assume the competitive and conflictive situation to be the principal condition of humanity, Hōnen considers the human condition to derive from cooperation and collaboration based on mutual reverence. This is a significant difference in terms of our discussion of egalitarianism. Unlike the conflict situation in which one party triumphs, a cooperative situation makes it difficult to identify who can help others most. In truth, if we consider our own communities, it becomes apparent that it is beyond our ability to measure the contribution of one or another participant or to say to what extent equality prevails. In other words, the ideas of equality or egalitarianism are ideals constructed on the recognition that individual human beings are too complicated and diverse to assess, evaluate, compare or rank fully.

Hōnen ultimately advocates the realisation of a complete egalitarian society in which the weak and the evil are never penalised. We have noted that, if we follow Hōnen's insistence, we must also alter the value standard which judges the strong as strong, and the weak as weak, the good as good, and the evil as evil. If, as Hōnen insists, we should aspire to a society which does not distinguish between either the strong and the weak or the good and the evil, and which regards all members as being beyond assessment, what form would such a society take? In Hōnen's ideal world, as well as in Marx's, the weak are as valuable as the strong; that is to say, the individual is in-valuable. Therefore, we can no longer say that the weak are disadvantaged. This position, however, invites at least two problematic conditions: stagnation and indifference. We shall examine this point later in the discussion of *The Tale of the Heike* in Chapter 4, and also of *The Eight Dog Chronicles* in Chapter 5.

2.4. Egalitarianism in a secluded class-based society: Itō Jinsai's (1627–1705) concept of *Jin*

According to Buddhist teaching, including the teaching of Hōnen, any expression of worldly desire, be it appetite, sexual desire, or desire for fame and fortune, always brings with it the fear of being consigned to hell after death. Confucianism liberated people from this kind of fear. Yamazaki Ansai (1618–82), who converted from Buddhism to Confucianism, criticises the former by noting that if, as Buddhism insists, we were to discard our sexual desire, the human race would surely be extinct in fifty or sixty years. Thus, concludes Ansai, it is apparent that Buddhist thought is flawed (Nishi et al. (eds) 1980: 83–4). Confucianism is undoubtedly emancipative in that it liberates people's desire from Buddhist asceticism. However, among Confucians there are those who support a "respect for the strong" ideology and those who support an ideology of "sympathy with the weak". Itō Jinsai's (1627–1705) thought is an example of the latter, while Yamazaki Ansai and Ogyū Sorai (1666–1728) adhere to the former.

From previous studies into the work of Jinsai we know that this thinker opposes the notions of idealistic study or transcendental truth propagated by Sung Neo-Confucianism. Rather, Jinsai advocates absolute humanism based on the concept of *jin* (compassion), first presented by Confucius and later interpreted by Mencius.[24] Najita Tetsuo points out that Jinsai emphasised the "horizontality" of universal human values rather than conventional distinctions between "high" and "low", that is, between those who govern and those who are governed. Thus, Jinsai's conceptual strategy was orientated towards circumventing the authoritative presence of immediate hierarchic politics in favour of an alternative, horizontal moral premise on which to base a definition of human society. For Jinsai, Najita continues, all human beings could be thought of as morally equal in some absolute sense without having to resort to definitions of power or knowledge. Najita concludes his argument by saying that Jinsai denied the ultimate relevance of conventional distinctions between the wise and the foolish, the powerful and the weak, the wealthy and the poor, or the aristocratic and the common people (Najita 1987: 28, 35–6, 40).[25] For the purposes of this book, Jinsai is the Tokugawa Era Confucian thinker who exemplifies the ideology of "sympathy with the weak".

24 *The strong and the weak in Japanese writings*

2.4.1. Inherent ability

As we have repeatedly seen, egalitarianism has two opponents – inherited distinction at birth between those with intellectual gifts and those without, and the distinction based on the alleged difference in effort between the hard-working and the idle. Let me discuss the inherited distinction first. Jinsai's egalitarian humanistic tendency, which attempts to treat people of both high and low social rank equally, is well demonstrated in his annotation of a passage from Mencius. In *The Meaning of Terms in the Analects and Mencius* (*Gomō jigi*), Jinsai cites Mencius as follows: "The Way is like a wide road. It is not at all difficult to find" (Mencius 1970, 6B (2): 172).[26] Jinsai then interprets the passage to mean that a wide road travelled by kings, nobles and great men can also be travelled by commoners, merchants and servants. Roads would not be called "roads" if only kings, nobles and great men could use them, and common men and women could not. Similarly if only worthies and wise men could practise the teachings of the sage, and ignorant and un-worthy people could not, then those teachings would not be referred to as the Way. Jinsai notes that Mencius therefore concludes that "The Way is like a wide road" (Itō Jinsai 1970: 70–1; Yoshikawa and Shimizu (eds) 1971: 28; Tucker 1998: 96).[27]

Yamazaki Ansai, however, presents a quite different interpretation of the same passage. It is well known that Ansai's study-hall was located in Kyoto just across the Horikawa river opposite Jinsai's *Kogidō* (hall of the study of ancient truthfulness), and that the two were apparently rivals. Citing the excerpt from Mencius ("The Way is like a wide road"), Ansai explains that loyalty (*chū*), filial piety (*kō*), compassion (*jin*) and righteousness (*gi*) are the ways of the human being; if we do not practise these, we are not human beings; if we do not know these, we cannot go anywhere; therefore the Way is like a wide road. Ansai further continues that there is a distinction between shallow and profound knowledge, as well as between a near and a distant destination of travel. To control oneself and maintain one's family is like reaching a near destination in that it requires no more than shallow know-ledge. To govern a country and rule the state, however, is like travelling to a distant destination and accordingly demands profound knowledge. Thus, the travel of those with only shallow knowledge is limited to nearby destinations, whereas those with profound knowledge can go much farther (Yamazaki 1936: 65–6). Such an understanding is similar to the Buddhist theory of "one vehicle of unification" which distinguishes between those who have the ability to undertake Buddhist practice and those who do not. This theory teaches that people should choose their own proper means to be born in the Pure Land, whether through arduous ascetic practice or simply by chanting the name of Amida Buddha, the nembutsu. As we have noted, Hōnen and, later, Taira Masayuki and Hakamaya Noriaki criticise this interpret-ation as discriminatory in the sense that it approves of the current social struc-ture based on ideology and desire.

Ansai elsewhere maintains that sages and worthies, on the one hand, and ordinary people, on the other, inherit the same human ability to recognise virtue, which he calls *kokoro*, and that in this regard there is no difference between people regardless of ability. But Ansai also argues that the sage, the worthy, the ignorant and the unworthy are distinguished by a further inherent characteristic, which he calls *kihin*. It is the different measure of *kihin* which results in sages and worthies having the inborn ability to concentrate seriously, while ignorant people must work hard in order to focus on serious thoughts. The unworthy are those who are blind to the need for sincere concentration (Nishi et al. (eds) 1980: 81).[28] At first glance, Ansai may seem to insist that all people have inherited the same basic human ability. However, ultimately he does distinguish between the sage, the worthy, the ignorant and the unworthy by highlighting the inherent ability to concentrate. That is, Ansai perceives two types of inborn human ability – a basic substructure shared by all human beings whether superior or inferior, and a superstructure related to the ability to concentrate which marks the difference between the superior and inferior. Though the inborn ability element in Ansai's thought has this dual structure, the fundamental idea is similar to Tokuitsu's position. We can perceive in Ansai's thought both a distinction between the strong and the weak in terms of inborn ability and acquired power, and also reverence for the strong and the superior.

Ogyū Sorai explains the concept of the Way in a more authoritative manner. Jinsai's relation with Sorai is often the subject of anecdotes. Sorai, almost forty years younger than Jinsai, was attracted by Jinsai's work and wrote to him seeking scholarly dialogue. Unfortunately, since Jinsai was ill and died soon after, he did not reply. A couple of years after Jinsai's death, Sorai found the unanswered letter published without permission in a collection of Jinsai's bibliographical documents. It is said that these unfortunate incidents made Sorai severely critical of Jinsai.[29] But Sorai's criticism actually helps us understand the difference between these two thinkers. After criticising Jinsai's interpretation of Mencius' Way, Sorai says:

The Way was constructed by the Ancient Kings. It is not natural. Possessing extraordinary intelligence and wisdom, these Kings received Heaven's mandate to be rulers. With total dedication, they set forth to establish peace under Heaven, and, committing their enormous spiritual and mental powers to the task, created the Way to guide the actions of later generations.

Sorai further confirms the inherent character of human beings as follows:

Great wisdom and intellectual power were given *at birth* to the Ancient Kings by Heaven. Human beings do not ordinarily achieve this kind of virtue with their own strength.

(Yoshikawa et al. (eds) 1973: 14–15; Najita 1998: 6–7; my italics)

26   *The strong and the weak in Japanese writings*

Sorai here strongly emphasises the inherent distinction between wise, intellectual kings and the common people, who lack wisdom or intellectual capacity. For Sorai, the Way was established by these talented kings, thus giving them the ability to lead and guide commoners.

In contrast to this, we have seen that in his annotations to the works of Confucius (*The Analects*) and Mencius (*Mencius*), presented in *The Meaning of Terms in the Analects and Mencius* (*Gomō jigi*), Jinsai does not fundamentally differentiate between the worthy, the ignorant or the unworthy. Elsewhere in this work, Jinsai cites and annotates Mencius' words:

> The heart of compassion is the seed of benevolence (*jin*); the heart of shame, of dutifulness (*gi*); the heart of courtesy and modesty, of observance of the propriety (*rei*); the heart of right and wrong, of wisdom (*chi*). All people have these four seeds just as they have four limbs.
>
> (Mencius 1970, 2A (6): 83)

According to Jinsai, this passage suggests that people have these "seeds" as part of human nature. Since everyone is endowed with them, none need look outside himself for they are as natural as four limbs are to the human body (Yoshikawa and Shimizu (eds) 1971: 39; Tucker 1998: 116–17).[30] Thus, Jinsai argues that anyone with human nature can achieve the virtues of benevolence, dutifulness, observation of propriety and wisdom. One of the differences between Ansai, Sorai and Jinsai is that, while Ansai and Sorai emphasise inherent distinction, Jinsai basically does not distinguish between great men and commoners. Ansai, however, rigorously and hierarchically differentiates between commoners, whose shallow knowledge only permits them to control themselves and maintain their families, and kings endowed with the profound knowledge necessary to govern the country and rule the state. Though he supposes a common inborn ability which is shared by all human beings, whether superior or inferior (*kokoro*), Ansai also presents the idea of distinct inborn ability to concentrate, which differentiates between the superior and the inferior (*kihin*). In contrast, Sorai admires the more authoritative great wisdom and intellectual power given by Heaven *at birth* to the Ancient Kings.

2.4.2. Individual endeavour

In *A Child's Inquiries* (*Dōjimon*), Jinsai repeatedly insists that the truth is simple and the difficult is false (Ienaga et al. (eds) 1966: 57, 62, 73, 76, 78). Concerning this point, Mencius says:

> The Way lies at hand yet it is sought afar; things lie in the easy yet are sought in the difficult. If only everyone loved his parents and treated his elders with deference, the Empire would be at peace.
>
> (Mencius 1970, 4A (11): 122–3)

Jinsai follows Mencius' words in advocating that the Way is easy to attain. Jinsai's point here must be not only that the Way is easy but also that humans are equal. It is because the Way is easy that Jinsai believes it can be attained by all, given that all are equal.

Sorai severely criticises this kind of egalitarianism by saying that, though Jinsai equates human nature with virtue, they are not the same thing. Otherwise, Sorai argues, people could be virtuous without any endeavour. Sorai describes the Way as difficult to comprehend and says:

> The Way was created over hundreds of years by a number of brilliant Sages and was not the achievement of a single individual over one lifetime. Confucius himself understood the Way only after much study. Regardless [of this] how could one say that the Way of the Ancient Kings is located in nature?

He also says:

> In general, the Way of the Sage is as though vast and distant. It cannot be known by ordinary people. Thus Confucius said, "The people should rely on it. It cannot be taught to them".
>
> (Yoshikawa et al. (eds) 1973: 10, 14, 43, 50;
> Najita 1998: 1, 6, 38, 45–6, 69)

It is apparent from the above comparison that Sorai highly values human talent and endeavour, whereas Jinsai does not.

The contrast between Jinsai's egalitarianism and Sorai's distinction between able diligent men and incompetent idle men is clearly seen in the difference between Jinsai's and Sorai's understanding of *jin*. In *The Meaning of Terms in the Analects and Mencius* (*Gomō jigi*), Jinsai interprets *jin* (compassion) as the "virtue of compassion and love", *gi* (righteousness) as "doing what should be done, and not doing what should not", *rei* (propriety) as "not overstepping the distinction between superiors and inferiors, as well as the higher and the lower", *chi* (wisdom) as "perceiving the principles of the world clearly", and *kei* (reverence) as "respect and veneration". He insists on *jin* (compassion) against *gi* (righteousness), and *ai* (love) against *kei* (reverence), as the organising principles of human communities (Yoshikawa and Shimizu (eds) 1971: 38, 71; Tucker 1998: 115, 177).[31]

In contrast, Sorai understands *jin* as the great virtue of the sages and the virtue of the head chief who brings peace to the people (Yoshikawa et al. (eds) 1973: 53; Najita 1998: 48). This indicates that the concept of *jin* for Sorai is a sort of paternalistic caring mind or generosity rather than the compassion perceived by Jinsai. Najita argues that inherent in Sorai's concept of *jin* is the theory that the underlying intent of the Ancient Kings in creating society was to establish peace and well-being among humankind. While in nature the strong overcame the weak, and strife and struggle were

28   *The strong and the weak in Japanese writings*

intrinsic to the very order of things, in the society ruled by kings all would be protected and nourished so that each human being could realise virtue to the fullest. This ethical purpose to nourish all, argues Sorai, is what the sages called *jin* (benevolence), the great virtue possessed only by the creative Ancient Kings (Najita 1987: 32–3).[32]

The difference between Jinsai's and Sorai's understanding of *jin* is obvious. Though both aim at a peaceful and stable society, Sorai's concept of *jin* is clearly formed in a hierarchical system in which the idea of *jin* itself is reciprocally reinforced. In contrast, Jinsai's idea of *jin* is rather contradictory and inconsistent with class distinction. Sorai's thought requires the master, the father, the elder brother and the husband to have a paternal caring mind and to demonstrate generosity (*jin* in Sorai's sense). In response, the retainer, the child, the younger brother and the wife must harmoniously respond to the care of the stronger with loyalty, respect and gratitude. Jinsai, in contrast, replaces all these distinctive sentiments with a simple sense of compassion (*jin* in Jinsai's sense). Furthermore, by claiming that the Way is easy to attain, Jinsai's thought diverts attention away from the notion of effort. By asserting that everybody can be treated equally, he eventually, if unconsciously, points at disrupting the consciousness of social hierarchy. Ultimately, however, he leaves the social class system intact.

Jinsai's insistence that the truth is easy to attain is equivalent to Hōnen's teaching that only the easiest means of the nembutsu will bring people to the Pure Land. There are certainly clear differences between the basic theories of the Pure Land Buddhist Hōnen and the Confucianist Jinsai. While Hōnen seeks salvation in the Pure Land after death, Jinsai is mainly concerned with human relations in the present world. A second significant difference between Hōnen, who taught in the twelfth to thirteenth centuries, and Jinsai, who wrote in the seventeenth century, relates to the different intellectual standards of the common people in those two periods. The Tokugawa period witnessed a great increase in literacy, with education becoming available not only to aristocrats, scholars and samurai, but also to merchants and farmers (Hall (ed.) 1991: 715–25; Dore 1984: 1–3, 14–32). Hōnen's work, however, was an almost desperate attempt to help the poor, who had no means to endeavour on their own behalf. It is for this reason that he offers entry to the Pure Land by means of the easiest nembutsu. In contrast, Jinsai operates on the assumption that people have the chance to educate themselves by their own effort. Thus, he confidently encourages the common people to achieve the Way themselves, because it is easy to attain.

2.4.3. Jinsai's class distinction

As we have seen above, Jinsai's egalitarian position is apparent in his opposition to the discriminatory notions of hereditarily transmitted ability and the capacity to endeavour. However, as we have also seen, Jinsai interprets the term *rei* (propriety) to mean not overstepping the distinction between either superiors and inferiors, or the higher and the lower (Yoshikawa and Shimizu (eds) 1971: 38; Tucker 1998: 115). Thus, Jinsai's thought is ultimately framed by the idea of class distinction. Since Confucianism is formed on the basis of class distinction – between master and servant, father and son, elder and younger brother, and husband and wife – it is little wonder that Jinsai supports such a hierarchy. But this leads us to conclude that Jinsai's thought is as contradictory as that of Genshin. One of the differences between the thought of Genshin and of Jinsai is that, while there are inconsistencies in Genshin's support both for egalitarianism and respect for endeavour, the conflict in Jinsai's thought is between egalitarianism and having one's position in the social order inherently transmitted. By insisting that the Way is easy to attain, Jinsai denies the importance of hard work, which Genshin respects. However, though Jinsai asserts equality among all people, he does not attempt to dismiss the distinction between the social classes which hinders the realisation of a non-hierarchical society in which all are equal.

Jinsai's class distinction can be partly related again to the historical circumstances of Tokugawa society. Following the Genpei war (1180–5), Japan was in a state of intermittent political turmoil until social stability was finally established in 1600 with the battle of Sekigahara. Jinsai was born twenty-seven years after this turning-point at a time when people were unlikely to have wanted to overturn the established social order yet again. Jinsai almost certainly shared this sentiment, and this is surely one of the reasons why he declined to subvert the notion of social rank. However, this assumption is insufficient to explain fully Jinsai's preference for a stable society based on the concept of *rei* (propriety) as "not overstepping the distinction between superiors and inferiors, as well as the higher and the lower". Nor does it explain his idea of *jin* (compassion) as the "virtue of compassion and love". While Hōnen regards a cooperative and collaborative situation as the ideal, Jinsai, too, idealises compassionate human relations in a well-ordered stable situation. We shall return to this point again later.

To summarise, the significance of Jinsai's thought is that, first, as is evident in his interpretation that the Way is like a road, he values the equality of the individual human over a distinction between the hereditary ability of the noble and the absence of ability in the vulgar. This assertion is also seen in his insistence that the Way is easy, which goes against a distinction between the capabilities of those who work hard and those who do not. Second, by insisting on the importance of *jin* as compassion, rather than *jin* as paternal caring mind or generosity, his thought introduces the latent possibility of subverting the consciousness of the existing social order. However, because he does retain some notion of class distinction which is incompatible with his own interpretation of *jin*, he ultimately leaves the system as it is. But, although Jinsai's thought is emancipative, it contains a certain inherent danger. This danger, as I have mentioned in reference to Saichō's *Commentary on the Protection of the Nation* (*Shugo kokkai shō*), and as we

30 *The strong and the weak in Japanese writings*

shall soon see in the discussion to follow, is that egalitarianism or "sympathy with the weak", as advocated by Hōnen and Jinsai as well as by Saichō, has the potential to develop into the nationalism of Fukuzawa Yukichi. A similar danger can also be seen in Kyokutei Bakin's *The Eight Dog Chronicles*. Shinoda Jun'ichi argues that there was interaction between Jinsai and Bakin, and that the concept of *jin* in *The Eight Dog Chronicles* is deeply influenced by the thought of Jinsai.[33] This examination of the differences between Hōnen's "selection of the one vehicle" and Jinsai's concept of *jin*, both of which are grounded in the egalitarian notion of "sympathy with the weak", prepares us for the analysis of the unity of the people evident in the egalitarianism of Saichō and Bakin and in the nationalism of Yukichi. These latter points will be explored in detail in the next section and also in Chapter 5.

2.5. Equality in battle and equality before God: Fukuzawa Yukichi (1835–1901) and Kitamura Tōkoku (1868–94)

2.5.1. Fukuzawa Yukichi

In the opening lines of *An Encouragement of Learning* (*Gakumon no susume*, 1872–6), Fukuzawa Yukichi declared his notion of egalitarianism in the well-known phrase "heaven does not create one man above or below another". His repeated assertions of the need for individual freedom, independence and self-respect pervaded the thought of modern Japan (Fukuzawa 1969: 1; 1980: 57; 1981c: 248–9, 264–7). Yukichi's message presented strikingly bright hope for the people of the early Meiji period, who, until then, had no means of emancipation from the strict class society of Confucian thought and thus no means of self-promotion in the feudal hierarchical system. As discussed in the previous section, although Jinsai's concept of *jin* suggested a subversion of the existing social order, in reality people in the Tokugawa era remained fettered by the Confucian principle of strict social ranking given at birth. In the sense that he rejected the notion of inherited social rank, Yukichi was without doubt emancipative, and his thought did at least liberate people from the oppressive power of the feudal hierarchical system in which those of low social rank were discriminated against without any hope of freeing themselves from their pregiven blood-family background. However, in the final instance, Yukichi's thought invited a new capitalist class distinction between the rich and the poor, and the strong and the weak.

Yukichi's early works, such as *An Encouragement of Learning* and *An Outline of a Theory of Civilization* (*Bunmei ron no gairyaku*, 1875), supported individual freedom and independence. However, critics have noted that later works, like *On the Nation's Right for the Common People's Understanding* (*Tsūzoku kokken ron*, 1878) and *Parting from Asia* (*Datsua ron*, 1885), are characterised by a problematic nationalism which includes support for the Sino-Japanese War and contempt for other people in Asia. Various arguments and controversies

The strong and the weak in Japanese writings 31

surround Yukichi's nationalism and contemptuous attitude towards Asia. Maruyama Masao, for instance, argues that in Yukichi's early work the Japanese people's individual freedom and their resultant independence, on the one hand, and the Japanese nation's independence and what should ideally have been its resultant treatment as an international equal by the great powers such as the United States and Great Britain, on the other hand, are related to the same principle of rationality and therefore equilibrated. Maruyama further claims that, though it was destined to be short-lived, the nationalism featured at this stage of Yukichi's writing was well balanced both for the author and for Japan. In contrast to this well-balanced nationalism, however, Maruyama notes that Yukichi's later work was produced in the context of the absolute irrational reality of international power relations of the time. Thus, although Yukichi regards rationality as superior to irrational force, he has no other choice than to argue for the realisation of Japan's independence by means of irrational power (Maruyama 2001: 119–61).[34]

In *Modern Japan and Liberalism* (*Kindai nihon to jiyūshugi*), Tanaka Hiroshi argues that Yukichi's nationalism is different from the ultra-nationalism which later led to Japan's aggressive expansion. He nevertheless points out that there are weaknesses in the understanding of liberalism and democracy presented in Yukichi's writings (Tanaka Hiroshi 1993: 107–8, 138, 147). In a different discussion, Tanaka notes that Yukichi's nationalism, and his advice to strengthen the forces of national defence, resulted in his eventual support for Japan's policy of "enriching the country and strengthening the army" (*fukoku kyōhei*). However, Tanaka argues that this insistence was permissible given the circumstances of the time (Tanaka Hiroshi 2000: 111).

Yasukawa Junosuke challenges Maruyama's and Tanaka's views, and argues that Yukichi's advocacy of individual independence is presented solely in the name of the independence of the Japanese nation-state. That is, in Yukichi's thought the purpose of human rights is to strengthen nationalism. Yasukawa further insists that Yukichi's contempt for other Asian people, his blind respect for loyalty and his understanding that the decisive factor in international relations is power all paved the way to Japan's wars of aggression against Korea, China and other Asian countries.[35] Yasukawa concludes his argument by saying that Yukichi emphasised the independence of the individual as a means of achieving national independence. Thus, his promotion of individual advancement comes with a demand for patriotic loyalty which requires the individual to lay down his life for the country (Yasukawa 1989: 26–7, 34).

In a recent detailed textual analysis, Ida Shin'ya and Hirayama Yō argue that the more discriminatory sections of Yukichi's writings were, in fact, not the work of Yukichi himself (Ida 2001; Hirayama 2004). Hirayama presents the hypothesis that many anonymous articles compiled in *The Complete Work of Fukuzawa Yukichi* (*Fukuzawa Yukichi zenshū*) (Tokyo: Iwanami, 1958–64), considered the most reliable edition of Yukichi's work, were written by Ishikawa Mikiaki, one of Yukichi's disciples and editor of an earlier collection

32 *The strong and the weak in Japanese writings*

of writing entitled *The Complete Work of Fukuzawa* (Tokyo: Kokumin Tosho, 1925–6). Hirayama argues that, after Yukichi's death, Ishikawa selected his own writings from the range of anonymous articles published in *Jiji shinpō*, a journal whose chief editor was Yukichi, and compiled them in *The Complete Work of Fukuzawa* (1925–6) under Yukichi's name. The current version of *The Complete Work of Fukuzawa Yukichi* (1958–64), edited by Keio University and published by Iwanami Shoten, closely followed the Ishikawa edition without any authentication of authorship. Hirayama claims that writing published under Yukichi's name features almost no discrimination against other Asian peoples. Thus, there is doubt as to whether Yukichi's attitude was, in fact, discriminatory; and it is, therefore, safer to argue on the basis of works published clearly under Yukichi's name.

It is on this understanding, and with reference to the studies cited above, that I shall examine Yukichi's writings. The discussion will focus on the relationship in Yukichi's thought between egalitarianism and endeavour, and egalitarianism and nationalism. First, if we look carefully at his view on individual equality, we see that Yukichi neither advocates egalitarianism itself nor wishes to console the weak as they are; rather he encourages the weak to become strong and win the power game. As Yasukawa Junosuke points out, Yukichi's famous statement from *An Encouragement of Learning* to the effect that "heaven does not create one man above or below another man" is, in fact, prefixed by the phrase "it is said that" (Yasukawa 2003: 256–72). Thus, the full sentence reads:

> *It is said that* heaven does not create one man above or below another man. . . . *Nevertheless*, as we broadly survey the human scene, we see the wise and the stupid, the rich and poor, the noble and lowly, the difference between whose conditions seems to be as great as that between the clouds and mud.
>
> (Fukuzawa 1969: 1; 1980: 57; my italics)

Yukichi further argues that this distinction depends on whether one has learning or not. As the title unmistakably indicates, and as Koizumi Shinzō also points out, rather than advocating the equality of man, Yukichi's purpose is to encourage people to study harder and learn more (Koizumi 1951: 377).[36] With the end of Tokugawa feudal society, all, ideally speaking, had an equal opportunity to participate in competition. However, it was those with greater learning who became stronger, defeated the weaker and won the power struggle. It is apparent that this message in Yukichi's writing was based on the principle of "respect for the strong".

On the issue of nationalism, I should like to focus on the claim made by Yukichi in *An Encouragement of Learning* that, for the purpose of the nation's independence, it is wiser to encourage the freedom and the independence of the people than to oppress them. In that work, Yukichi argues that a despotic nation controlled by a small number of rulers must be weaker

The strong and the weak in Japanese writings   33

than a nation which grants its people freedom and independence. This is because, while in the former people are forced by the ruler to fight unwillingly, in the latter people willingly fight to protect themselves and their nation. In his *An Outline of a Theory of Civilization*, Yukichi writes that the main objective of civilisation is to comfort one's life (material well-being) and sophisticate one's spirit. Thus, the independence of the nation is no more than a small part of the ultimate aim of civilisation as a whole. This understanding of civilisation seems at first sight to be compatible with notions of support for the weak. But Yukichi continues by arguing that in the present age Japan's independence is an urgent issue and the development of a civilised nation-state should occur for this purpose. Yukichi considers that the present world is governed by a power struggle derived from the rule of the jungle. Though not a desirable condition, the priority must be to survive.[37] Carmen Blacker explains that, having encountered the enormously strong power of the West and witnessed China's defeat in the Opium War in 1840–2, there was agreement among influential Japanese scholars of the time that "the spiritual secret of the strength and wealth of the western nations lay in the fact that their people were equal and therefore free". Blacker argues that "it was because western people enjoyed freedom and equal rights and were hence imbued with the spirit of enterprise, initiative and responsibility that the western nations had succeeded in becoming strong, rich and united" (Blacker 1964: 30). In this situation it was natural for Yukichi to advocate freedom and equal rights in order to form a strong and rich nation-state in which the people were firmly united.

As early as 1950, Ienaga Saburō conducted a detailed analysis of Yukichi's writings. Ienaga challenged the positive evaluation of Yukichi that then pervaded with the claim that capitalism was the driving force behind Yukichi's enterprise to modernise feudal Japan. Ienaga further argued that at first Yukichi optimistically believed that, since it was based on free competition, capitalism would logically lead to a free society. He realised only later that capitalist society was discriminatory rather than emancipative, in the sense that it widened the distinction between the rich and the poor. But, Ienaga continues, Yukichi never attempted to liberalise the social position of poor workers, attempting instead to justify the capitalist position. Finally, Ienaga concludes that Yukichi's utilitarian and pragmatic thought prevented him from helping the labouring class (Ienaga 1998: 191–212).[38]

I should like to add one point to Ienaga's conclusion that "respect for the strong" must be a major factor underlying Yukichi's utilitarianism and pragmatism. Yasukawa Junosuke mentions that the perspective of "might is right" is a constant element in Yukichi's approach to international relations (Yasukawa 1989: 22). In actuality, "might is right" underlies not only Yukichi's approach to international relations but also his whole thought. As Earl H. Kinmonth points out, in *An Encouragement of Learning* Yukichi introduced notions of human equality and rights as the starting-point in the competition for entry to the ruling strata of society – a competition which

34 *The strong and the weak in Japanese writings*

ultimately results in social inequality (Kinmonth 1978: 685–6). By locating Yukichi in a wider modernisation movement which included Europe as well as Japan, Alan Macfarlane also argues that, in essence, for most of his life, Yukichi "proclaimed the Enlightenment message; wealth and power would follow a rise in equality, liberty and individualism" (Macfarlane 2002: 245). Here, again, we might note that between the starting-point in Yukichi's thought of equality, liberty and individualism and the goal of wealth and power there must be competition in which the strong defeat the weak. It seems that any assessment of Yukichi's thought must be closely related to perceptions of modernisation. If we focus on rationality and regard modernisation positively, we shall probably consider Yukichi's maxim of "might is right" as pertinent for the purpose of development and progress. However, if we take a negative view of modernisation and condemn the need in this system to sacrifice the weak, we are likely to judge Yukichi as an oppressor.

Since Yukichi regards equality as a basic human right, as well as a nation's right, he treats egalitarianism as an ideal both for the individual and for the nation-state. At the same time, he has a clear view that the present world is governed by power, both at the individual and the national level. Nevertheless, he does not attempt to realise an ideal society consistent with the ideal of equality; rather he approves of reality, at least for the time being, and thus endeavours to teach the people and also the rulers of the nation how to win the power game. In order to win this game, people must be properly educated and think rationally, while a nation must give its people freedom, independence and self-respect (Maruyama 2001: 142–9).

Yukichi's advocacy of individual independence, freedom and egalitarianism originally arose from a strong moral feeling against what he understood as the unreasonable wielding of violent and despotic authority in the Tokugawa period. Like all values, however, this kind of moral value has various faces. For instance, as we have seen, Yukichi's individual freedom is, on the one hand, emancipative from the blind determinism of feudalism; but, on the other hand, it paves the way to individual competition, sacrificing the defeated weak. Furthermore, Yukichi's assertion of egalitarianism clearly supports his advocacy of nationalism, which, as we have seen, is exactly the same process evident in Saichō's thought. An ideology of egalitarianism clearly serves to maintain social unity. Thus, when conflict with other societies is imminent, egalitarianism is often urged in order to survive. In other words, egalitarianism and assisting the weak can be used to cement the bond between people in a given society in order to compete with other societies. Yukichi's insistence well coincides with this formula (Fukuzawa 1981b: 71–6).

In the field of anthropology, Christopher Boehm's study supports a connection between egalitarianism and intergroup warfare. Boehm argues that, while the revolutionary process empowered groups with egalitarianism, the despotism often associated with this process merely strengthened the position of select individuals. Although the majority of scholars have rejected

The strong and the weak in Japanese writings 35

group selection as a viable level of natural selection, Boehm points to its possibilities in human society. He further notes the relation between egalitarianism and warfare as follows:

> As the egalitarian syndrome helped to reshape human nature in the direction of altruism over hundreds or thousands of generations, the probability of intensive warfare rose precisely because this risky activity is predicated on a strong capacity for patriotic self-sacrifice – and therefore on altruistic genes. Intensive warfare with genocide may not have affected the species greatly during the early development of innate altruism, but once altruistic genes had time to become well established in the human gene pool it was far more likely that intergroup conflict would rise to an intensive level, with territorial displacements and massacres.

Boehm eventually concludes that, had we not invented both morality and the egalitarian syndrome, the potential for intensive genocidal warfare would not have arisen (Boehm 1999: 222–3, 254).

This understanding of the relationship between freedom, egalitarianism, in-group competition and intergroup warfare reminds us of Pierre Clastres' claim that the uncivilised society declares war against other societies and that, in order to do so, it must maintain an undivided single totality. In contrast, Clastres continues, the state is a class society divided into those who exercise power and those who submit to it (Clastres 1994: 165–6).[39] This entails a transformation from the incessant war between societies to the diplomatic peaceful negotiation between states and also from the classless society of undivided single totality to the class society consisting of various collections of individuals. Among individuals, respect for the strong and sympathy with the weak doubtlessly emerge in the latter context. Intergroup war between primitive societies is replaced now with intragroup competition between individuals. Although the latter is presented under the cloak of the concept of freedom, it brings with it the notion of class distinction. At the same time, we can presume that, in order to maintain society, the concept of equality is urged. Thus, the idea of egalitarianism in civilised society emerges in order to retrieve the original undivided single totality lost in the process of forming the class divisions of the state.

As in Yukichi's case, freedom, requiring emancipation of the weak from the despotic oppression of the strong, and equality, demanding a lack of discrimination between the weak and the strong, originally emerged to emancipate weak people from a small group of despots. But ideas of freedom and equality might have also served to beautify the promotion of individual aggression (freedom) while at the same time maintaining the formation of a totalitarian society (equality) for the purpose of between-group warfare. In this paradigm, the demand for equal treatment may result in a certain degree of release from a politically discriminatory society. However, it also

36 *The strong and the weak in Japanese writings*

means the approval of the despot's compensatory pledge to lead a unified fight against other societies. That is to say, the acquisition of freedom from despotic oppression and equality against discrimination become the means to compete for progress through freedom for individual competition and equality for intergroup warfare. We can see here how skilfully and cunningly the urge to fight in order to evolve appropriates the concepts of freedom and equality.

As I mentioned in the introduction, the idea of equality introduced into Japan by Yukichi had been problematised from the seventeenth to the nincteenth centuries in Europe in conjunction with the emergence of notions such as "nation", "national character" and "nation-state".[40] The concepts of equality presented during this period by Thomas Hobbes's *Leviathan* (1651), John Locke's *Two Treatises of Government* (1689), Jean-Jacques Rousseau's *Discourse on the Origin of Inequality* (1754) and *Social Contract* (1762),[41] and Jeremy Bentham's *An Introduction to the Principles of Morals and Legislation* (1789) share at least three features that are important for our discussion. First, they generally consider that equality – regardless of whether it is natural or physical equality, or jurisdictional or political equality[42] – is defined as a fundamental and naturally given attribute of the human being.[43] While men (sic) were regarded as *born naturally different* in the despotic absolute monarchy, or aristocratic or feudal society, these thinkers regarded men as *naturally born free and equal*. Since, at the time they were writing, the notion of "culture" was regarded as innate rather than constructed, from a contemporary perspective the discourses proposed by these theorists naïvely underestimate the role of culture. For, as Hannah Arendt later cautioned, human equality is, like any other culturally constructed attribute, not given by nature; we are only bestowed and guaranteed equality as members of a cooperative group. For Arendt, the highest organisation bestowing and guaranteeing equality is the state (Arendt 2004: 378–83). However, the European definition of equality and freedom as grounded in human nature resulted in, intentionally or unintentionally, concealing the relationship between these concepts and the state. Nevertheless, as Arendt points out, equality and freedom are confined ultimately in the nation-state and cannot extend beyond its boundary. We need to be aware that freedom, equality and fraternity are culturally constructed in exactly the same way as notions such as class, race and ethnicity.

The second salient feature of European discourses of human equality concerns the "state of nature" – the hypothetical condition of humanity before the state's foundation. For instance, it is well known that Hobbes considered the original human condition as a state of every man at war against another (Hobbes 1996: 84–5). Locke, too, in the final analysis, asserted that we are governed by the "law of the jungle" or the "law of the strongest", and that we need to resort ultimately to the power of violence (Locke 1967: 289, 348–9, 368–9).[44] The idea of the social contract proposed by both Hobbes and Locke is grounded in the notion of conflict. Both regard the individual as fundamentally selfish and in a state of conflict. In order to protect one's property, he (sic) must unite with friendly others and form the nation-state. Conversely, in order to protect our nation, we have to unite with those in our community to fight against other communities. Here, the ideas of individual freedom, equality and fraternity are utilised in competition for the survival of the nation-state. As Mary Kaldor explains, the individual rights that citizens enjoy in peacetime are exchanged for the abrogation of those rights in wartime. This is because, in time of war, citizens become part of a collectivity – the nation – and must be ready to die for the state to which they belong (Kaldor 2003: 47). We have to fight for our nation-state at the risk of our lives, because it is our nation-state that bestows freedom and equality on us. The idea of equality is here exploited, so to speak, for the purpose of competition between like states.

The third point is that, in most cases, the realisation of equality and freedom that marks the change from absolute monarchy to the nation-state was brought about by violent revolution. The nation-state was born by means of accumulating this violence and concentrating it in the newly born national government while prohibiting its use by others. The purpose of this violence is to punish transgressors of the state's law and also to demonstrate force against other nation-states. According to Max Weber, "the state is the form of human community that (successfully) lays claim to the *monopoly of legitimate physical violence* within a particular territory" (Weber 2004: 33; Weber's italics).[45] Therefore, no sooner had the concepts of freedom, equality and fraternity been born than they served as justification for one nation-state to fight another. Thus, rather than being rendered obsolete, official violence was redirected in a manner that well explains the many wars of the twentieth century.[46] Although equality was originally intended to liberate the common people from the despotism of royalty and nobility, this was only achieved by confining ideas such as freedom, equality and fraternity within the boundaries of the nation-state for the purpose of declaring war against other states. Yukichi's egalitarianism, too, followed the above variety of European egalitarianism in the sense of being confined within the nation, being exploited for the purpose of competition between nation-states, and in relying upon violence and power to achieve the ideal society.

In our discussion to this point of the contrast between the thought of Hōnen and of Yukichi, we have noted that, while the former directs us towards social reformation as well as the reconfiguration of ideology and desire, the latter confirms and follows the current social model based on modernism and capitalism. There is one more important difference between the egalitarianism of Hōnen, and of Jinsai, and that of Yukichi and the associated ideas of Saichō. This is the fact that, while the former deny endeavour, the latter encourage people to work hard. By rejecting endeavour and effort, and regarding the human condition as grounded in cooperation and collaboration, Hōnen and Jinsai ultimately resist development and progress. And by rejecting development and progress they refuse to make egalitarianism a means to

38   *The strong and the weak in Japanese writings*

evolution or competitive victory, keeping it rather as a final goal. From this point of view, in order to break the relation between egalitarianism and nationalism, as well as between freedom and individual competition, it might be necessary, for other purposes, to reject the reification and appropriation of the idea of equality and freedom. But of course, as we have mentioned, by rejecting development and progress, Hōnen and Jinsai inevitably arrive at a position of stagnation. We need always to bear this problem in mind.

In the West, following the tradition of Hobbes, Locke and, especially, Rousseau,[47] Karl Marx further developed the idea of equality. In his *Critique of the Gotha Programme* (1875), Marx repudiates as a *bourgeois right* the "equal" right manifested in the formula that "the individual producer receives back from society – after the deductions have been made – exactly what he [or she] gives it" (Marx 1989: 85–6). This is because Marx sees this as a principle that evaluates humans as mere workers and producers, rather than as whole human beings. To receive from society resources equal to what one contributes inevitably results in a situation in which those who are stronger can give more and thus receive more. This formula creates a competitive situation in which only the strong can win and in which the strong will be rewarded more than the weak. Marx, however, opposes this model, seeking to shift "from each according to his abilities, to each according to his needs" (Marx 1989: 87). Thus, the ideal "state of nature" imagined by Marx is not the competitive society, but one in which all have access to wealth and peace. The problem faced by Marxists, however, is that, first, they hold that human equality can only be achieved through a process of class conflict and revolutionary struggle. Thus, the issue of violence remains. Marxism, of course, suffered considerable damage as a practical option with the fall of the Soviet Union and China's shift to a capitalist economy. We might note that Hōnen's and Jinsai's egalitarianism also resulted in stagnation and economic destruction. Nevertheless, the Marxist ideal of equality based on the assumption that the "equality" of any given individual is immeasurable by any single standard, and that all humans are naturally born to be respected equally, continues to hold sway with many thinkers throughout the world.

For instance, John Rawls, a more recent egalitarian thinker, insists that we must reconsider the principles of justice based on Hobbes's and Locke's "state of nature" on the grounds that these principles are selected behind a "veil of ignorance". According to Rawls, "no one knows his place in society, his class position or social status, nor does any one know his fortune in the distribution of natural assets and abilities, his intelligence, strength, and the like" (Rawls 1973: 12). Cognisant of the fact that we do not know how much any individual contributes to society, Rawls argues his general conception of justice as follows: "All social primary goods – liberty and opportunity, income and wealth, and the bases of self-respect – are to be distributed equally" (Rawls 1973: 303).[48]

The above discussion distinguishes at least two understandings of "equality". First is the equality of people in a nation-state, an entity born of the overthrow of the unequal aristocratic and feudal class society of the past. Equality in this sense ultimately serves to develop and preserve the nation-state, leading to a state of conflict with like states. Having been granted equality by the nation-state, individual members are obligated to fight on its behalf. The first variant of equality is apparent in the idea of egalitarianism propagated by Hobbes and Locke in the West, and by Saichō, Sorai and Yukichi in Japan. The second concept of equality is humanistic equality based on Marx's formula of "from each according to his abilities, to each according to his needs". This variety is also evident in John Rawls's notion of equality behind the "veil of ignorance", and in the work of Hōnen and Jinsai in Japan. As we shall soon see, it is also related to Tōkoku's ideas of egalitarianism derived from a denial of the value of endeavour and effort, resistance to development and progress, and an understanding that cooperation and collaboration are the basis of the human condition. This version of equality does not operate as a meritocratic tool for conflict with others, but as a tool with which to realise the emancipation of all humanity from discrimination. But, as I have cautioned a number of times, in this variety of egalitarianism, we must also be prepared for stagnation.

In addition to these two positions – egalitarianism for competition or for cooperation – we can also view egalitarianism from the perspective of globalisation. If we are confined to a limited community or, specifically, to the nation-state, we face the dilemma of whether to fight or to collaborate. Hence, broader emancipation might be realised by expanding the concept of society through globalisation to include all human beings. Notions of egalitarianism, then, would be transformed by a clear sense of equal and fair respect for human nature rather than by the need to fight others. However, this would not solve the problem of stagnation and would, moreover, lead to the human race being confined in a society pervaded by a single value with no expectation of change.

2.5.2. Kitamura Tōkoku

As noted previously, in contrast to Yukichi's adage of "might is right" and the advocacy of utilitarianism and pragmatism as a means of winning the social power game, Christianity was a system of thought which sought human emancipation in an ideal world. This position is typified in the writing of Kitamura Tōkoku. Janet Walker noted that in a letter dated 18 August 1887 to his future wife, Ishizaka Minako, Tōkoku wrote that he had decided in 1884 to sacrifice himself for the benefit of the people by devoting all his energy to politics. In order to achieve this, Tōkoku explained, he needed to become a great philosopher and destroy the new Social Darwinist school of "survival of the fittest" popular in Europe (Kitamura Tōkoku 1950–5, 3: 167–8; Walker 1979: 67).[49] In his short essay "Who Will Be the Final Victor?" ("Saigo no shōrisha wa dare zo", 1892), Tōkoku writes:

40 *The strong and the weak in Japanese writings*

> Life is a history of war. . . . The strong slaughter the weak; the powerful, the powerless; the clever, the dull; the productive, the unproductive. . . . Cold-hearted social scientists say: "Victory or defeat is a result of social class division. The loser has sufficient reason to be defeated, and there are good grounds for the victor to win. Negligence, mistakes, dullness and resourcelessness, these are the basis of the non-achiever. Industriousness, self-endeavour, intellect and strategy, these are the foundation of fame." I believe, however, that universal affairs are never only subject to social and economic rules.
>
> (Kitamura Tōkoku, 1950–5, 1: 317; my translation)

By clearly opposing Yukichi's assertion, Tōkoku here presents as the final victor the Christian God, who offers a harmonious reconciliation rectifying the inconsistencies of the phenomenal world. Tōkoku finds in Christianity an insistence on respecting the neglected common people more than highly acclaimed heroes. In Tōkoku's concept of harmonious reconciliation, we find some similarity with Hōnen's notion of reverence and with Jinsai's concepts of *rei* and *jin* – all of which idealise cooperation and collaboration. Janet Walker, however, finds a similarity between Yukichi and Tōkoku in that both are interested in promoting a spirit of freedom or independence among the Japanese of their day. Yet she points out the difference by saying that

> where Fukuzawa's interest was social and political, his theories influenced by Western social liberalism, Tōkoku's was primarily religious or spiritual. Where Fukuzawa wished to create good, responsible citizens, Tōkoku's desire was to awaken the spiritual selfhood of the individual.
>
> (Walker 1979: 69)

A further distinction which can be added to Walker's contrast is that, while Yukichi displayed "respect for the strong", Tōkoku demonstrated "sympathy with the weak". As Makibayashi Kōji has noted, by rejecting the utilitarian and materialistic view of Social Darwinist notions of "survival of the fittest" evident in Yukichi's thought, Tōkoku rejected discrimination against the socially disempowered and those stigmatised variously as negligent, full of mistakes, dull and lacking resourcefulness (Makibayashi 2000: 128–30).[50]

In this regard, it is useful to examine the controversy between Tōkoku and Yamaji Aizan (1864–1917).[51] Aizan insists that literature should be a form of "enterprise" (*jigyō*). In other words, literature should contribute to the good of the world and should benefit mankind. In order for this to be the case, Aizan insists that literature should portray the enterprise of the strong hero. The common people will show interest in this hero and thus be educated. This thinking is typical of "respect for the strong" and "might is right" ideologies. Tōkoku, taking the viewpoint of the common people, challenges Aizan's view of literature and criticises worship for the hero. He attacks the principle of respect for the strong hero and contempt for the weak

The strong and the weak in Japanese writings 41

or mediocre underlying Aizan's concept of "enterprise". Through debate with Aizan, Tōkoku, like Hōnen, sought to overturn the current value system which placed the heroic enterprise higher than the everyday lives of the common people.

But Tōkoku was surrounded at the time by the vast current of thinking influenced by the "might is right" maxim which characterised the early-modern period in Japan, a time when the weak were mercilessly colonised and oppressed by the strong. Thus, he had no other way to oppose the assertions of Aizan and Yukichi, each of whom advocated the growth of strength in the real world at the level of both the individual and the nation-state, than to imagine the ideal human relationship in a fictional world. Against Aizan, who insists that literature's mission is to benefit man in the real world, Tōkoku wrote a series of essays in which he claimed that literature has its own laws removed from the real world and is something which leads man to the "ideal world".[52] According to Tōkoku, sympathetic identification with the weak is realised only in literature and in the fictional world.

Tōkoku's ideal world is also found in his idea of love.[53] In a letter dated 4 September 1887, addressed to Ishizaka Minako, Tōkoku writes:

> Dearest,
> As you know, Japanese people's love is selfish. They love with and are in part led by their carnal desire. The easy-going way of their loving is just like playing with toys. But our love is different from our desire. We love each other with our hearts and our hopes. Our love is stronger than our desire. Our bodies are still not united, but we feel we are together.
> (Kitamura Tōkoku 1950–5, 3: 185; my translation)

Kinoshita Naoe (1869–1937), a journalist and novelist, revealed at a "Tōkoku Study Meeting" held in 1933 that there were two passages that deeply touched his heart in his younger days; one was Yukichi's "heaven does not create one man above or below another man", and the other was Tōkoku's "Love is a secret key which opens the door to life" (Kitamura Tōkoku 1950–5, 1: 254). Naoe continued that Tōkoku was the first thinker in Japan seriously to consider the meaning of love; until that time people regarded love between men and women as something unclean (Kinoshita 1972: 283–5). Love has at least two different aspects: carnal or physical desire and a lofty spiritual adoration of human qualities. Confucianism appears to focus on the first aspect, teaching people to avoid sexual love as far as possible by separating men from objects of desire.[54] However, inspired by Christianity, Tōkoku focuses on the beauty of the latter element of love, long obscured in Japan and the East by the importance accorded to the former. Looking at this issue from a slightly different perspective, as Janet Walker comments, the proper feelings between a man and his wife in pre-Meiji Japan had been generosity on the part of the husband and gratitude on the part of the wife. Tōkoku attempted to replace the ideal of vertical, reciprocal obligation that had been

42 *The strong and the weak in Japanese writings*

the basis of social relationships in the past with a new, horizontal, egalitarian ideal based on love (Walker 1979: 81–3). Interestingly, the contrast between Yukichi's high regard for the strong and Tōkoku's sympathy for the weak parallels Sorai's advocacy of respect for the strong and Jinsai's egalitarian attitude.

We have seen how the issues of "respect for the strong" and "sympathy with the weak" have long been discussed in Japanese religious, philosophical, political and literary thought. In fact, this division has been a subject of debate since the ninth century, as is evident in the contrast between the thought of Saichō and of Tokuitsu. With his high regard for inborn ability, Tokuitsu believed that, no matter how hard one practised, one could not attain enlightenment in the absence of innate ability. In contrast, Saichō and Ryōgen emphasise acquired ability and assert that, no matter how poor one's inherited ability, if one practises hard enough, Buddhahood can be attained. Against these three, each of whom focuses on either inborn ability or acquired ability, Genshin seeks to help those who lack both. Nevertheless, he is inconsistent and wavers between a desire to "admire the strong and the good" and also to "sympathise with the weak and the evil". In a challenge to Genshin's position, Hōnen argues that it is Amida's desire to help the weak. He consequently guarantees that all sentient beings, regardless of their birth origin, acquired ability or self-endeavour, can be reborn in the Pure Land after death merely by calling Amida's name ten times. In contrast, Myōe highly values human effort and hard work.

Against these Buddhist thinkers who attempt to help the weak and the infirm to find paradise in the afterlife, Confucian Itō Jinsai declares that a peaceful and stable society is attainable in this world if all people follow their humanistic emotions. But, like Genshin, there are contradictions in Jinsai's desire both to "admire the higher social classes" and to "sympathise with the lower social classes". Ultimately, although his interpretation of *jin* has the potential to threaten the social order, Jinsai declines to subvert the feudal hierarchical system. Fukuzawa Yukichi removes the shackles of Confucian class distinction and declares that all people are fundamentally equal and free. He emphasises, however, the importance of hard work, education, cleverness and the endeavour of the individual. Equality is necessary to Yukichi in order that fair competition can occur. Kitamura Tōkoku claims egalitarianism as his ideal and thereby challenges the realistic, pragmatic and utilitarian attitude represented by Yukichi and Aizan. But he can only locate his notion of harmonious human relations in an ideal Christian world or the imaginary and fictional world of literature.

To summarise, the tradition of respecting acquired strength, hard work and ability flows from Saichō to Myōe, Yamazaki Ansai, Ogyū Sorai, Fukuzawa Yukichi and Yamaji Aizan, and has parallels to the positions of Hobbes and Locke in Europe. Genshin's position in relation to "respect for the strong" and "sympathy with the weak" is characterised by contradiction. A stream of unconditional egalitarianism, similar to that of Marx and

Rawls in the West, originated in Hōnen and was partly followed by Itō Jinsai and Kitamura Tōkoku. Maruyama Masao has high regard for Ogyū Sorai and Fukuzawa Yukichi, and we might say that Sorai–Yukichi–Maruyama form a progressive modernist tradition of thought which gives value to rationalism, endeavour and strength. Hōnen's egalitarianism, partly adopted by Jinsai and Tōkoku, on the other hand, is currently subscribed to by a number of scholars, including Taira Masayuki and Hakamaya Noriaki. We might note that the champion of egalitarianism, however, although his interest is in Shinran rather than in Hōnen, is literary critic and social commentator Yoshimoto Takaaki.

3 Ugly ladies in *The Tale of Genji*

3.1. Two different views in *The Tale of Genji*

On the basis of the ideas established in Chapter 2, let me now examine *The Tale of Genji*, one of the highest achievements in the history of Japanese literature. Completed in the early eleventh century, this work focuses on relations between the strong, beautiful and sophisticated and the weak, ugly and indecent.

During the previous two decades, two major perspectives in the study of *The Tale of Genji* have developed both inside and outside Japan. The first is the perspective of narrative study and the second the study of power structures in the text, including the feminist viewpoint.[1] Celebrated achievements written in English by, among others, Haruo Shirane (1987), Norma Field (1987), Richard H. Okada (1991), Doris G. Bargen (1997), Edith Sarra (1999) and Tomiko Yoda (2004) all deal with at least one of these two perspectives. Prior to that, for about fifty years from the 1930s to the 1980s, many scholars investigated the order of writing of the first thirty-three chapters of the narrative. Although this kind of analysis, well documented in a number of previous English-language *Genji* studies, is now considered out of date, I should like to revisit it here.[2] As we shall see as the discussion proceeds, the order of writing of the first thirty-three chapters, especially in relation to the two different groups of characters in the story which scholars suppose were written at two different times, is, in my view, closely related to the strong–weak issue. Let me first briefly summarise scholarship addressing the order in which the early chapters of *Genji* were written. The focus will be on the likelihood or otherwise of a change in the author's philosophy of life – an issue which I regard as related to the strong–weak binary. Abe (Aoyagi) Akio and Takeda Munetoshi each separately identified two distinctive streams in the early *Genji* chapters.[3] Taking the title of the first chapter of each stream, Abe called the former the Wakamurasaki group and the latter the Hahakigi group. Takeda identified the groups according to the principal heroine, naming the former the Murasaki group (Abe's Wakamurasaki group) and the latter the Tamakazura group (Abe's Hahakigi group).

Abe and Takeda independently demonstrated that each group had its own storyline and its own major characters, and that the newly introduced characters in the Hahakigi/Tamakazura group rarely appeared in the Wakamurasaki/Murasaki group. Based on this and other evidence, they concluded that the author, Murasaki Shikibu, wrote the Hahakigi/Tamakazura chapters after the Wakamurasaki/Murasaki group, inserting the former into the text later.[4] The two scholars then both raised the question: Why did the author, Murasaki Shikibu, choose to undertake such a complicated process of text production? Why write the new chapters featuring new stories of the Hahakigi/Tamakazura group and add them to the completed stories of the Wakamurasaki/Murasaki group? Both Abe and Takeda concluded that a dramatic change occurred in the thought of Murasaki Shikibu and, therefore, in her basic attitude towards *Genji*. Abe, for instance, sees the author becoming more mature both as a person and as a writer. He argues that the notion of beauty in the Wakamurasaki group is superficial, while that in the Hahakigi group is more humanistic. In the first group, symbols of beauty predictably include elements of the gorgeous, such as cherry blossoms, autumn leaves and the palace. Symbols of beauty in the second group, however, are simple and quiet, as exemplified by a rainy night, a provincial governor's mansion, or a poor shabby house in a dirty cluttered street. Similarly, while the Buddhist knowledge promulgated in the Wakamurasaki group is shallow, that in the Hahakigi group is profound; and where the main Wakamurasaki stories are sanitised love-affairs between good-looking aristocratic ladies and gentlemen, notable for their lack of complexity, those in the Hahakigi group are complicated by the subtle ambiguities of human psychology (Abe Akio 1969–82, 3: 41–51). Takeda similarly argues that, while the Murasaki sequence is an optimistic story of Genji's loves and successes with a mostly happy ending, the Tamakazura sequence is a pessimistic account of characters in the throes of various agonies. He argues that, by adding the Tamakazura sequence to the Murasaki material, the author attempted to make a simple tale complex, a mediocre story excellent, and a superficial view of life profound (Takeda 1950b: 71–80).[5]

I should like to suggest here that the coexistence of the Wakamurasaki/Murasaki and Hahakigi/Tamakazura groups demonstrates the contrast between the two contradictory ideologies underlying the tale. Thus, we shall see that "admiration for the strong, young, beautiful, decent and sophisticated" resides in the former group while "sympathy with the weak, infirm, old, ugly, indecent and unsophisticated" is evident in the latter. It will also become apparent that the different themes and motifs variously associated with the Wakamurasaki/Murasaki and Hahakigi/Tamakazura groups are in the final analysis synthesised into the polyphony of the whole story. In the body of this chapter I shall focus on the "sympathy with the weak, ugly, old and indecent", and examine how characters with these attributes are depicted in the tale.

46   The Tale of Genji

3.2. The weak, low and fragile

The Tale of Genji first introduces the Kiritsubo (Paulownia) lady in the "Paulownia" chapter as a weak, defenceless woman lacking strong backing (I 4–5; S 3; T I: 3). The narrative leads the reader to sympathise with this ailing and powerless heroine. After the death of her father, a grand councillor, the Kiritsubo lady was raised by her old-fashioned mother. Nevertheless, she carries the burden of her father's longing that she rise in the world. In the words of her mother, the family's hopes all reside in the girl (I 13; S 9; T I: 9). As a concubine of the emperor, the Kiritsubo lady finds herself in competition at court with the Kokiden lady, the emperor's principal wife and a daughter of the Minister of the Right. Kokiden is also the mother of the emperor's first son (Suzaku). From a family of the highest social class, she is depicted as wilful, abrasive, arrogant and intractable (I 17; S 12; T I: 11). Given the strength of her antagonist, the Kiritsubo lady is destined to be defeated. She disappears from the narrative following her premature death after giving birth to the infant Genji, the tale's hero. We can read the story of Kiritsubo as the story of a beautiful young woman who ultimately fails in her attempt to promote her family. She eventually dies in a power struggle with ladies of a higher rank while trying to raise herself from her lowly social position by means of attracting the emperor.[6] Even here, at the outset of the tale, there is a strong sense of the strong–weak struggle that develops as the tale progresses.

Following the story of Kiritsubo, the narrative tells of the young Genji's marriage to Aoi, a daughter of the Minister of the Left. This section of the *Tale of Genji* highlights the conflict between the powerful Kokiden lady/Minister of the Right faction and the Genji/Minister of the Left group. There is also an introduction to the activities of the Hahakigi/Tamakazura group, which operates outside the sphere of the main political power struggle. This introduction occurs through an account of Genji's love-affair with Locust Shell (Utsusemi), a wife of the vice-governor of Iyo. Utsusemi is portrayed as nothing remarkable and thus nicely represents a woman of the middle grade (I 71, 87, 228; S 45, 51, 126; T I: 41, 49, 126). She is the daughter of a deceased guards officer who had once planned to send his daughter to the court. For a time she had also come to the attention of Emperor Kiritsubo. Utsusemi's son-in-law, the governor of Kii, regards her subdued demeanour as the result of her failing to gain a place at the court (I 64, 71; S 41, 45). In this sense she is, like the Kiritsubo lady, also burdened by her failure to fulfil her father's wish to raise her family's standing in the world. As Haruo Shirane points out, Utsusemi regrets having married an elderly provincial governor, believing that, were she not his wife, she might well be happy. In her heart of hearts, she feels that she might receive Genji gladly, however seldom, if only she were still at home with the memory of her late parents rather than settled in a marriage for life. However, it is too late now for such thoughts, and she makes up her mind to remain stubbornly unresponsive to Genji until the end (I 75–6; S 48; T I: 44; Shirane 1987: 64–6).

The Tale of Genji 47

Some scholars and critics highlight the importance of Utsusemi's suppressed pride, and of her grief and agony at not being able to be loved by Genji, a man of higher social rank. They consider Utsusemi the archetype of similarly blighted women in the story, including the Kiritsubo lady, the Fujitsubo lady, Suetsumuhana, Orange Blossoms (Hanachirusato), the Akashi lady, and Murasaki. Some include Ōigimi from the later Uji chapters in this group.[7] However, I would argue that commentary of this nature overly emphasises the feelings of frustration common to these women. Although each woman in the group suffers from being suppressed by a man of higher rank, we can detect subtle differences in their responses. For instance, while Kiritsubo assumes the mantle of her family's ambition and remains at court, Utsusemi has not been at court and remains very modest. Though she is regretful, she does not have a strong personal ambition to rise in the world.

In conjunction with the conflation of the frustration experienced by the women listed above, previous discussions on Utsusemi have focused on the perspective of romantic desire represented by Kiritsubo, Murasaki and other ambitious ladies. Commentary of this kind has therefore focused on Utsusemi's agony at having her romantic desire suppressed. It seems to me that the point of Utsusemi's story is not so much her regret and resentment as her final decision to satisfy herself with her present situation. She repeatedly rejects Genji's love, knowing that her present situation and her social rank cannot match his. Thus, rather than being the story of a weak young woman's frustrated ambition, Utsusemi's tale is one of a middle-rank lady who acknowledges her limitations and resolves to satisfy herself with her present situation. The subtle but significant difference between the Kiritsubo and Utsusemi stories is that, while the point of the former is Kiritsubo's wish to rise, albeit through parental pressure, the latter relates Utsusemi's acceptance, albeit unwilling, of her own social position. These are important points of difference related to the strong–weak issue to which we shall later return.

The next heroine to appear in the tale is Evening Faces (Yūgao) (Hahakigi/ Tamakazura group) whose father was a captain in the guards. Both Yūgao's parents are dead, and she is considerably lower in rank than the other ladies featured in the opening chapters of *Genji*. Yūgao's father adored his daughter, but his career did not go well, and his life came to an early and disappointing end. She somehow came to the notice of Genji's companion, Tō-no-chūjō, while he was still a lieutenant. Although Tō-no-chūjō was very attentive for about three years, his visits ended one autumn following a rather awful threat from his wife's father's house, but not before he had fathered Yūgao's child, later named Tamakazura. Here, again, is the story of a power struggle disguised beneath the tale of a young woman's romance. Yūgao is often portrayed as having a fragile beauty. Besides the expression *rōtashi* ("precious", "dear" and "pathetic"), which Haruo Shirane reports as frequently used to describe this retiring young woman (Shirane 1987: 68), the adjectives used in reference to Yūgao include *wakabi* ("childlike", "girlish", "young", or "naïve") (I 113, 115, 124; S 65, 67, 72),

48   The Tale of Genji

komekashi ("girlish", or "naïve") (I 116; S 67; T I: 63), *aeka* ("delicate" or "frail") (I 140; S 79; T I: 76) and *hakanage* ("weak" or "frail") (I 140; S 80; T I: 76). She is timid and frightened when there is no need to be afraid (I 122; S 71; T I: 67), and as frail and defenceless as a child (I 122, 124; S 71, 72; T I: 67, 68). In his comparison of Yūgao and Utsusemi, Masuda Shigeo regards Utsusemi as a clever woman who knows her place well, while he finds in Yūgao a feminine beauty which sexually attracts men. Masuda regards these two women as archetypes of the two kinds of women featured in *Genji*. He further argues that the Murasaki lady is a combination of the two (Masuda Shigeo 1980b: 1–22). Although his argument has merit, I should like to focus on the similarity of Utsusemi and Yūgao, rather than on the difference between them. As characters in the Hahakigi/Tamakazura group, they should have characteristics in common with other members of the same group and which contrast with characters in the Wakamurasaki/Murasaki group. Once we adopt this perspective, it becomes clear that the two women are depicted in a very similar manner in the sense that Utsusemi reconciles herself to a low position in the social hierarchy while Yūgao refuses to become mature. Unlike the Kiritsubo lady, who endures and resists the threat from her rival, the Kokiden lady, finally dying as if defeated in battle, Utsusemi and Yūgao decline to fight the social forces aligned against them. In the same way that Utsusemi distances herself from a romantic love-affair with Genji, Yūgao runs from Tō-no-chūjō and hides herself at her nurse's house in the western part of the city (I 138–9; S 79). Lacking the ambition to be strong, these women are content to remain weak.

The "Lavender" (Wakamurasaki) chapter (Wakamurasaki/Murasaki group) introduces the young Murasaki, who is charming, perfectly beautiful and, at 10, still very young. Murasaki's mother was the daughter of a lord inspector, a prince who took great pains with his daughter's education. He had hoped to send the girl to court, though he died before that ambition could be realised. Later, Prince Hyōbu began visiting this fatherless daughter in secret, and they had a daughter (Murasaki). But his formal wife was jealous and tormented Murasaki's mother until the latter wasted away from worry (I 162; S 90). Here is yet another story of a middle-ranking lady who, like Kiritsubo, Utsusemi and Yūgao, is burdened by her family's ambition but who fails in her attempt to attain a higher social rank. While these are the circumstances into which Murasaki was born, she is, like Kiritsubo, a woman who certainly aspires to strength.[8]

It is useful to note that underlying the stories of Kiritsubo, Utsusemi, Yūgao and Murasaki is the struggle by these young women to raise themselves and their families in the world in response to the desire of their fathers. Therefore, we can say that one of the motifs in the early chapters of *Genji* is that of a lower-rank woman in a weak position, or married to a provincial governor, or fragile and childish, or still very young, who shoulders the ambitions of her father or maternal grandfather and thus seeks to raise her family's social standing through the love of a higher-ranking man. However, as I have suggested, there is at least one striking difference between the heroines in the Wakamurasaki/Murasaki group and those in the Hahakigi/Tamakazura group. This is the fact that, while the former – Kiritsubo and Murasaki – are ambitious, the latter – Utsusemi and Yūgao – are modest. Murasaki may appear on the surface still too young to be ambitious. However, in addition to the maternal grandfather's expectations placed upon her mother, the bud of hidden ambition is often seen in the clever character of the child Murasaki herself. Although still very young, she is depicted as having a talent for playing musical instruments (I 255; S 142) and composing poems (I 298; S 164). This competence reveals her ambition without which it would be difficult to develop her talents. We also know that she is decidedly ambitious in her later life with Genji. In contrast, Utsusemi and Yūgao have in common an unpretentious and tranquil character completely lacking in ambition, aggressive spirit, or the wish to compete with others.

This distinction corresponds with the conclusion of the "rainy night critique" (*amayo no shina sadame*) – a discussion depicted in the "Broom Tree" (Hahakigi) chapter that takes place one rainy night in Genji's own palace quarters. Present at this notorious forum canvassing the merits and demerits of women are the Chief Left Equerry (Hidari-no-uma-no-kami), Fujiwara Aide of Ceremonial (Tō-shikibu-no-jō), Tō-no-chūjō and Genji. As I shall discuss in more detail later in this chapter, a number of scholars caution that the criticism of women presented in the "rainy night critique" is made not from the author's viewpoint, but from the perspective of the male characters. Even so, the view of women presented in this section is important in any consideration of the strong-and-weak issue not only in terms of evaluating those being discussed but also in assessing each of the characters in the story.

Richard H. Okada argues that the "rainy night critique" focuses on women who resist reification into types, since each instance discussed by the men involved redefines how women should be grouped. Thus, no description or judgement can ever be exhaustive or final (Okada 1991: 212). Abe Akio, on the other hand, argues that the most critical point in this critique is encapsulated by the Chief Left Equerry's general comment to the effect that, rather than being of a certain rank, it is more important that the perfect woman be steady (*monomameyaka*), quiet (*shizuka*), trustworthy (*ushiroyasuku*) and calm (*nodokeshi*) (I 41; S 25; T I 25).[9] Highlighting the fact that the Chief Left Equerry's general comments focus on middle-rank women, Abe regards the overall point of the "rainy night critique" as the notion that there are good women in the middle and low ranks rather than in the high rank (Abe Akio 1959: 971). I agree with Abe that the Chief Left Equerry's comments summarise the gist of the argument presented in this famous discussion. But, while Abe focuses on the comment that there are good women in the middle and low ranks rather than in the high rank, I would like to draw attention to the insight offered that the admirable woman is defined as being steady, quiet, trustworthy and calm. Until now, discussion of the "rainy night

50   The Tale of Genji

critique" has focused on ladies of the middle rank. Middle-rank women in this story can certainly evoke curiosity and a romantic desire in high-ranking men. They also represent the author's position, as well as an anti-authoritarian attitude. But we should stress once more that the important points made in the Chief Left Equerry's comments relate to the fact that desirable women not only come from the middle-low ranks but are also steady, quiet, trustworthy and calm. In other words, they are modest anti-progressive women without ambition. In the sense that these women lack the unattractive aggression or progressiveness of the more strong-willed ladies featured in the tale, they orientate reader sympathy towards the weak.

Furthermore, the women regarded as undesirable according to the personal experience of the men taking part in the "rainy night critique" are: (1) a jealous woman, determined not to seem inferior even in matters for which she has no great aptitude, and who therefore insists on doing things for which she is unsuited through either talent or nature (I 46; S 27–8); (2) an unfaithful woman, highly skilled in cultural matters such as poems, handwriting and *koto*-playing (I 50; S 30); and (3) a remarkably wise woman (I 56; S 35). Each of these three is very ambitious and hardworking. In contrast, the one exceptional woman regarded favourably, and who later appears as Yūgao, is described as being quiet and calm (*nodokeki ni odashiku*) (I 54; T I 31).

Opinions differ concerning the author's attitude towards the "rainy night critique". As briefly mentioned, a number of scholars caution that the criticism of women presented is made not from the author's viewpoint, but from the perspective of the male characters.[10] Suzuki Kazuo, for example, argues that the criticism of women in this section is well contrasted to the story of Utsusemi which immediately follows the critique. While, in the former, women are superficially criticised through the collective gaze of various male characters, in the latter the author describes Utsusemi and her responsible attempts to live according to her modest wishes (Suzuki Kazuo 1994: 13–14). As Suzuki's argument suggests, it is not useful to infer that the author presents her own view on women in the "rainy night critique". But, regardless of either the author's own or the male characters' views on women, it is undeniable that two types of women are presented. There are, first, ambitious and progressive women, and, second, modest and tranquil women. Furthermore, these seem to correspond with the two types of feminine characters in the first part of *Genji*, namely the women in the Kiritsubo and Murasaki group, and the women in the Utsusemi and Yūgao group. We can therefore clearly identify here the strong–weak contrast attributed to two groups of characters in the early *Genji*, as well as the two types of women criticised in the "rainy night critique".

We should note, however, the need to distinguish the attributes "modest", "quiet" and "calm" from the Confucian moral standard for woman of submission to men. Although these two partly overlap, Utsusemi and Yūgao are not exactly submissive. Utsusemi rejects Genji and prefers her own calm life. Rather than being obedient to men, Yūgao is an escapist who avoids

The Tale of Genji   51

confrontation with the world. Thus, we can surmise that the middle-ranking women of the "rainy night critique" represent the "modest" and anti-progressive groups who generate sympathy for the weak.

However, as the plot gradually unfolds, a group of new ladies appear whom the narrator seems to ridicule and mock. These are exactly the women I should like to analyse in this chapter. Three of the best-known of this category are the ugly lady (Safflower/Suetsumuhana), the old lady (Gen-no-naishi)[11] and the indecent lady (Ōmi-no-kimi). Interestingly, each of these three is considered to be related to the Hahakigi/Tamakazura group. At first sight, their function in the tale seems to be to provide comparison with and thus enhance the younger, more beautiful and elegant ladies. For example, in her discussion of Suetsumuhana and Gen-no-naishi, whom she labels as "weird", Aileen Gatten argues that these women

> give variety to the first section of the novel, make the admirable female characters seem even more tasteful and talented, and give the radiant Genji the opportunity to exhibit his magnanimous nature to the full. Weird ladies are welcome additions indeed to *Genji monogatari*.
>
> (Gatten 1986: 47)

Haruo Shirane, from a different perspective, sees in Genji's relations with these ladies a deepening and broadening of his personality. He argues that in each episode involving women of lesser rank, such as Utsusemi, Yūgao, Suetsumuhana, Gen-no-naishi and, later, Tamakazura, the otherwise glorious hero Genji is sent down a road to private and unexpected defeat. This depiction of his private difficulties and suffering, Shirane concludes, makes Genji more "human" and gives him far more psychological depth than his literary predecessors (Shirane 1987: 71–2). However, if we look at these women from the perspective of contrast between the weak and the strong, the beautiful and the ugly, and the modest and the ambitious, a series of different insights are gained. In fact, the narrative itself seems to become a multilayered discourse of the conflict between admiration for the beautiful, the strong and the ambitious, and sympathy with the ugly, the weak and the modest.

3.3. Princess Safflower (Suetsumuhana)

In his old age, the late Prince Hitachi fathered a daughter. This child was known as Princess Safflower or Suetsumuhana. The princess enjoyed every comfort from her doting father before his death, but once alone she was forced to live in sad and straitened circumstances (I 205; S 113). Suetsumuhana's physical attributes result in her becoming an object of mockery in the story. Her figure is described as being most uncommonly long and attenuated; and, although her skin is whiter than snow, her nose is also long, pendulous and red. Her forehead bulges, and her full face is very long (I 224–5; S 124). At

52   The Tale of Genji

first, she does not answer Genji's poem, responding only with "Mmm" and a smile (I 226; T I 125). However, in spite of her uncanny appearance, this unprepossessing woman has a love-affair with Genji. Genji often returns from Suetsumuhana's mansion to Murasaki's Nijō mansion. Thus, in the story, the ugly and uncanny princess, Suetsumuhana, is compared ironically with the beautiful young Murasaki, now on the eve of womanhood (I 233; S 130). At the end of the "Safflower" (Suetsumuhana) chapter, Genji draws a picture of an ugly lady with a long red nose for Murasaki, also giving himself a bright red nose. Looking at him, Murasaki laughs merrily. Genji's mockery is merciless, and the reader is unable to avoid the conclusion that Suetsumuhana is a hopelessly ugly and definitely unsuitable partner for the beautiful Genji. Her role seems to be to highlight Genji's kindness – he does not discard even an ugly lady, caring for her to the end. Indeed, the author confirms that "Genji was a generous man" who "did not abandon women to whom he had been even slightly drawn" (II 332; S 387).

However, it is useful also to focus on a comment made at the end of the scene in which Genji draws an ugly lady with a long red nose. Here the narrator asks: "I wonder what happened to all these people in the end" (I 235; T I: 131). It is not entirely clear who "these people" (*kakaru hitobito*) are. Commentators usually identify them as Suetsumuhana, Utsusemi and Nokiba-no-ogi.[12] But it is more logical to assume that, since it comes immediately after an exchange between Genji and Murasaki, the term also refers to this couple. Thus, we can read this sentence as referring both to the later agony of Genji and Murasaki in the "New Herbs: Part One and Part Two" chapters, and to the manner in which Suetsumuhana and Utsusemi maintain their dignity and spend calm and comfortable lives. Thus, in hindsight, it is possible to see the narrator's musings as a lament for, expression of pity for, or even criticism of Genji and the young Murasaki, both of whom merrily mock the ugly lady. The narrator's comments can also be seen as praise and admiration for Suetsumuhana and Utsusemi.[13] In other words, the last sentence of the chapter suggests that embedded in the tale is a critical view of those who ridicule the ugly appearance of others.

It is not only Suetsumuhana's figure which is the target of ridicule. Her poems and letters are also the subject of contempt.[14] Many of her poems are composed on the topic of the Chinese robe. Genji criticises these as outdated by saying: "Her conservative style is unable to rid itself of Chinese robes and wet sleeves" (II 370; S 407). Furthermore, in an age when a love-letter written on thin beautiful paper is a mark of refinement, Suetsumuhana writes her letters on heavily perfumed thick Michinoku paper, yellowed with age, or so old that the purple has faded to an alkaline grey (I 220; S 121). Except for the scent, heavily burned into the stationery, there is nothing to suggest feminine elegance (I 229; S 127). Rather than indicating seductive sexuality, the thick yellow or alkaline-grey aged Michinoku paper suggests the official, the ceremonious and the old-fashioned (II 369–70; S 407). In addition to her choice of writing material, Suetsumuhana's handwriting is also criticised as lacking feminine sexuality. The lines are straight and prim (I 220; S 121), or cramped, rocklike, stiff and angular (III 78; S 478). Fujii Sadakazu argues that Suetsumuhana's initial refusal to answer Genji's poems indicates an absence of sexuality (Fujii 1980, 2: 142). Certainly, with the exception of her fair skin and beautiful hair, there is little that is alluring about this unfortunate woman, and it is likely that this sexlessness is also being ridiculed when Genji and his other, more sensual partners make fun of Suetsumuhana. In the "Royal Outing" (Miyuki) chapter, for example, after reading yet another poem sent to him on the topic of the Chinese robe, Genji responds: "A Chinese robe, a Chinese robe once more/And yet again a Chinese Chinese robe." When he shows this verse to Tamakazura, she breaks into a smile and says: "The poor thing! You're making fun of her" (III 78; S 478; T I: 509).[15] Suetsumuhana is mocked here because her old-fashioned poem lacks the requisite charm of a woman's letter to a man.

Suetsumuhana is used by Genji as a buffer or alibi between pairs of jealous ladies, including Murasaki and Akashi, and Murasaki and Oborozukiyo. In the "First Warbler" (Hatsune) chapter, having spent a night with the Akashi lady, Genji hesitates to return immediately to Murasaki. Instead he visits Suetsumuhana (and also Utsusemi, who is now a nun) (II 385–6; S 413). In the "New Herbs: Part One" ("Wakana: Jō") chapter, Genji has Murasaki believe that he will visit Suetsumuhana when, in fact, he goes to see Oborozukiyo (III 251; S 560). Because she lacks sexuality, and thus will not be an object of jealousy, Genji is able to use this unattractive woman to cover-up secret love-affairs. Suetsumuhana may well be less overtly sexual. However, a careful reading of the text reveals that she nevertheless demonstrates features of traditional femininity. She is, for example, described as being "stricken with embarrassment" (I: 215; T I 119), as someone who "shrank from Genji's presence" (II 149; T I 310) and as "shy" when she meets Genji (II 150; T I 310). It is also useful to take note of the narrator's comment after Genji's mockery of the Chinese-robe poem in the "Royal Outing" chapter: "I (the narrator) talk far too much nonsense [of Genji's mockery]" (III 78; T I 509). This comment makes it clear that it is Genji and not the narrator who is displaying contempt. The comment thus ensures that Genji's ridicule is here again objectified by a third-party perspective. Furthermore, we should not neglect the comments of the old women serving Suetsumuhana concerning this poem. They say: "Our lady's poem is honest and to the point. Genji's is merely clever" (I 231; S 129).[16] The words of these old women clearly conjure up before our eyes the image of a sincere, honest and faithful Suetsumuhana, while Genji and his other ladies appear clever but nonetheless frivolous, sexual and insincere.

In addition, Suetsumuhana becomes the object of mockery as a result of her old-fashioned character and an overly keen sense of social ceremony and duty.[17] On many occasions she sends Genji items of old-fashioned clothing he declines to wear. In the "Suetsumuhana" chapter, Genji receives a remarkably lustreless pink singlet of an old-fashioned cut, and a deep-red

54   The Tale of Genji

informal court robe lined with the same colour to wear on New Year's Day (I 230; S 127). On the occasion of Tamakazura's moving into Genji's mansion, and with the approach of the New Year, Genji sends Suetsumuhana a white robe lined with green and decorated profusely with Chinese vignettes. Prim and proper as she is, Suetsumuhana follows the dictates of etiquette by giving something to the messenger who delivers the gift. However, the best she can produce is a yellow lady's robe rather discoloured at the sleeves (II 369; S 407). In the "Royal Outing" chapter, which revolves around Tamakazura's initiation ceremonies, Suetsumuhana remains inflexible in her allegiance to good form and is unable to let the occasion pass without acknowledgement. However, although delivered in a beautifully wrought wardrobe with elaborate wrapping, her gift is a graceless robe of drabbish green, lined trousers of a dusty rose or some such colour much admired by the ancients, and a faded purple jacket of minute weave (III 77; S 477–8). In each case she is ridiculed as both vulgar and old-fashioned.

Suetsumuhana's old-fashioned character is somehow related to her wish to live in the past.[18] She is always looking back to the time when her father protected her and insists on retaining the mansion she inherited from her father. No matter that it is now in a state of frightening disrepair; the house is a comfort to her, for she still feels her father's presence (II 134; T I 302). She will not part with the least utensil and bravely persists in living exactly as before (II 140; T I 305). Underlying these sorts of preferences are personal features very similar to the characteristics of Utsusemi and Yūgao – modesty and a lack of ambition for future progress. Concerning her old-fashioned preferences, the narrator defines her as *ohodoka* (I 216–17),[19] which refers generally to an unpretentious and tranquil character lacking ambition, aggressive spirit or the wish to compete with others.

In her diary, Murasaki Shikibu writes that she is thought by others to be *oiraka*, which means meek. The word, therefore, is similar in meaning to *ohodoka*. In addition, Murasaki followed her father as far as Echizen province where she spent more than two years. Later she married Nobutaka, a man about twenty years her senior and, therefore, almost her father's age. Nobutaka left her a large cupboard full of Chinese books, and whenever loneliness threatened to overwhelm her she took out one or two to read. In her diary she writes that her women whisper: "It's because she goes on like this that she is so miserable. What kind of lady reads Chinese books?" In addition to the Chinese classics, she also read the *Chronicles of Japan*, and was given the nickname "Our Lady of the Chronicles" (Bowring 1982: 133–41). It is hard to believe that Murasaki Shikibu did not see any shadow of her own character in Suetsumuhana.[20]

Related as it is to the past and to memory, scent is used in the story as a key to understanding Suetsumuhana. When Genji first approaches her, he catches a faint, pleasing scent (I 217; S 120). When Jijū, Suetsumuhana's foster sister, leaves Kyoto to go to Kyūshū with her aunt, Suetsumuhana gives her a jar of old fragrant clothing incense (II 144; T I 307). In the

"Wormwood Patch" ("Yomogiu") chapter, after coming back to Kyoto from Suma and Akashi, Genji goes in the Fourth Month to see the Lady of the Orange Blossoms. Making his way by memory to her dwelling, he by chance passes Suetsumuhana's ruined mansion. As he does, a vague nostalgic perfume of Wistaria blossoms, similar to but somehow different from orange blossoms, wafts on the breeze, reminding Genji that he should also visit Suetsumuhana. The perfume evokes a well-known poem: "When I breathe the fragrance of the mandarin orange blossoms that await the Fifth Month/it brings back the scented sleeves of one I loved" (*Kokinshū*, 139; Rodd with Henkenius 1984: 88). In many cultures, not just Japan, the olfactory sense is often associated with nostalgic memories of the past. Suetsumuhana is a nostalgic figure. When she meets Genji again after long lonely years, he is welcomed by the fragrance of the scented Chinese chest in which the robe she wears has been stored (II 149; S 300). The scented Chinese chest, like the Chinese robe previously, is here used as something both nostalgic and old-fashioned. When Genji leaves the mansion, the narrator mentions the faint perfume of Suetsumuhana's sleeves that comes to him from behind the curtains. Again, her fragrance makes past memories vividly return to Genji's mind, and he can visualise the furnishings in her chamber which remain as they have always been. Her stoicism in the face of poverty gives her a certain dignity, so that, upon meeting her, Genji "hated to think of his own selfishness through the years" (II 152; S 301). Sigmund Freud relates the uncanny both to something which is secretly familiar and to a regression to a time when the ego had not yet marked itself off sharply either from the external world or from other people (Freud 1964: 236, 245). Referring to Freud's insight, it is evident that what creates Suetsumuhana's uncanniness and nostalgia is a tendency to regression or at least to something that is the opposite of progress.

It seems to be clear now that one of Suetsumuhana's roles in the narrative is to make both Genji and the reader aware of how selfish, ugly, poor and shabby is a life dedicated to love and glory, and driven by ambition and the desire to progress. This is not necessarily the role of either Utsusemi or Yūgao. Since Genji is attracted to these women, there is a different ideology of the "modest" operating which clearly does not constitute a criticism of Genji. But, because Genji ridicules and mocks Suetsumuhana, the ideology of regression, retrospection and anti-ambition which informs her character provides the narrative with a critical space against which to judge Genji and other courtiers.

There is good justification here for paying special attention to the scented Chinese chest and the Chinese robe used in the Suetsumuhana story as symbols of the nostalgic and the old-fashioned. Behind these images, though different from the modern sentiment of the people of the nation-state, we might detect an upsurge of Japanese national sentiment and a desire for the development of a national consciousness which, as we have seen in our discussion on Saichō in Chapter 2, appeared as early as the ninth century.

56 The Tale of Genji

Ultimately, however, in the superficial ridicule evident in Genji's response to Suetsumuhana's modest and retiring character we can detect the respect of both the author and of people in general for effort and social responsibility, and an associated criticism of Genji's cavalier and irresponsible approach. It is now apparent that the narrative does not simply present the single perspective of Genji's mocking attitude to Suetsumuhana. The reader is given multiple viewpoints, including the comments of the old serving women on the poems of Suetsumuhana and Genji (I 231; S 129), the inference contained in the last sentence of the "Suetsumuhana" chapter – "I wonder what happened to all these people in the end" (I 235; T I: 131), and the narrator's disclaimer later in the "Royal Outing" chapter that the mocking tone is Genji's rather than her own (III 78; T I 509). There is undoubtedly a consistent viewpoint here which, on the one hand, supports Suetsumuhana's modest character and her longing for the past, and which, on the other hand, laments, feels pity for, and even criticises Genji, Lady Murasaki, Tō-no-chūjō and the other good-looking people who ridicule and mock Suetsumuhana.[21] This viewpoint is admittedly hidden beneath the base of the narrative and is often overshadowed by an overt perspective which both praises the beautiful, young, elegant and ambitious characters of Genji and Murasaki and ridicules the ugly, outdated, modest and regressive tendencies of Suetsumuhana. Since admiration for the strong and the beautiful dominates the surface of the narrative, the reader in many instances only retrospectively discovers sympathy for the ugly and the weak. But, still, it certainly exists. Once we notice it, we no longer laugh at Suetsumuhana. And, having once made even a slight change of perspective, the reader will find that, in spite of Genji's mockery, Suetsumuhana's lofty and dignified attitude looks perfectly respectable. Moreover, from the revised point of view, this "ugly" lady can appear beautiful, elegant and even desirable. However, we are accustomed to the modernist reading of *The Tale of Genji*, which presents from this perspective as a story of beautiful romantic love, progress, power struggle, future and hope. We therefore find it difficult to adopt the anti-modernist stance which rejects the valorisation of the elements listed above in favour of sympathy for ugly, regressive, old-fashioned, and anti-progressive characters. These respective approaches are, in general, materialised separately in the characters in the Wakamurasaki/Murasaki and Hahakigi/Tamakazura groups.

Both Nomura Seiichi and Mori Ichirō have noted an ostensibly dramatic change in Suetsumuhana's character between the "Safflower" ("Suetsumuhana") chapter and the "Wormwood Patch" ("Yomogiu") chapter. While in the former the lady is portrayed as an ugly, old-fashioned and unsophisticated princess lacking the skills to compose an acceptable poem, the latter emphasises the beauty of her soul (Nomura 1969: 98–101; Mori 1965: 1–17). Mori argues that the change in attitude towards Suetsumuhana's character from that of an object of mockery to that of a holder of an admirably unchanging mind corresponds with a shift of her role in the story. Thus, this peculiar woman loved by Genji is presented in a remarkably different light in the

"Suetsumuhana" chapter from the faithful lady contrasted with other faithless people in the "Yomogiu" chapter which follows Genji's return to Kyoto after his exile to Suma and Akashi (Mori 1965: 2–5).

Suetsumuhana's role as a contrast against other ambitious people, including Genji himself, is faintly discernible, as we have already seen, even in the "Suetsumuhana" chapter. She furthermore remains an object of mockery even after the "Yomogiu" chapter. Therefore, rather than changing dramatically between the "Suetsumuhana" and "Yomogiu" chapters, it seems to me that Suetsumuhana's modest beauty, which longs not for the future but for the nostalgic past, is consistently hidden behind the more overt scenes of ridicule.[22] Thus, rather than seeing her apparent transformation as a change of character from ugly and old-fashioned in the "Suetsumuhana" chapter to unchanging and faithful in the "Yomogiu" chapter, we should perhaps regard this as a change of emphasis on the part of the author from "respect for the ambitious" to "sympathy with the modest".

The analysis to this point leads us to presume that it is not merely Suetsumuhana's ugly appearance that makes her an object of scorn. More damning are her regressive tendencies manifested in a lack of sexuality and her retrospective and old-fashioned character. Her ugliness is in a sense used as a place where the real reason of mockery – her regressive and retrospective tendencies – can comfortably reside. In other words, two axes of ridicule operate in the case of this woman. The first is that between beauty and ugliness. In this sphere, the beautiful Genji and Murasaki laugh at the ugly Suetsumuhana. The second is that between progression and retrogression, or between the strong-orientated and the weak-orientated. On this axis, the progressive and ambitious Genji and Murasaki ridicule the regressive and retrospective Suetsumuhana. Ridiculing the ugly, regressive and retrospective Suetsumuhana might well release the reader's desire to despise and discriminate against the weak, the ugly and the old-fashioned. As mentioned previously, in addition to an authorial observation on human nature, this can also be interpreted in the context of the Japanese people's urge since the ninth century towards national development and an accompanying contempt for weakness. On the other hand, as we have seen, there is a sympathetic perspective towards Suetsumuhana underlying the whole narrative. The fact that the narrative maintains these multiple perspectives and presents both sides indicates a simultaneous presence in the text of the two opposing ideologies – respect for the strong and sympathy with the weak.

3.4. Gen-no-naishi

Gen-no-naishi ("Dame of Staff") is described as a well-born, talented, cultivated and widely respected lady. Although rather advanced in years (57 or 58), she is still coquettish and dissolute (I 258; S 143; T I 145). In this sense she is categorised as an ambitious woman, and therefore different from Utsusemi, Yūgao or Suetsumuhana. Many scholars and critics, however,

58   The Tale of Genji

judging from a similarity to the Suetsumuhana narrative, consider that the Gen-no-naishi story belongs with the Hahakigi/Tamakazura group, although there is dispute over chronology. For example, Abe Akio suggests that the Gen-no-naishi episode was added before Suetsumuhana was created, while Iwashita Mitsuo surmises that this occurred after the completion of the "Suetsumuhana" chapter (Abe Akio 1954: 148–60, esp. 158; Iwashita 1967: 92, 134–6).[23] In any case, the general consensus among *Genji* scholars is that Gen-no-naishi's character seems to have some relation to that of Suetsumuhana. What, then, is the relationship between this pair?

Fujimura Kiyoshi considers that the Gen-no-naishi story is a prelude to the Oborozukiyo story, given that both tell of an illicit love-affair in the palace. This is in spite of the fact that one is comical and the other serious (Fujimura 1971: 118–46). Fujimura argues that, in order to emphasise the realism of the love-affair of Genji and Oborozukiyo in the palace, the author first tells a similar story with a comical flavour. Mitani Kuniaki goes one step further and argues that, by presenting a similarly illicit love-affair with Oborozukiyo, the role of the Gen-no-naishi story is to foreground Genji's crime against kingship through his adulterous love-affair with Fujitsubo. Concerning the comic episode of the affair between Genji and Gen-no-naishi, Mitani argues that by placing this story, which also conceals a crime against kingship, between two narratives of serious adulterous liaisons, Murasaki the author ensures that Genji's crime becomes more vivid and doubly serious. She thus provides a reasonable background for his self-exile (Mitani 1980: 212–32).

When Tō-no-chūjō hears about the affair between Genji and Gen-no-naishi, he says to himself that, while he had thought his own love-life varied, the possibility of a liaison with an old woman has not occurred to him. Thus, the story of Gen-no-naishi can in fact be viewed as an adventure for both Genji and Tō-no-chūjō, both of whom are amused by the thought of an inexhaustibly amorous old woman (I 260; S 145). By reading the story as one of Genji's (and also Tō-no-chūjō's) prohibited and marginal love-adventures, we can compare this story with other similar *Genji* love-stories, including those of Fujitsubo and Oborozukiyo. As we have seen, Utsusemi is someone's wife; Yūgao is a woman of low rank; Lady Murasaki is too young to be loved; Fujitsubo is Genji's father's consort; Suetsumuhana is ugly; and now Gen-no-naishi is old. All are either prohibited or marginal. In addition to these women, Genji's affair with Oborozukiyo, a lady from a hostile family, is also presented as an example of prohibited love (I 281; S 155). There is, furthermore, the hint of an illicit relationship with Princess Asagao, who becomes the high priestess of Kamo shrine (I 63, 292, 357; S 40, 159, 194). The liaison with Gen-no-naishi is but one example from the long list of adventurous relations with marginal and prohibited women in which Genji and Tō-no-chūjō indulge.

The mutual love-affair with Gen-no-naishi plays the role of cementing the friendship between Genji and Tō-no-chūjō. Previously, the pair have also been in competition for the hands of Yūgao and Suetsumuhana. These various women are used to bond the two young men whose rivalry in their careers and love-affairs is one of the threads weaving together the story of *Genji*. Our concerns, however, are with the contrast between the narrative position accorded to the senile old lady and the beautiful young lady. From the viewpoint of the strong–weak issue, then, what significance can we find in the Gen-no-naishi story?

Unlike the Suetsumuhana episode, there is no clear criticism of Genji or the aristocratic court system by the narrator or other characters in the story of Gen-no-naishi. However, a careful reading of the Gen-no-naishi story reveals that a number of voices can be heard behind the scenes, thus providing an example of the kind of polyphonic narrative found throughout the entire text of *Genji*.[24] For instance, the original sentence structure at the beginning of this story reads as follows:

> There was an aging Dame of Staff, of impeccable birth, witty, distinguished, and well respected by all, nevertheless very *coquettish* (*adameitaru koko-rozama*) and *of easy virtue* (*sonatani wa omokaranu*). (Genji) was curious to know why she should be so dissolute even in her declining years. (He) jokingly tested her, but (she) did not think his proposition at all incongruous.
>
> (I 258; S 143–4; T I: 145; my italics).[25]

In this sentence there is some ambiguity concerning whether the moral judgement which includes the criticism of Gen-no-naishi's character and behaviour as "coquettish" or "of easy virtue" is that of the narrator or of Genji. While the voice which makes accusations of coquettishness and easy virtue in old age seems initially to be that of the narrator, it seamlessly merges into Genji's musings concerning why Gen-no-naishi behaves thus. The passage ultimately results in an amalgamation of both consciousnesses into one voice.

Another example can be found in the description of Gen-no-naishi's appearance. The text relates:

> Hiding (her) face with a fan on which a beautiful picture is painted, (she) turns around (to Genji) and casts *a seductive glance*, but *a pair of dark and muddy eyelids* emerge from above it, and (her) hair, which of course the fan can not hide, is *rough and stringy*. *A very poorly chosen fan for an old lady*, (he) thinks, giving her his and taking the other from her. (It is) decorated with a gold painting of a tall grove and so bright a red that (his own) face must be red from the reflection. In one corner, written in a hand that is *old-fashioned* but not displeasingly so, is a line of poetry: "Withered is the grass of Oaraki." *Of all the poems (she) could have chosen!*
>
> (S 144; my italics).[26]

60   The Tale of Genji

Judgements such as "a seductive glance", "the dark and muddy eyelids", "hair is rough and stringy", "a very poorly chosen fan for an old lady", "a hand that is old-fashioned" and "Of all the poems she could have chosen!" are all ostensibly made from Genji's perspective and sensibility. However, in each case, the consciousness of criticism against Gen-no-naishi is skilfully presented through a polyphonic narrative which blurs the voices of the narrator and Genji.

As readers, we usually tend to share Genji's feelings, and to suppose that the narrator does the same. However, in spite of the polyphony which characterises the *Genji* narrative, as I read the Gen-no-naishi story, there is only one clear narratorial criticism of this elderly woman, as follows: "He (Tō-no-chūjō) was a promising catch who might (she thought) make up for Genji's unkindness, but apparently it was only Genji she wanted – *a terrible choice (utate no konomi ya)!*" (I 260; T I: 146; my italics).[27] The critical comment "*utate no konomi*" ("a terrible choice") is apparently made by a lady-in-waiting narrator and thus conveys her judgement. However, the meaning is ambiguous. Is it a terrible choice because it is over-reaching for Gen-no-naishi to choose between Genji and Tō-no-chūjō, or because it is an insult to Tō-no-chūjō, or because Genji is a terrible man? The reader is inclined to suppose that Genji cannot be a terrible man, and, therefore, it must be Gen-no-naishi who is a terrible woman. Accordingly, we do not imagine that this criticism could be directed at Genji in the sense that to choose Genji is a terrible choice, since he is just making a fool of her. Nevertheless, the possibility remains that the narrator might consider Genji to be a terrible man. It is significant that the narrator's rare criticism of Gen-no-naishi allows various different interpretations of the whole episode.

In addition to the polyphonic narrative underlying the story of Gen-no-naishi, a significant point of this section for our discussion is, as Tabata Chieko suggests, the influence of the traditional story of love typically depicted in *Tales of Ise* between the hero of a narrative and an old woman (Tabata Chieko 1991, 2: 135).[28] Let me briefly introduce the relevant section of the *Ise* narrative. Ariwara (no) Narihira, famous for his indiscriminate love, half-glimpses an old woman with whom he has slept only once peeping at him through the window of his house. He then recites a poem: "The lady with thinning hair – but a year short of a hundred –/Must be longing for me, for I seem to see her face." Having heard the poem, the woman rushes home. Narihira follows her and, upon arrival at her house, begins to peep into her window from a sheltered spot, as the old woman herself had done. She then recites: "Must I again tonight/Spread a single sleeve/On the narrow mat/And sleep without/My beloved?" Upon hearing this, Narihira is moved by pity (*aware to omoite*), and spends the night there with the old woman. The narrator of *Tales of Ise* says: "Most men show consideration for the women they love and disregard the feelings of the ones who fail to interest them. Narihira made no such distinction" (McCullough (trans.) 1968: 110–11). Following Narihira's tradition, Genji is also described thus: "Genji

The Tale of Genji   61

was a generous man and he did not abandon women to whom he had been even slightly drawn" (II 332; S 387).

There is a striking difference, however, in the attitude to old women adopted by Narihira and by Genji. While Narihira is obviously sympathetic, Genji, rather, ridicules Gen-no-naishi. Narihira is told by the old woman's son that she wishes to meet with a good man, and he (Narihira) therefore is asked to come to see her. Genji, on the other hand, first jokingly approaches Gen-no-naishi out of curiosity, but is then shocked to find that she does not believe such a pairing to be incongruous. In fact, having seduced her, he finds her attachment irritating and disgusting, and he keeps his distance for fear of starting gossip about a liaison with an old woman (I 258; T I: 145). Nevertheless, the adventure amuses him (I 258; S 144). Gen-no-naishi is saddened (*ito tsurashi to omoeri*) by Genji's attitude (I 258–9; S 144). He, in contrast, laughs at her, but continues to send his poems, although he is troubled when she replies (I 258; S 144). Indeed, Genji's attitude to Gen-no-naishi is consistently contradictory. It is related that Gen-no-naishi's age so arouses Genji's pity that he wishes to console her; but here, again, the narrator notes that in practice Genji finds this idea too depressing (I 261; T I: 146). Although the language of her poetry is described as "extremely seductive" (*koyonaku iromekitari*), Genji feels it would be disgusting (*utomashiku*) to reply to her poem (I 259–60; S 144), and he is troubled (*wabishi to omoi ariki tamau*) by her seduction (I 266; S 148). On a later occasion in the "Heartvine" ("Aoi") chapter, when Gen-no-naishi happens to meet Genji at the Kamo festival, she writes a poem on a fan and sends it to him. Recognising the handwriting, Genji is irritated and frowns (*nikusani hashitanau*). Nevertheless he replies, and Gen-no-naishi feels bashful upon receiving this reply (I 299; S 164; T I: 170–1). When the pair meet again by chance in the the "Morning Glory" ("Asagao") chapter, Gen-no-naishi's heart palpitates, and she feels young again. But Genji, though nostalgic, remains repulsed (*utomashikute*) upon hearing her poem (II 262–4; S 354–5).

Narihira's sincerity and kindness to the old woman puts Genji's ridicule and mocking of Gen-no-naishi in a very bad light. As a direct result of Genji's response, their relationship becomes ugly and the entire incident farcical. Without this mockery, the affair would result, as it does in the case of Narihira, in a beautiful love-story. Unlike that of Narihira, Genji's unfaithful, insincere and arrogant behaviour operates to make the reader feel pity for and to sympathise with Gen-no-naishi, and to despise and detest Genji and his ridicule. Like the Suetsumuhana story, the tale of Gen-no-naishi is constructed in a way that allows two interpretations. On the one hand, it highlights Genji's beauty and strength and, as a function of the admiration of youth and beauty, releases the reader's desire to ridicule the weak and the old. However, at the same time, it highlights Genji's coldness and thus arouses reader sympathy for this old woman.

It is worthwhile here to see how Narihira and *Tales of Ise* are dealt with in other sections of *The Tale of Genji*. The "Picture Contest" ("Eawase")

62   The Tale of Genji

chapter describes a contest held at the court of the emperor Reizei between Genji and Akikonomu's left group and Tō-no-chūjō and Kokiden's right group. The first match is between an illustration for *The Bamboo Cutter* (left) and a scene centring on Toshikage from *The Tale of the Hollow Tree* (right). One of the views supporting *The Bamboo Cutter* (left) is that the moon princess avoided sullying herself with worldly affairs. Against this, the right group criticises *The Bamboo Cutter* on the grounds that, since the moon princess lived in a stalk of bamboo, she must be of dubious lineage. In the second contest, *Tales of Ise* is matched against *The Tale of Jōsanmi*. A lady-in-waiting, Hei-naishi (left), makes a waka supporting *Tales of Ise*: "In rank ignorance of the great Sea of Ise's magnificent depths/must the waves now wash away words thought merely old and dull?" She goes on to criticise *The Tale of Jōsanmi*, saying that it is a tale of worldly common licentiousness tricked out in pretty colours (II 177; S 312; T I 326).[29] Daini, a lady-in-waiting from the right, replies in support of *The Tale of Jōsanmi*: "To the noble heart that aspires to soar aloft, high above the clouds/depths of a thousand fathoms appear very far below." Finally Fujitsubo supports *Ise* and declares: "At first glance, indeed, it may all seem very old, but despite the years/are we to heap scorn upon the fisherman of Ise?" (II 177; T I: 326). It is related that in both matches the pictures offered by the right are bright, lively paintings of contemporary life with much to recommend them, including details of the palace (II 177; T I: 326).

Since the competition is very close, the contestants decide to make the final judgement in the emperor's presence. On this occasion, the left wins the contest with Genji's scroll depicting his secluded life in Suma. Throughout the picture contest, *Tales of Ise* and Narihira are associated with ignorant, humble and old fishermen, in contrast to the elevated nobility of *The Tale of Jōsanmi*. It is interesting to note that, in each picture contest, the narrative prefers the secluding (left) to the worldly (right), the humble and old (left) over the high and noble (right), and old-style nostalgic and philanthropic love (left) rather than the modern high-ranking worldly life (right). These features of the left correspond with the conclusions of the "rainy night critique" and are shared by the ladies in the Hahakigi/Tamakazura group – Utsusemi, Yūgao and Suetsumuhana.

Akiyama Ken highlights the suppressed emotion that resulted from Narihira's unsatisfactory career as one of the significant artistic features of *Tales of Ise*, and further argues that this is an element *The Tale of Genji* borrowed from the earlier narrative (Akiyama 1964: 64–7). Thus, we might argue that the different degree of sympathy shown towards old ladies by Narihira and Genji exactly reflects the degree of satisfaction each has with his respective career. While Narihira's prospects remained hopeless throughout his life, Genji's career ultimately was more satisfactory in that he was finally accorded benefices equivalent to those of a retired emperor.

Returning once more to the story of Gen-no-naishi, it is clear that at least two different value standards operate. If we admire Genji and Tō-no-chūjō,

The Tale of Genji 63

and read *Genji* as their coming-of-age tale, Gen-no-naishi will probably be judged as an old lady who loves Genji, in spite of the incongruity of this, and who thus annoys and torments the story's hero. Her sole role then becomes one of a bond which cements the intimate friendship between the two young men. She is therefore a catalyst who releases the reader's desire to ridicule and laugh at the weak, the ugly and the old, and conversely to admire the strong, the beautiful and the young. In contrast, if we turn a critical eye to Genji's unfaithful, narcissistic, arrogant and irresponsible seduction, and make an intertextual reading comparing Genji with Narihira in *Tales of Ise*, Gen-no-naishi becomes an old lady who loves Genji with all her heart. Unlike Narihira, Genji makes fun of this old woman with whom he makes love. Nevertheless she loves him sincerely, if not exclusively; and, in spite of his mockery, attempts to help him. Thus, the Gen-no-naishi tale has contradictory readings similar to the contrasting readings of the Suetsumuhana episode.

However, we should also note the differences between the objects of ridicule and laughter in the Gen-no-naishi story and in the Suetsumuhana story. In Suetsumuhana's case, as we have seen, the scorn shown by the progressive and ambitious characters towards her ugly figure cloaks a scorn for her regressive and retrospective character. However, in the case of Gen-no-naishi, it is her aggressive, progressive and ambitious features that are scorned behind the disguise of age. The features which become a target of contempt in the case of Gen-no-naishi are, in actuality, shared by Genji, Tō-no-chūjō and other aristocratic ladies and gentlemen, especially the members of the Wakamurasaki/Murasaki group. Thus, laughter at an aggressive, progressive and ambitious woman is, as a matter of fact, the reverse side of praise for the regressive, retrospective and modest characters possessed by Utsusemi and Yūgao. Let me explore this point further in the case of Ōmi-no-kimi.

3.5. Ōmi-no-kimi

Ōmi-no-kimi is a daughter of Tō-no-chūjō, described as a serving woman with an indecent laugh who comes from the country to the capital (III 13–25; S 448–53). She embarrasses her father and her sisters by saying that in order to promote herself she will do any job, even carrying water or emptying chamber pots containing excrement. As early as 1953, Sugiyama Yasuhiko argued that, although Ōmi-no-kimi herself is the butt of laughter, the story attracts the reader less because of this laughter and more because of the manner in which the people around Ōmi-no-kimi are upset by her refusal to adhere to social values such as sophistication, morality and custom (Sugiyama 1953: 36). Masuda Katsumi also argues that, although Ōmi-no-kimi's conduct is out of place, it has a certain truth and that, even as we laugh, we therefore feel sorry for her (Masuda Katsumi 1954: 20). With reference to Sugiyama's and Masuda's analysis, Nomura Seiichi and Akiyama

64   The Tale of Genji

Ken argue that Tō-no-chūjō's authoritarian character is revealed when he mocks Ōmi-no-kimi. They furthermore argue that Genji's mockery of Tō-no-chūjō makes the former a perfect authority, because it demonstrates that Genji has the power to mock whoever he chooses (Nomura 1969: 108–9; Akiyama 1964: 135–49).[30, 31] Against the arguments of Nomura and Akiyama, Abe Yoshitomi refutes the claim that the Ōmi-no-kimi story strengthens Genji's authority, arguing instead that it is exactly the authority of Genji that is objectified by his accusing his opponent (Abe Yoshitomi 1979: 18).

With these arguments in mind, I should like first to consider the intertextual relations operating. Some scholars support the view that the Ōmi-no-kimi story is based on *The Lotus Sutra*. Misumi Yōichi, for example, finds a similarity between the Ōmi-no-kimi story and the story of "Belief and Understanding" in chapter 4 of the well-known Buddhist text. He argues therefore that the former derives from the latter (Misumi 1996: 89–102). I shall briefly introduce the story of "Belief and Understanding" as it appears in *The Lotus Sutra*. There was a young man who abandoned his father and ran away to live for a long time in another land. After searching unsuccessfully for his son, the father took up residence in a certain city and became very wealthy. After wandering, the young man came by chance to the same city, unaware that his father was living there. When they happened to meet, the father immediately knew his son, although the son did not recognise the father. The young man raced from the spot, fearing to be seized. The father sent his men to follow, whereupon they caught the son and brought him back to the father's mansion. Here the young man started work clearing away excrement without knowing that he was working at his father's house. The old man watched his son and noticed that, when working, the young man was never deceitful or lazy and never spoke angry or resentful words. The father kept his son clearing away excrement for the next twenty years until he fell ill and knew that he was about to die. The old man then disclosed his identity and asked his son to take charge of his wealth. However, the son continued to live in the same humble hut, unable to cease thinking of himself as mean and lowly. *The Lotus Sutra* concludes by noting that this old man with his great riches is none other than the Thus Come One (Buddha), and that we are all like the Buddha's sons. Although we may have no mind to covet or seek such a thing, the great treasure of the Dharma King will come to us of its own accord (Watson (trans.) 1993: 81–96).[32]

Misumi points out associations between the story of Ōmi-no-kimi and the "Belief and Understanding" section of *The Lotus Sutra*. There is an extract from the "Simile and Parable" chapter of the Buddhist work which reads:

> If a person fails to have faith but instead slanders this sutra. . . . If he should become a human being, his faculties will be blighted and dull, he will be puny, vile, bent, crippled, blind, deaf, hunchbacked. . . . If he should become a human being, he will be deaf, blind, dumb.

(pp. 74–7)

The Tale of Genji   65

This passage is evoked in the following words spoken by Tō-no-chūjō: "*The Lotus Sutra* tells us that dumbness and stammering are punishment for blasphemy" (III 20; S 450). Given the similarity between the tale of Ōmi-no-kimi and both the "Belief and Understanding" chapter and the section cited from the "Simile and Parable" chapter, we can strongly argue that the Ōmi-no-kimi story is written under the influence of the *Lotus Sutra*.

As Misumi notes, common points found in Ōmi-no-kimi and the "Belief and Understanding" stories are: (1) a father and his child live separately for a long period; (2) they meet, and the father welcomes the child; (3) the child does not mind performing a job involving cleaning excrement; (4) the father advises the child; and (5) the child is thankful for his father's advice (Misumi 1996: 90). But differences also abound. While in the "Belief and Understanding" narrative the son's mind is not greedy while the father is merciful, in the Ōmi-no-kimi story the daughter is covetous while this father ridicules his daughter. The points being made in the "Belief and Understanding" story are: (1) the mercy shown by the father to his son is equivalent to Buddha's mercy towards all sentient beings; and (2) just as the son who sincerely worked without coveting is helped by his father, if we work without greed we shall some day be helped by the Buddha. In contrast, the Ōmi-no-kimi story reveals the ugly aspects of Ōmi-no-kimi and Tō-no-chūjō. Furthermore, the rich man in the "Simile and Parable" chapter thinks to himself: "These little boys are all my sons and I love them without partiality. I have countless numbers of large carriages adorned with seven kinds of gems. I should be fair-minded and give one to each of my sons. I should not show any discrimination" (p. 58). In contrast, Tō-no-chūjō apparently loses his capacity for fair-mindedness and discriminates against Ōmi-no-kimi in favour of his other daughters. Thus, this section of the *Genji* narrative once again reveals the ugly face of Tō-no-chūjō.

In addition to the criticism evident in the intertextual comparison given above, the narrator of *Genji* also clearly criticises Tō-no-chūjō, both commenting on the latter's unfatherly mockery and disapproving of the manner in which Tō-no-chūjō feels ashamed of and thus torments Ōmi-no-kimi (III 85; T I 512). This criticism of Tō-no-chūjō's mockery, as well as the comparison between the Ōmi-no-kimi story and *The Lotus Sutra*, helps the reader to acquire a critical perspective. In the story of Ōmi-no-kimi, like that of Suetsumuhana, there is a viewpoint that criticises the mockery in which a sophisticated character engages. Thus, once again the reader is aware of a polyphonic voice advocating different values in the narrative – not only ridiculing Ōmi-no-kimi's indecency but also criticising Tō-no-chūjō and his sons and daughters who ridicule Ōmi-no-kimi. In other words, we can say that the text demonstrates both admiration for the strong and sympathy with the weak. As Sugiyama Yasuhiko and Masuda Katsumi argue, even while laughing at Ōmi-no-kimi, readers also identify with her, if only unconsciously. They thus begin to see things through her eyes and therefore become aware of the farcical elements in aristocratic society.

66   The Tale of Genji

Besides the intertextual and intratextual analysis, we have further evidence which supports a critical assessment of the aristocratic Tō-no-chūjō and a sympathetic view towards the rustic Ōmi-no-kimi, in spite of her willingness to do such demeaning tasks as carry water and empty chamber pots. In her diary, Murasaki Shikibu writes about palanquin-bearers. On the occasion of the imperial visit to Tsuchimikado mansion where she served Fujiwara Michinaga's daughter, Shōshi, Murasaki Shikibu noticed the bearers of low rank kneel beneath the palanquin and hoist it up the steps. She writes that as she watched she thought to herself: "Are we really that different? Even those of us who mix with nobility are bound by our rank. How difficult life is!" (Bowring 1982: 77). If Murasaki Shikibu was able to write in this way, it is unlikely that she sympathised with those in the nobility who, because they were so beholden to their rank, could despise a serving girl merely because she fetched water and emptied chamber pots.

Throughout the narrative, Ōmi-no-kimi is clearly compared with another of Tō-no-chūjō's daughters – Tamakazura. As the daughter of Yūgao, Tamakazura is modest. Her life of modesty and contentment without ambition accords with the genealogy of Utsusemi, Yūgao and Suetsumuhana. This is confirmed by her marriage to Higekuro. Being assigned a role contrasted to Tamakazura, Ōmi-no-kimi is the focus of a story which, as we have seen, is a burlesque of worldly people pursuing mundane prosperity. If we read this story from the ideology of the Wakamurasaki/Murasaki group, that is, from an ideology of admiration for the beautiful characters featured, we shall regard Ōmi-no-kimi as a weak, unsophisticated and indecent woman ridiculed and mocked by the strong, sophisticated and decent. The reader's desire to discriminate against the weak again finds release in this story. But if we read this episode from the ideology of the Hahakigi/Tamakazura group, that is, from the point of view of sympathy with the ugly, the aged, the unsophisticated and the insulted, it becomes apparent that the strong, sophisticated and decent people in the story are objectified and criticised by their accusations against the weak. As is the case with Suetsumuhana, we might also note that Ōmi-no-kimi's mockery operates along two axes: first, the decent Tō-no-chūjō and his children laugh at the indecent Ōmi-no-kimi; and, second, while the modest Tamakazura is praised, the aggressive Ōmi-no-kimi is ridiculed. However, it is important to note that, with respect to the latter, it is actually the aggressive attitude of Tō-no-chūjō, Genji and the other courtiers which becomes the object of mockery.

If we compare the stories of Suetsumuhana, Gen-no-naishi and Ōmi-no-kimi, we notice differences in the object of mockery being targeted in each episode. In the first story, it is Suetsumuhana's retrogressive and retrospective character that is scorned by those who are considered progressive and ambitious, while the progressive and ambitious character of Lady Murasaki is praised. In contrast, because of Gen-no-naishi's age, it is precisely her progressive and ambitious character that is mocked by those considered progressive (Genji and Tō-no-chūjō). Thus, this story can have a self-reflective irony. Finally, in a reversal of the Suetsumuhana-and-Murasaki balance, the Ōmi-no-kimi story admires Tamakazura's modest character while ridiculing Ōmi-no-kimi's progressive and ambitious traits.

To summarise, the *Genji* narrative features two types of woman – the first is ambitious and progressive while the second is modest and calm. These traits are distinctly represented by Kiritsubo and Murasaki in the Wakamurasaki/Murasaki group and by Utsusemi and Yūgao in the Hahakigi/Tamakazura group. Each of the three ugly, elderly and indecent ladies dealt with in this chapter – Suetsumuhana, Gen-no-naishi and Ōmi-no-kimi – has links to the Hahakigi/Tamakazura group. We have also identified a polyphonic narrative in the three stories of Suetsumuhana, Gen-no-naishi and Ōmi-no-kimi. These episodes present the voice of the Genji, Murasaki and Tō-no-chūjō side, while also creating a space for the perspectives of the Suetsumuhana, Gen-no-naishi and Ōmi-no-kimi side. Thus, the text gives the viewpoint of the beautiful, the young and the decent (admiration for the beautiful and the strong), while also ensuring the reader understands the viewpoint of the ugly, the old and the indecent (sympathy with the ugly and the weak). Though, on the superficial level, ugly, old and indecent characters are mocked, a strong current of sympathy for these marginalised characters flows beneath the surface of the narrative.

Suetsumuhana's ugly figure is used as a cloak beneath which the progressive Genji and Lady Murasaki laugh at her regressive character. In Gen-no-naishi's case, Genji and Tō-no-chūjō mock her elderliness as a means of ridiculing her aggressive sexuality. Ōmi-no-kimi's story reverses Suetsumuhana's case, in that it is the former's progressive character that is laughed at by the progressive Tō-no-chūjō, while Tamakazura's modest character is praised. The ambitious, progressive and even aggressive features criticised are, however, shared by other people in the tale, especially Genji, Murasaki and Tō-no-chūjō. Thus, by laughing at Gen-no-naishi and Ōmi-no-kimi, the reader has an impression of also laughing at Genji, Tō-no-chūjō and other ambitious courtiers.

Polyphonic narrative does not occur coincidentally. It is a strategy that has been deliberately constructed by writers of narrative. Murasaki Shikibu was an innovator in this respect and uses a variety of strategies to achieve a polyphonic effect in the *Genji* text. As an author, Murasaki was at pains on some occasions to distinguish between the consciousness of the narrator and the other characters or deliberately to blur the line between the consciousness of one character and of another. In this style of fictional language it becomes impossible to tell whether the judgement made in the text originated with the narrator, with character A, or with character B. Thus, the authorial voice which carries a strong monistic authority of thought, philosophy or ideology disappears. This is a characteristic highly developed in *The Tale of Genji* in the typical tradition of Japanese fictional language.

A polyphonic effect is also realised by the narrative thread being taken up at different times by different narrators. The role of narrator of *The Tale*

68   The Tale of Genji

of Genji is taken by various ladies-in-waiting. That is, while the narrator of the "Paulownia" chapter and of the "Hahakigi" chapter are both ladies-in-waiting, they are, in fact, different women. By making the different voices of different narrators tell the story, the text acknowledges the coexistence of conflicting views. This is a strategy repeatedly used by Murasaki Shikibu in *The Tale of Genji*. Third, in fiction, different characters can make different judgements of the same issue. Although this strategy can be deployed in any fictional language, if the authorial narrator controls the whole text, the effect is diminished or lost. *The Tale of Genji* lacks this sort of authorial narrator. Murasaki Shikibu instead creates spaces in which her characters speak in their own voices. Finally, a polyphonic tone in *Genji* is realised through the use of intertextuality and references to previous traditional stories. By contrasting Genji to *Ise monogatari*'s Narihira, or by comparing Tō-no-chūjō and Ōmi-no-kimi to the father and son in *The Lotus Sutra*, the reader can obtain a perspective different from the most apparent meaning of the insulated original text. By using these techniques, *The Tale of Genji* is able to reveal simultaneously, and rather remarkably in a single text, "admiration for the strong, beautiful, young and decent" and "sympathy with the weak, ugly, old and indecent".

From the ideological perspective, it is important to note the two contradictory views coexisting in the story. For instance, as we have seen in Chapter 2, although Genshin has multiple viewpoints, in *Essentials of Rebirth* (*Ōjōyōshū*) his writing is, as might be expected, narrated in a monologic narrative. Therefore, contradiction becomes inevitable. But, as we have seen, since it is polyphonic in tone, the style of narration in *The Tale of Genji* permits the simultaneous existence of two or more different views. It is only fiction that allows us to overcome the restrictions of a single mode of thinking and thus to express the coexistence of multiple and contradictory thoughts without any inconsistency. This issue is not just one of literary appreciation; it also has important implications in fields such as identity. At present, individuality or identity is regarded as being constituted mainly by philosophical, religious, political and everyday language which requires a monistic voice clearly dividing the narrator and the character. If language and narrative play a crucial role in forming identity, then fictional language perhaps has the potential to initiate a radical change in the manner in which identity is conceived.[33]

4 Women, humble men and insulted people in *The Tale of the Heike*

4.1. Introduction

In this chapter we shall discuss the contrast between "respect for the strong" and "sympathy with the weak" in the war tale *The Tale of the Heike*, compiled in the thirteenth to fourteenth centuries. In the previous chapter on *Genji*, I discussed the "admiration for the strong", associated with the Wakamurasaki/Murasaki group, and "compassion for the weak", associated with Hahakigi/Tamakazura group, as contradictory themes and motifs which then synthesise into the polyphony of the story as a whole. In this chapter, however, I shall contribute to text-based comparative research by examining how the strong–weak binary is differently narrated in the different texts of *The Tale of the Heike*. In terms of the great narratives of Japanese literature, *The Tale of the Heike* is regarded as being second only to *The Tale of Genji* (Miner, Odagiri and Morrell 1985: 49; Miller 1996: 313) and comparable only to that text in terms of its immeasurable influence on later Japanese literature. Helen Craig McCullough suggests that no single Japanese literary work has influenced so many writers in so many genres for so long a time as the *Heike* (McCullough 1988: 9). However, compared with the detailed attention given to *The Tale of Genji* in English-language scholarship, study of *The Tale of the Heike* is very limited.[1] One of the obstacles hindering research was the existence of widely differing texts of the narrative. There was tacit agreement among scholars that before research, including English-language research, into the *Heike* could proceed it was necessary to clarify the relationship between extant texts and to reconstruct the original form of the narrative.

The *Heike* texts are roughly divided into two categories: recited texts dictated by a blind lute-playing reciter known as *biwa hōshi* and texts originally composed for reading. Previous scholarship assumed that the short version of the text composed for reading, the *Shibu kassenjō* text, was the oldest extant form of the *Heike*.[2] The much longer version, the *Engyō* text (also called *Enkyō* or *Enkei*),[3] was thought to have been compiled later, on the supposition that additional stories were successively added during the copying process.[4] But, following Mizuhara Hajime's 1970s studies on the *Engyō* text, this position

70   The Tale of the Heike

has shifted, with critics now agreeing that the longer text, in fact, preserves the old form. Accordingly, Saeki Shin'ichi declared in 1999 that the controversy over the original form of *Heike* had finally come to an end.[5] Evidence in support of this privileging of the *Engyō* text includes the digressive style of narration, the lack of literary refinement and the inclusion of historical record in addition to purely literary material by the original compilers (Mizuhara 1979: 17–18, 295). However, while the *Engyō* text may now be recognised for its age, the *Kakuichi* text, which scholars agree has been subject to extensive revision, has long been regarded as the most artistically refined final version of the recited *Heike* text.[6] There have been three major English translations of *Heike monogatari*. The first was made by Kitagawa Hiroshi and Bruce T. Tsuchida, and published by University of Tokyo Press in 1975. The second was Helen Craig McCullough's translation, published by Stanford University Press in 1988. The third was Burton Watson and Haruo Shirane's abridged translation, published by Columbia University Press in 2006. All are based on the *Kakuichi* text. It is often said that, rather than the *Engyō* text, it has been the *Kakuichi* version that has specifically refined the *Heike* literarily and artistically, and unified the whole text under a cohesive rubric.

Concerning differences between the *Engyō* and *Kakuichi* texts, Matsuo Ashie argues that the *Kakuichi* text consistently evokes its thematic emotion of *mujō* (impermanence) by describing human emotion in terms of corresponding landscape depictions. In contrast, she continues, the *Engyō* text embeds various writings such as records, anecdotes, historical documents and memoir, and is proud of its wide range of information. She sees artistic narrative as the basis of the *Kakuichi* text, on the one hand, and the intellectual activity of collecting records of religious sermons, official documents and documentary diaries as the foundation of the *Engyō* text, on the other (Matsuo 1998: 74–93). Some scholars, nevertheless, also see artistic value in the *Engyō* text. Kobayashi Yoshikazu, for example, searches for a polyphonic voice in this work (Kobayashi Yoshikazu 1991: 64–8), while Ubukata Takashige tries to find a coherency in the *Engyō* text's multivariant modes (Ubukata 1996: 132–9). However, in spite of the arguments advanced by researchers such as Kobayashi and Ubukata, *Heike* scholarship still tends to evaluate the *Engyō* text, notwithstanding the fact that this version preserves the old form, as inconsistent, incongruous and lacking serious editorial work, and the *Kakuichi* text as well organised and coherent. From this point of view, the latter is assessed as having greater literary and artistic value than the former.[7] How this process from the *Engyō* to the *Kakuichi* text has unfolded is a question that has recently been explored by many Japanese specialists. I would argue that the strong–weak issue is also related to comparative studies of the *Heike*. Certainly, in the chapter that follows we shall see how the *Engyō* and *Kakuichi* texts deal differently with "admiration for the strong" and "sympathy with the weak". First, however, I shall briefly review the previous literature relating to our study.

While vast effort has been dedicated to textual criticism, scholars have examined many other aspects of the *Heike* narrative. Extensive discussion, for example, has been devoted to Buddhist elements, including the concept of impermanence (*mujō*) and the manner in which Hōnen's Pure Land Buddhist teaching is depicted.[8] There is also a lengthy history of research into literary aspects of the text, such as the style of fictionalising historical characters.[9]

Haruo Shirane has argued in favour of two general canons of literary criticism. The first centres around tropes of dominance, including authority, masculinity, the nation-state and the elite. The second is associated with subordinate groups, such as the colonised, women, and the common people (Shirane and Suzuki (ed.) 2000: 1–18). Citing Shirane's notion, David T. Bialock writes that, from its earliest beginning, *The Tale of the Heike* has always straddled these two canons. This has produced an official canon that is associated with the vested interests of particular centres of power and authority, and which reproduces the values of the dominant group. It has also led to the emergence of a popular canon which is sympathetic towards those deprived of power (Bialock 2000: 165).

In a 1980 study examining the *Heike* from the perspective of power structures, Hyōdō Hiromi suggests that *monogatari* is actually derived from the words *mono*, meaning dead spirits, and *gatari*, meaning to talk. He thus argues that *Heike monogatari* is a tale told by the spirits of the dead defeated in a battle for kingship. Hyōdō's work draws on both Orikuchi Shinobu's etymological study of *monogatari* and Tsukudo Reikan's view that the *Heike* is a tale to placate and appease vengeful spirits (Orikuchi 1985: 102–3; Tsukudo 1976: 299). By overlaying the work of these scholars with the new concept of power structure, Hyōdō's ground-breaking study effectively expanded the nature of *Heike* scholarship (Hyōdō 1985: 25; 1989: 8).[10] For instance, in a book published almost simultaneously with Hyōdō's study of *monogatari*, Ubukata Takashige argued for the *Heike* as a story of a heretic family centred on Emperor Antoku which resisted and was finally defeated by the political power of the family of the authentic emperor (Ubukata 1984: 15, 122–3). Akasaka Norio also sees the *Heike* as a tale of power structures. Drawing on Yamaguchi Masao's study of kingship, Akasaka argues that the king in a non-Japanese context is destined to be destroyed as a scapegoat by outsiders. The *Heike*, however, depicts a Japanese style of power transfer. Here, the outsider (in this case, the Heike family) presents a threat to, although never overthrows, those holding the power of kingship (in this case, the emperor's family). Instead, the outsider manipulates the king as a puppet figure and is then in turn overthrown by a newcomer (the Genji family) (Akasaka 1986; Yamaguchi 1979: 203–25).

Borrowing from René Girard's theory of violence, Ōtsu Yūichi proposes three functions of the war tale. The first is to narrate the failure of the hero's rebellion against the king, and thus both confirm the power of kingship and teach the reader about royal strength. The second is to narrate the tragic hero and thereby provide the reader with the opportunity to release her or

72 The Tale of the Heike

his own desire to rebel. The third function is to conceal the system in which the story of rebellion is in actuality the story of the absoluteness of kingship. Consequently, Ōtsu sees in the tale of warfare a discourse designed to maintain kingship itself (Ōtsu 2005: 7–81, 177–223).

Drawing on Foucault, Derrida and also Ōtsu, Takagi Makoto notes the importance in any analysis of symbolic power in the *Heike* of analysing the relationship between the function of the text and its reader. He discusses three types of reader. These are the reader who accepts at face value without criticism the "grand narrative" produced by the text, the reader who adds new hidden meanings to the text by referring to knowledge outside the text, and the reader who produces new significance by criticising the text and identifying inconsistencies and discrepancies. Takagi insists that a study of textual power structures should begin with the first type of reader and move through to the third. That is, the reader's job is not only to find the apparent form of power in the text but also to add new meanings to the power presented and finally to create a new significance by deconstructing the text (Takagi 2001: 118–41).

To summarise the previous research focusing on the power structures of the *Heike*, we can confirm that this narrative is now regarded as a tale to placate defeated heroes. Insisting as it does, perhaps unintentionally, on the absoluteness of kingship, the text ultimately entrenches the pervading power system. In other words, much current scholarship makes it incumbent upon the reader to attempt to find new meanings in the power structures presented in the *Heike* and to create new significance by deconstructing the text. This perspective focuses on the struggle, which may or may not be successful, of a strong hero seeking the right to hold power.

However, not all *Heike* scholarship has emphasised the kingly hero. Although their work has less of a profile, a number of scholars have also examined the perspective of the weak, the mediocre and the common presented in the text. This is, in fact, the perspective I intend to probe in the discussion that follows. Mizuhara Hajime and Imanari Genshō (Motoaki) are two critics whose research focuses on this aspect.[11] Mizuhara argues that the *Heike* advocates an ethic of the weak, who criticise but ultimately validate the strong (Mizuhara 1971: 329). Imanari's interest is in women, children and the weak, with particular emphasis on their rebirth in the Pure Land paradise of Buddhism (Imanari 1971: 210–36). To date, however, there has been no significant study which compares the *Engyō* and *Kakuichi* texts from the perspective of the manner in which they portray the weak. In the following sections I shall explore how the two texts differ with regard to the representation of this group.

4.2. Women, humble men and insulted people

It is useful to begin with a summary of the issues raised in the studies conducted by Mizuhara Hajime and Imanari Genshō. First, Mizuhara argues that one of the principal themes of the *Heike* is that of the sad woman.[12] This theme is exemplified in three narratives as follows. (1) In the first, Lady Tashi (a consort of the late Retired Emperor Konoe) is forced against her will, at the command of the Emperor Nijō, to become the latter's consort (*Engyō* I: 47–51, *Kakuichi* I: 29–32, McCullough 37–9). [13] (2) In the second, Gotokudaiji Sanesada, Lady Tashi's brother, journeys from the new capital, Fukuhara, to Kyoto and visits his sister's palace in order to comfort her in her loneliness (*Engyō* I: 417–19, *Kakuichi* I: 272–4, McCullough 169–71). (3) In the final narrative, Retired Emperor Go-Shirakawa visits Ōhara to console Kenreimon'in (*Engyō* II: 513, 533, *Kakuichi* II: 399, 407, McCullough 432, 437). Since Gotokudaiji Sanesada is involved in each of the above incidents, Mizuhara suggests that Sanesada plays a vital role in creating the theme of the sad woman. On each occasion, Tashi, Kenreimon'in and Sanesada respectively compose poems on the topic of the moon. Thus, Mizuhara argues that the moon functions as a metaphor of the glorious high rank of women of pathetic fate (Mizuhara 1979: 399–406).

Second, Mizuhara argues that the nameless women's viewpoint can be clearly found in the passage "The forty or more women, to whom no punishments had been meted out, had turned to relatives for assistance or gone to stay with other connections" (not found in *Engyō*, *Kakuichi* II: 408, McCullough 437). This comment, which, as noted, is absent from the *Engyō* version, is made by the narrator in the "Initiates' Chapter" when explaining the situation after the battle at Dan-no-ura. While this brief passage may appear to be an insignificant anecdote, Mizuhara interprets it as a counter-theme contrasted against the war tale's theme of violent fighting (Mizuhara 1995: 103–10).

Third, Mizuhara argues that one of the literary viewpoints of the *Engyō* text is, in fact, that of the weak. However, recited texts such as the *Kakuichi* text might modify and thus supersede this (Mizuhara 1971: 105–6; 1979: 93–4). As a specific example of the *Engyō*'s presentation of the viewpoint of the weak, Mizuhara points to the fact that the sad story of the suicide of the pathetic and timorous Koremori is narrated in that text as many as four times. These narrations appear in chapter IV, section 35 (II: 178), chapter V-1, section 17 (II: 231–3), chapter V-1, section 30 (II: 286) and chapter V-2, section 10 (II: 320).

Fourth, Mizuhara points out that attention to people of the lower social classes is apparent in the "Dedication of Tokujōjuin" section of the *Engyō* text. Here, a poor, nameless monk of humble origin with merciful heart and virtuous conduct is appointed leader at the dedication service (Mizuhara 1979: 407–29). In addition, continues Mizuhara, there is a focus on the Fudaraku Temple and its belief in Yakushi Nyorai and also in Hakusan (Shirayama). Each of these is associated with a deep concern for the poor, the humble and those discriminated against (Mizuhara (ed.) 1992–7, 4: 7–24).

Imanari Genshō, in contrast to Mizuhara, insists that those in the *Heike* designated for rebirth in the Buddhist Pure Land paradise are mostly

74   The Tale of the Heike

women, children and the weak. He lists twenty-six examples, namely the sisters Giō and Ginyo, their mother Toji, Hotoke, Senju-no-mae, Kenreimon'in, Awa-no-naishi, Dainagon-no-suke, Narichika, Shunkan, Yorimasa, Shigemori, Kiyotsune, Tadanori, Kozaishō, Koremori, the Hyōe Novice, Ishidōmaru, the Nun of the Second Rank, Emperor Antoku, Munemori, Kiyomune, Shigehira, Tomotada, Kii-no-Jirōbyōe Tamenori and Rokudai (Imanari 1971: 226–8).

A review of the above five points, with special emphasis on the comparison between the *Engyō* and *Kakuichi* texts, raises the following issues. First, since the stories of Tashi, Kenreimon'in and Sanesada are each found in the *Engyō* and *Kakuichi* texts, we cannot say that the sad story of women is characteristic of either one of the two texts. In fact, both texts have sympathy for glorious women of high rank who fall down on their fate.

The comment on forty or more women who seek assistance from relatives and other connections after the battle at Dan-no-ura is in the *Kakuichi* text, and not in the *Engyō* text. Hence, on this occasion, it is the *Kakuichi* text that is concerned with the fate of these nameless women. On the other hand, however, following the stories of the many Heike warriors killed after the battle at Ichi-no-tani, the *Engyō* text says: "The wives of people killed in this battle pathetically altered their appearance by wearing the black robes worn by nuns and then recited Amida's name for their husbands' enlightenment" (*Engyō* II: 274). This remark is not found in the *Kakuichi* text, although that text does describe the aftermath of the battle at Ichi-no-tani (*Kakuichi* II: 181–2, McCullough 320). This leads us to conclude that both the *Engyō* and the *Kakuichi* texts similarly express sympathy with the sad fate of nameless women or wives, although on different occasions.

Concerning the suicide of Koremori, both the second and the fourth examples cited above are found in the *Kakuichi* text (*Kakuichi* II: 224–5, McCullough 341; *Kakuichi* II: 145, McCullough 299). Besides the above four anecdotes, the section on "The Parade of Heads", which is in both the *Engyō* and the *Kakuichi* texts (*Engyō* II: 290, *Kakuichi* II: 198–9, McCullough 327), describes Koremori's mind in the process of deciding on suicide. That is to say, of those sections which depict Koremori's weak and vacillating mind, the first and third examples cited above are unique to the *Engyō* text, while the second and the fourth, and the account of Koremori's decision to commit suicide in the section on "The Parade of Heads", are each in both the *Engyō* and the *Kakuichi* texts. Thus, we are able to say that the *Engyō* text shows more concern for Koremori's weakness than the *Kakuichi* text.

With respect to attention paid to those of the lower classes, Mizuhara is right in pointing out this aspect of the "Dedication of Tokujōjuin" section of the *Engyō* text. In this passage, Retired Emperor Toba remarks: "The leader at the dedication service is not necessarily intelligent, nor good at preaching. Even if he is a man of humble origin, I wish the poorest monk in this world with a merciful heart and virtuous conduct to be the leader" (*Engyō* I: 19; not found in the *Kakuichi* text). This comment well shows the *Engyō*

The Tale of the Heike   75

text's emphasis on lower-class people of humble origin. Regard for the lower classes in the *Engyō* text can also be seen in the story of Emperor Ninmyō as reported by Chōken. When famine and epidemic visited various parts of the country, Emperor Ninmyō, concerned for the welfare of the common people, ordered Enryakuji Temple to pray for good weather and to overcome disease. While the *Engyō* text reports this story (*Engyō* I: 98–100), the *Kakuichi* text does not.

Lastly, concerning the issue of rebirth in the Pure Land paradise, we can distinguish two categories among the twenty-six persons listed by Imanari. The first are those whose rebirth in the Pure Land is clearly mentioned in the text. There are, for example, passages such as the following: "I have heard that all of those nuns achieved their goal of rebirth in the Pure Land, each in her turn" (*Kakuichi* II: 409, McCullough 37), or "[Shigemori] breathed his last soon afterward, on the First of the Eight Month, maintaining correct thoughts in his final hour (*Rinjū shōnen ni jūshite*)" (*Engyō* I: 291, *Kakuichi* I: 172, McCullough 117).[14] In this category we might also include those rebirths that are clearly indicated as oracles in the dreams of other characters. Thus, the passage "Then, he (Mongaku, alias Moritō) dreamt of lotus flowers blooming on [Wataru's wife's] grave and cried for joy" (*Engyō* I: 467) is clearly an indication of the rebirth of Wataru's wife. In the *Kakuichi* text, mention is found of the rebirth of Senju-no-mae (*Kakuichi* II: 224, McCullough 341), Kenreimon'in (*Engyō* II: 534, *Kakuichi* II: 409, McCullough 438), Awa-no-naishi (*Kakuichi* II: 409, McCullough 438), Dainagon-no-suke (*Kakuichi* II: 409, McCullough 438), Shigemori (*Engyō* I: 291, *Kakuichi* I: 172, McCullough 117) and Koremori (*Engyō* II: 354, *Kakuichi* II: 248, McCullough 353). Besides these six characters, some versions of the *Kakuichi* text include the story of Giō, Ginyo, their mother Toji, and Hotoke in which all four are also described as having been reborn in paradise. If this latter group is added to the original group of six, it results in a total of ten rebirths in the Buddhist Pure Land paradise referred to in various versions of the *Kakuichi* text. The second category consists of characters who, although their rebirths are not clearly described, express the wish to be reborn in the Pure Land. For instance, Yorimasa's death is depicted as follows: "Yorimasa turned toward the west, chanted ten Buddha-invocations in a loud voice . . . thrust the tip of his sword into his belly and fell forward, his vitals pierced" (*Engyō* I: 381–2, *Kakuichi* I: 247, McCullough 157). Similarly, the end of Shunkan's life reads: "(Shunkan) ceased to consume even his former meagre fare, continuously chanted the name of Amida Buddha and prayed for correct thoughts in his final hour (*Rinjū shōnen o zo inorare keru*). On the twenty-third day after Ariō's arrival, he died in his rude shelter at the age of thirty-seven" (*Kakuichi* I: 167, McCullough 114).

It is important to distinguish here between to die while *maintaining or staying in correct thoughts* in his/her final hour (*Rinjū shōnen ni jūshite*) and to die while *praying for correct thoughts* in his/her final hour (*Rinjū shōnen o zo*

76   The Tale of the Heike

inorare keru) (emphases are mine). The former can be considered as a sign of rebirth in the Pure Land paradise, whereas the latter only shows the person's desire for rebirth.[15] Thus, those in the *Kakuichi* text whose rebirth in the Pure Land paradise is not featured in spite of their expressing the wish to be reborn are Narichika, Shunkan, Yorimasa, Kiyotsune, Tadanori, Kozaishō, the Hyōe Novice, Ishidōmaru, the Nun of the Second Rank, Emperor Antoku, Munemori, Kiyomune, Shigehira, Tomotada, Kii-no-Jirōbyōe Tamenori and Rokudai. This is a total altogether of sixteen persons.

Of the two categories mentioned, it is reasonable to regard only the first as a clear case of rebirth in the Pure Land. That is, although Hōnen teaches that the invocational nembutsu is sufficient to achieve rebirth in the Pure Land, the text's intention to save the characters in the Pure Land is obvious in the first category but not in the second. A comparison of the manner in which the ten persons in the first category are featured in the *Engyō* and *Kakuichi* texts shows that three – namely Shigemori, Koremori and Kenreimon'in – are designated for rebirth in the Pure Land in both versions, while the Pure Land rebirths of Senju-no-mae, Awa-no-naishi and Dainagon-no-suke are described only in the *Kakuichi* text. In fact, these three women's deaths are simply not mentioned in the *Engyō* text. In addition, the rebirths in the Pure Land of the four women Giō, Ginyo, their mother Toji, and Hotoke are described in the *Engyō* text and in some editions of the *Kakuichi* texts.

It is important to notice that, besides the above ten persons in the first category, the *Engyō* text clearly tells of the Pure Land rebirth of a number of other characters. I shall introduce them one by one. The first is Kiyomori's father, Tadamori. The text notes that he

> died facing the west, as if sleeping. In his life, he lived in the splendour derived from the benefit of dedicating a thousand and one Buddha statues. Having come to his end, he was led by three Buddhas and reborn on a lotus flower in the Pure Land of Nine Grades.
>
> (*Engyō* I: 29)

The *Kakuichi* text, on the other hand, merely refers to Tadamori's death with no mention of rebirth:

> Tadamori died at the age of fifty-eight, on the Fifteenth of the First Month in the third year of Ninpei, after having attained the office of Punishments Minister.
>
> (*Kakuichi* I: 11, McCullough 27)

The second and third cases are those of Wataru's wife and her mother. The *Engyō* text lengthily explores the well-known story of Moritō's (Mongaku's) religious awakening. In the *Engyō* text, the Pure Land rebirth of Wataru's wife is suggested in Moritō's dream:

The Tale of the Heike   77

Moritō . . . gathered her ashes and buried them in a grave in a back garden. In the first three years he continued to perform memorial services for her by practising Buddhist austerities and praying to Amida Buddha more sincerely than anyone else. Then, he dreamt of lotus flowers blooming on her grave and cried for joy.

(*Engyō* I: 467)

Following Wataru's wife being mistakenly killed by Moritō, her mother prays to be reborn in the Pure Land in order to meet her daughter again. The text subsequently recounts:

on the Eighth of the Tenth Month in the following year, [the mother of Wataru's wife] at last achieved the goal of rebirth in the Pure Land at the age of fifty-five.

(*Engyō* I: 467)

This element is not featured in the *Kakuichi* text.

The fourth case of rebirth referred to in the *Engyō* text only is that of Kogō, who was loved by the emperor Takakura but hated by Kiyomori, who eventually forced her to become a nun. The text recounts that Kogō was finally reborn in the Pure Land at the age of 80 (*Engyō* I: 592). In contrast, the *Kakuichi* text merely relates her last years as follows: "Thus at the age of twenty-three she went to live at Saga, a shabby figure in deep black robes. A sad story, indeed!" (*Kakuichi* I: 337–8, McCullough 206). The contrast between Kogō's Pure Land rebirth in the *Engyō* text and her sad and shabby last days in the *Kakuichi* text is striking.

The fifth case is Kōkamon'in Fujiwara no Seishi. She is a daughter of Fujiwara no Tadamichi and a wife of Emperor Sutoku. The *Engyō* notes that after her death a marvellous fragrance permeated the air (*Engyō* I: 665). This story does not appear in the *Kakuichi* text. The sixth is Kako Shinnyo. The daughter of an Usa Shinto shrine priest, she wishes to sleep with an emperor. Her wish comes true when she is invited, although only once, to the bed of Emperor Go-Toba. She is said then to be reborn in the Pure Land without marrying any other man (*Engyō* II: 124–5). This story is also not found in the *Kakuichi* text.

The seventh is Kumagae Naozane. After the Genpei War, Naozane visits the priest Hōnen, practises Buddhist austerities and finally achieves the goal of rebirth in the Pure Land (*Engyō* II: 202). There is no mention of Naozane's rebirth in the *Kakuichi* text's discussion of this character (*Kakuichi* II: 164–76, McCullough 283–90). The eighth and final case is that of Retired Emperor Go-Shirakawa, who maintains correct thoughts in his final hour (*Rinjū shōnen midarezu*) (*Engyō* II: 549). Go-Shirakawa's rebirth in the Pure Land is not mentioned in the *Kakuichi* text.

A comparison of the two texts thus makes it clear that three women (Senju-no-mae, Awa-no-naishi and Dainagon-no-suke) are destined for rebirth in

78 The Tale of the Heike

the Pure Land only in the *Kakuichi* text, whereas nine women (Giō, Ginyo, their mother Toji, Hotoke, Kogō, Seishi, Wataru's wife and her mother, and Kako Shinnyo) and three men (Taira Tadamori, Kumagae Naozane and Retired Emperor Go-Shirakawa) are destined for Pure Land rebirth only in the *Engyō* text. (There are also some *Kakuichi* editions that feature the story of Giō, Ginyo, their mother Toji, and Hotoke, including their rebirth in the Pure Land.) In addition, three persons (Shigemori, Koremori and Kenreimon'in) are destined for rebirth in the Pure Land paradise in both texts.

There are a number of features common to some of the above persons. Hattori Kōzō argues that the role of the women reborn in the *Kakuichi* text (Kenreimon'in, Senju-no-mae, Awa-no-naishi and Dainagon-no-suke) is to placate the dead. Kenreimon'in appeases the spirits of the Heike family, Senju-no-mae comforts the spirit of Shigehira, while Awa-no-naishi and Dainagon-no-suke console Kenreimon'in. This, argues Hattori, is the reason for their rebirth. This critic further suggests that, since Giō, Ginyo, Hotoke and Toji have no placatory role in the original *Kakuichi* text, their rebirths are not narrated (Hattori 1983). Mizuhara Hajime, on the other hand, argues that Awa-no-naishi and Dainagon-no-suke are reborn in the Pure Land by virtue of their roles in passing down Kenreimon'in's story to the next generation (Mizuhara 1971: 144–63). Both Hattori's and Mizuhara's interpretations are feasible; and, since there can be plural reasons for one phenomenon, they are neither exclusive of nor incompatible with each other.

However, a comparison of the *Engyō* and *Kakuichi* texts suggests another possible interpretation. First, it will be useful to examine the case of Kenreimon'in, who is the only woman destined for Pure Land rebirth in both the *Engyō* and the *Kakuichi* texts. While this event is one of the highlights of both versions of the *Heike*, it is interesting to note that Kenreimon'in's character is portrayed quite differently in each of the two texts. Chō Munju (Jo Mun Joo), for example, has noted that only the *Engyō* text suggests Kenreimon'in's sexual relations with Go-Shirakawa and her incestuous relations with her brothers, Munemori and Tomomori. According to Chō, this woman's miserable fate helps to placate the Heike family (Chō 2001). Chō correctly suggests that the Kenreimon'in of the *Kakuichi* text is depicted as more gentle, modest and ladylike than the *Engyō* character. Conversely, the *Engyō* Kenreimon'in is stronger and more rigid than the woman depicted in the *Kakuichi* text. For instance, in the latter, Kenreimon'in confides to Retired Emperor Go-Shirakawa:

> But, never, in all the lives to come, shall I forget the Former Emperor's [Antoku's] face. I try to forget, but forgetting is impossible; I try to control my grief, but that is also impossible. Nothing causes such sorrow as parental affection: that is why I pray faithfully for the Emperor's enlightenment, morning and evening.
>
> (*Kakuichi* II: 401–2, McCullough 434)

Kenreimon'in here displays a degree of maternal affection and devotion that is lacking in the *Engyō* text. In contrast, the *Engyō* Kenreimon'in, although initially demurring, openly suggests the incest transacted between her and her brothers, Munemori and Tomomori, at the urging of Retired Emperor Go-Shirakawa. Arguing that everything is karma set in the former life, she declares that she need not grieve too much at the death of her son (*Engyō* II: 527). She clearly and candidly explains her experiences and her chagrin at being unable to regain her past glory (*Engyō* II: 531).

Here it can be said that the *Kakuichi* text depicts Kenreimon'in as a devoted, modest, ladylike woman who is also a nurturing mother to her deceased son, Emperor Antoku. Thus, it advocates her Pure Land rebirth. In contrast, the *Engyō* Kenreimon'in is presented as a woman insulted and injured by men. Mortified though she is by her helplessness, she has no option but rigidly to endure her ill fate. Her own wish to be reborn in the Pure Land is much stronger than that of the *Kakuichi* character. In fact, one of the significant features common in all four women whose rebirth in the Pure Land is related in the *Kakuichi* text is their devotion and sense of service to someone of a higher rank. Kenreimon'in devotes herself to the Emperor Antoku, Awa-no-naishi and Dainagon-no-suke to Kenreimon'in, and Senju-no-mae to Shigehira. Each of these women cares for and helps a higher-ranked party. Given that neither text relates the Pure Land rebirth of men who devote themselves to others, such as the Takiguchi Novice or Ariō, we can assume that a message of the *Kakuichi* text is that devotion to others is the path to Pure Land rebirth for women only. Thus, the *Kakuichi* text intentionally sets out to advocate the Pure Land rebirth of the devoted woman, whereas the *Engyō* text does not have such a concern.

In contrast to the *Kakuichi* text, among the nine women in the *Engyō* text destined to be reborn in the Pure Land, Giō, Ginyo, Toji, Hotoke (I repeat that some of the *Kakuichi* texts have the story of their rebirth in the Pure Land) and Kogō are all women insulted and injured by Kiyomori. Although they do not directly resist Kiyomori's power, they are never obedient. They patiently endure their helpless fate and wait to be freed from the mundane world. Lee Sun-Young (I Son'yon) argues that the *Engyō* text emphasises the stouteartedness of Giō, Ginyo, Toji, Hotoke and Kogō, and the manner in which their courageous characters take pride in knowing their shame and fighting against the fates (Lee 1994; 2002). Lee's argument is applicable not only to these five women but also to the other four women whose rebirth in the Pure Land is related only in the *Engyō* text. It will be useful to explore this matter further.

The other four women whose Pure Land rebirth is only related in the *Engyō* text are Wataru's wife, Wataru's wife's mother, Kako Shinnyo and Seishi. Kako Shinnyo, for example, is described as a stubborn girl who does not obey her parents' wish that she marry a Shinto priest. She has her own strong desire to become a high-status woman by marrying a man of high rank. When her fiancé spreads a rumour that the couple have slept together, she curses

80   The Tale of the Heike

him to death. Her wish for a partner of high rank comes true with an invitation to the bed of Emperor Go-Toba. However, she leaves the palace soon after and becomes a nun. Although it is unclear from the text whether her departure is forced or voluntary, it is apparent that she is a strong-willed woman who is insulted by a man.[16]

Wataru's wife is in a sense obedient to the concept of chastity and she deliberately permits herself to be killed by Moritō in order to help her husband. While her devotion to her husband is clear, she also has the will to oppose Moritō's intentions. She therefore has two different sides – sacrificial devotion and strength of will, with the *Engyō* text emphasising the latter. Her mother is depicted as a frivolous woman who leads Moritō to and permits him to have her daughter. Thus, it is rather difficult to understand why the mother is destined to be reborn in the Pure Land. But it should be noted that Wataru mentions that his wife must be an incarnation of Kannon, the Goddess of Mercy, who came to them in order to help them find enlightenment (*Engyō* I: 465). Wataru's wife herself writes in her will that when she attains Buddhahood she will surely lead her mother and husband to the Pure Land (*Engyō* I: 466). Thus, we can presume that the mother of Wataru's wife is guided to and redeemed in the Pure Land by her daughter. We shall return to the matter of relations between parents and their children as depicted in the *Engyō* text later in the discussion.

Seishi is the last woman whose rebirth in the Pure Land is related only in the *Engyō* text, which notes that: "When Emperor Sutoku was exiled to Sanuki, how deep was [Seishi's] sorrow!" (*Engyō* I: 665). Since she is a wife of the vengeful Emperor Sutoku, we can classify her as a woman insulted and injured, if not by authority or by men, then at least by fate. Regardless of the source of this woman's tribulations, we can confirm from the above that it is the *Engyō* rather than the *Kakuichi* text that supports the Pure Land rebirth of women who must persistently endure the hardship of Buddhist austerities after being humiliated by authority, by the strong, by males or by fate.

The Pure Land rebirth of nine women – Giō, Ginyo, Toji, Hotoke, Kogō, Seishi, Wataru's wife and her mother, and Kako Shinnyo – is related only in the *Engyō* text; three women – Senju-no-mae, Awa-no-naishi and Dainagon-no-suke – have their rebirth related only in the *Kakuichi* text. Making a comparison of these, it becomes clear that, while the *Kakuichi* text shows concern for and a desire to see the Pure Land rebirth of women of devotion, the principal focus of the *Engyō* text is women who are insulted and injured or who are forced to endure a helpless fate. It is these latter women that the *Engyō* text seeks to have reborn in the Pure Land paradise. This position is confirmed by the differing emphasis in the depictions of Kenreimon'in in both texts. Thus, the omission of any reference to Giō, Ginyo, Toji and Hotoke in some *Kakuichi* texts may be intentional, given that these women do not fit the required model of devotion. As Tomikura Tokujirō notes, it is generally assumed that the original twelve-volume *Kakuichi* text does not contain sections mentioning these characters (Tomikura 1966: 116). The compilers of these volumes may well have hesitated to include narratives relating the rebirth in the Pure Land of disobedient, strong-willed women.

We have previously noted that, in addition to the women characters mentioned, there are three male characters whose Pure Land rebirth appears in the *Engyō* text. They are Taira Tadamori, Kumagae Naozane and Retired Emperor Go-Shirakawa. In addition, there are two male characters, Shigemori and Koremori, whose rebirth in the Pure Land is related both in the *Engyō* and the *Kakuichi* texts. It will be useful to examine each of the first three cases in more detail.

First, Tadamori is insulted by courtiers as being a man of humble origin who attains high rank. His rebirth is a clear indication of the *Engyō* text's sympathy with humiliated people of humble origin and its wish to allow them to live happily in the Pure Land. The case of Tadamori, in addition to the section on "The Dedication of Tokujōjuin" mentioned previously, indicates that the *Engyō* text's wish to give Pure Land entry to those who are poor and humiliated is not restricted to women. Second, when Kumagae Naozane is walking on the beam of the Uji Bridge, his son, Naomune, follows in order to help. Suddenly realising that nothing is more important than his child, Naozane is overcome by the desire to help his son. This wish leads him eventually to believe in Amida and finally to attain rebirth in the Pure Land. Kumagae Naozane's story emphasises the importance of father–son relations and the value of family in general. The *Engyō* text makes it clear that love for his family led Naozane to the Pure Land (*Engyō* II: 201–2). In this way, the story is similar to that of Wataru's wife and her mother. This point will be discussed later in relation to the *Engyō* text's concern for family.

Lastly, we should not forget that the Pure Land rebirth of Retired Emperor Go-Shirakawa is related only in the *Engyō* text. Rather than being manipulated as a puppet of fate, Retired Emperor Go-Shirakawa skilfully manipulates his own fate. He is one of the strongest authorities in the *Heike*. From this point of view, the *Engyō* text's narration of the Pure Land rebirth of Go-Shirakawa might be seen as contradictory. That is to say, on the one hand, it narrates the rebirth of a strong authority while, on the other hand, it advocates the rebirth of powerless women and men who are humiliated by others, especially those in authority. This point will be explored in the following section, which examines the polemic character of the *Engyō* text.

4.3. Polemical *Engyō* and moderate *Kakuichi*

The previous section has noted the *Engyō* text's special concern for the weak, the lower classes and those who are insulted, discriminated against and humiliated by the strong. It has also noted the presence of some contradiction to this, exemplified by the narration of Retired Emperor Go-Shirakawa's rebirth in the Pure Land. Although it features special concern for the weak, it is also true that the *Engyō* text sometimes expresses blunt contempt for women and for men of humble origins (*onna to gesen*). In contrast, the *Kakuichi*

82   The Tale of the Heike

text tends to avoid both extremes. These differences become evident, for instance, when comparing citations from the "Execution of Saikō" section of each text. The first is from the *Engyō* text while the second comes from the *Kakuichi* text.

> Saikō and his sons were Retired Emperor Go-Shirakawa's favourite men (*kirimono*). They did not respect the world and the people, and had a noble and guiltless man (the Tendai Abbot) banished. Thus they were subject to the Sannō god's divine and mysterious punishment and perished in an instant. People said to each other "Look! I told you this would happen!" *In general, women and men of humble origins, even if they look clever, are thoughtless people. Saikō was a man of humble origins.* However, it seemed that, after obtaining the Retired Emperor's special care, the good karma of this man and his sons apparently ran its course. They caused serious consequences in the world and were therefore punished in that way. It was a disgraceful happening.
>
> (*Engyō* I: 163; my italics)

> Saikō and the others were *insignificant men* (*ifukahi naki mono*, literally means "men who are not worth mentioning") who rose in the world, meddled in affairs of no concern to them, caused the banishment of the guiltless Tendai Abbot, and perished in an instant through the Sannō god's divine and mysterious punishment, their good karma having apparently run its course.
>
> (*Kakuichi* I: 80, McCullough 66; my italics)

It is, first, significant that the sentences "In general, women and men of humble origins, even if they look clever, are thoughtless people" and "Saikō was one of the men of humble origins" appear in the *Engyō* text but have been deleted from the *Kakuichi* text. In addition, the *Engyō* text's expression "Saikō and his sons were the Retired Emperor's favourite men" is modified in the *Kakuichi* version to "Saikō and the others were insignificant men (men who are not worth mentioning)". We see here that the *Engyō* text's accusation against and aversion towards women and men of humble origins is eliminated in the *Kakuichi* text where those who are of humble origins but nonetheless the favourites of a retired emperor become "insignificant men". Concerning these changes, there are two points to be raised. One is that, although the *Engyō* text criticises Retired Emperor Go-Shirakawa with the comment "Saikō and his sons were Retired Emperor Go-Shirakawa's favourite men", the *Kakuichi* text does not. This point will be discussed later. The second point is that, while the *Engyō* text assesses the characters on the basis of gender and social origin, the *Kakuichi* text does this on the basis of individual personality or ability.

To summarise, the *Engyō* text considers that Saikō and others were punished because they were men of humble origin who were favoured by Retired

Emperor Go-Shirakawa, did not respect the world and people, and caused the banishment of the noble and unblemished Tendai Abbot. In contrast, the *Kakuichi* text considers that Saikō and others were punished because they were insignificant men who rose in the world and caused the banishment of the guiltless Tendai Abbot. The *Kakuichi* text's assessment is more individualistic, whereas the *Engyō* text's judgement relates more to the men's origins.

It is also interesting to examine the case of Hitachibō Shōmei's capture of Minamoto Yukiie, whose disposal was ordered by Yoritomo. Hitachibō Shōmei took his trophy to Kamakura, only to find himself banished to Kasai. In Yoritomo's words, the *Engyō* text justifies this as follows: "The reason why a man of humble origin who attacks a Commander-in-Chief is punished is that he has no divine protection. In order to ask for divine protection, I have banished you" (*Engyō* II: 504). However, in the *Kakuichi* text, Yoritomo says: "There is no divine protection for a man who attacks a Commander-in-Chief. That is why I was obliged to discipline you for a time" (*Kakuichi* II: 375–6, McCullough 419). The *Kakuichi* text clearly omits any reference to humble origins as a cause of Yoritomo's actions.

Concerning women and men of humble origins, one point which can be reconfirmed here is the *Engyō* text's contradictory treatment of this group. As pointed out in the previous section, the *Engyō* text shows apparent sympathy for the lower social classes as exemplified in the "Dedication of Tokujōjuin" section and in Chōken's telling of the story of Emperor Ninmyō. We have also seen in the previous section that the *Engyō* text is concerned for people who are insulted and injured, and who endure a helpless fate. This text advocates much more than the *Kakuichi* version for this group to achieve Pure Land rebirth. However, it is also apparent from the above that the *Engyō* text can be bluntly contemptuous towards women and men of humble origin. That is to say, while the *Engyō* text can sometimes show this group sympathy, it can also show them derision and disdain, with some sections being candidly contemptuous. In contrast, the *Kakuichi* text avoids either extreme.

In order to illustrate this contradictory aspect of the *Engyō* text, it will be useful to examine the Retired Emperor Go-Shirakawa's rebirth in the Pure Land, which appears only in that version of the *Heike*. In addition to the "Execution of Saikō" section mentioned above, criticism of Go-Shirakawa is also found in the "Battle at Hōjūji" section (*Engyō* II: 170–1). This battle between Go-Shirakawa and Kiso Yoshinaka results in the death of many noble persons, including the Tendai Abbot. The *Engyō* text reads:

> The noble and the poor, as well as the high and the low, said that "Retired Emperor Go-Shirakawa did not learn from previous failure. Because he ventured into this meaningless battle which caused the deaths of tens of thousands, he was caught and confined. This shows how deep his crime is, and his afterlife must be disgraceful."
>
> (*Engyō* II: 170–1)

84   The Tale of the Heike

In contrast to this harsh criticism, the text also praises Go-Shirakawa, noting that no other emperor has practised Buddhist austerities more diligently (*Engyō* I: 221). At the same time, however, Go-Shirakawa's pride is severely criticised by the Sumiyoshi deity (*Engyō* I: 225). Nonetheless, as I have mentioned earlier, the *Engyō* text beautifully describes Go-Shirakawa's rebirth in the Pure Land Buddhist paradise. Thus, we can conclude that high praise and severe criticism of Go-Shirakawa coexist in the *Engyō* text, whereas in the *Kakuichi* text neither extreme is depicted. This corresponds to the coexistence of deep sympathy with and blunt contempt for women and for men of humble origins in the *Engyō* text and the absence of either extreme in the *Kakuichi* text. To understand this contradiction, we might refer to the study by Ōtsu Yūichi. Concerning the contradictory views on Emperor Go-Daigo made in the tenth century, Ōtsu hypothesises that this results from the emergence of a notion of the sacredness of the king. Both the praise and criticism of Go-Daigo, he argues, confirm an ideal of the king as the best and most sacred being. Thus, praise or criticism of the real-world emperor is conducted against the benchmark of an ideal figure (Ōtsu 2005: 50–1). Similarly, the praise and accusations of Go-Shirakawa are based on an assumption of kingly sacredness. This point alone, however, is insufficient to explain the full range of contradiction apparent in the *Engyō* version. Ultimately, we must acknowledge that the coexistence of contradictory factors is one of the characteristics of this text. Before we proceed to explore this point further, let me first examine some parts of the *Kakuichi* text which seemingly contradict the above contrast between the depiction of women and men of humble origin in the *Engyō* and the *Kakuichi* texts. This is necessary in order to avoid possible misunderstandings.

While it is true that the *Kakuichi* text does not go so far as to accuse women or men of humble origin, it is nevertheless sometimes contemptuous towards these two groups. Both the *Engyō* and *Kakuichi* texts, for example, feature characters who express regret at being a woman. Before Ariō goes to Kikai-ga-shima to see Shunkan, Shunkan's daughter writes a letter to her father which she asks Ariō to deliver. In the letter she writes: "Nothing is worse than being a girl. I would certainly go to that island of yours if I were a boy" (*Engyō* I: 276–7, *Kakuichi* I: 165–6, McCullough 113). Although the sentiment "Nothing is worse than being a girl" is expressed by Shunkan's daughter, it nevertheless expresses the judgement of the narrator. Rather than narratorial contempt, however, the declaration is better-regarded as an acknowledgement of how miserably women of the time were situated.

In this context it is also useful to mention that the reader is told in the "Matter of the Six Paths" section in chapter VI-2 of the *Engyō* text that "In India, China and Japan, whether among the noble or the humble, nothing is more miserable than the woman" (*Engyō* II: 527). This passage is not found in the *Kakuichi* text (*Kakuichi* II: 405–6, McCullough 436).[17] I have mentioned before, and shall mention again shortly, that this position can be related to the *Engyō* text's suggestion that Kenreimon'in has an incestuous relationship with

The Tale of the Heike   85

each of her brothers (*Engyō* II: 527), since the statement given above is part of that anecdote – an anecdote omitted from the *Kakuichi* text (*Kakuichi* II: 405–6, McCullough 436).

Both the *Engyō* and the *Kakuichi* texts demonstrate contempt for men of humble origin in the respective accounts given of Koremori's suicide. At Mount Kōya, Koremori asks his servant Takesato to convey a message to Yashima. The former thereupon ends his life by jumping into the Sea of Kumano with the Hyōe Novice and Ishidōmaru. When, unable to bear being left alone, Takesato tries to enter the water to follow them, the Takiguchi Novice says: "It is base to ignore His Lordship's dying injunctions. A man of humble origin (*gerō*) is a worthless lot!" (*Engyō* II: 347, *Kakuichi* II: 284, McCullough 350). This comment is common to both the *Engyō* and the *Kakuichi* texts. However, in spite of the Takiguchi Novice's admonition, the narration avoids condemning Takesato, declaring instead: "Takesato flung himself into the bottom of the boat and wailed in an agony of grief, too miserable at having been left behind to turn his thoughts to pious exertions for the dead." The sympathetic tone of the text is also evident in a comparison made between Takesato's misery and that of Prince Siddhārtha's groom, Chandaka. These examples confirm that it is a characteristic of the *Kakuichi* text to avoid contempt for woman and for men of humble origin.

4.4. The *Engyō* text's love between men and women, husbands and wives, and other family members, and the *Kakuichi* text's indifferent individualism

There are other points to mention regarding the depiction of women in *The Tale of the Heike*. The "Genbō" section in chapter 7 of the *Kakuichi* text, and in chapter III-2, section 16, of the *Engyō* text, introduces the story of Fujiwara no Hirotsugi in the reign of Emperor Shōmu. Hirotsugi imperilled the nation and was put down by court forces. Later, when Archbishop Genbō was leading the dedication service for the Dazaifu Kannonji Temple, the sky suddenly clouded over. The *Kakuichi* text says that then a mighty thunderclap roared and the archbishop's head was taken off into the clouds by a lightning bolt that came down upon him. The *Engyō* text, on the other hand, relates that a dragon king came down from the sky and took Genbō's body into the clouds. People said that this event was caused by Hirotsugi's violent spirit.

According to the *Kakuichi* text, Hirotsugi's evil spirit killed Genbō because the latter performed a prayer for Hirotsugi's defeat when Hirotsugi imperilled the nation (*Kakuichi* II: 27–8, McCullough 235–6). In contrast, the *Engyō* text claims the reason for the archbishop's demise to be an illicit love-affair between Genbō and Hirotsugi's wife. The *Engyō* text continues:

> *Taihei kōki*[18] says: "Woman is the messenger of a country's ruin (the woman causes the collapse of the nation). Do not love her. To love a

86　The Tale of the Heike

woman is to commit ten charges of offence." It is true that Archbishop Genbō was bewitched by an illusionary appearance, and killed because of a woman. It is miserable.

(Engyō II: 48)

There is no criticism of women of this kind in the *Kakuichi* text.

Both the *Engyō* and the *Kakuichi* texts feature sections in which the Higo Governor, Sadayoshi, encounters the imperial Heike procession fleeing the capital, Kyoto. Springing down from his horse, Sadayoshi asks Munemori, head of the Heike, to stop and return to Kyoto. Munemori explains that the Heike must leave the capital since they cannot bear to let Kenreimon'in and the Nun of the Second Rank suffer a tragic fate (*Kakuichi* II: 58–9, McCullough 252–3). Although both texts note a response to Munemori from Sadayoshi, only the *Engyō* text includes the following comment: "If a man who takes up a bow and arrow has deep compassion for his wife and children, he can never venture to fight" (*Engyō* II: 83). This is further recognition of the claim that "woman is the messenger of a country's ruin" and that the collapse of the Heike was, to some extent, caused by women.

The understanding that "woman is the messenger of a country's ruin" is also found elsewhere in the *Engyō* text. For instance, the *Engyō* text introduces Yang Kuei-fei's story that the nation collapsed because of the emperor's deep love for a woman with connections through her family to political power (*Engyō* II: 6–9). As mentioned in the previous section, the *Engyō* text also provides a lengthy account of the tale of Moritō and Wataru's wife (*Engyō* I: 449–68), a story of how a man's life changes dramatically because of his obsession with a woman. In other words, the *Engyō* text argues, rightly or wrongly, that women are the cause of the collapse of nation, family and man. The *Kakuichi* text, in contrast, makes no such inference.

Notwithstanding the suggestion that "woman is the messenger of a country's ruin", the *Engyō* text also emphasises the importance of love between men and women, and husbands and wives. This is evident, for instance, in the account of Shigemori's death. After the death of Shigemori, *Engyō* readers are given an emotional written memorial composed by his wife emphasising the importance of depth of feeling between a married couple (*fūfu no nasake*), desire between a man and a woman (*nannyo no kokorozashi*) and between people who are sexually united (*dōkin no chigiri* and *icchin no katarahi*). The memorial emphasises how lonely a wife becomes after her husband's death (*Engyō* I: 291–2).[19]

The *Engyō* text also features sections not mentioned in the *Kakuichi* text which emphasise the importance of the man–woman or husband–wife bond. When Saikō is killed by Kiyomori, Saikō's wife informs her son, Morotaka, of his father's death in order that the younger man might flee (*Engyō* I: 162–3, *Kakuichi* I: 80, McCullough 66).[20] Morotaka, however, is nonetheless caught and beheaded, following which his lover personally returns the beheaded body to his home where she cremates and buries it (*Engyō* I: 163).

The Tale of the Heike   87

This account of the actions of Morotaka's lover is absent from the *Kakuichi* text. In addition to emphasising the importance of man–woman and husband–wife relationships, the *Engyō* text also focuses on the love between a parent and a child, between siblings, and between family members generally. Some examples, which are not found in the *Kakuichi* text, are: a description of how the late Emperor Takakura grieved over his mother's death (*Engyō* I: 576–7); brotherly love between Shō no Saburō and Shirō in the Kodama League (*Engyō* II: 220–1); Atsumori's mother's grief upon seeing her son's severed head (*Engyō* II: 267); the grief of the Heike family (*Engyō* II: 273–4); mention of the importance of the relationship between parents and children (*Engyō* II: 527–8; a similar passage is found in Shigemori's wife's memorial writing); Kumagae Naozane's rebirth in the Pure Land, as mentioned previously, being the result of his love for his son, Naomune (*Engyō* II: 201); and the story, also mentioned previously, of Wataru's wife and her mother (*Engyō* I: 466–7).

It is true that, as in Kenreimon'in's case discussed at some length earlier, the *Kakuichi* text also gives value to love between parents and children, and regards family love generally as a precious human relationship. However, compared to the *Kakuichi* text, the *Engyō* text provides more detailed and extended narrations of love of this kind. Examples include narrations of: relations between the father, Narichika, and his son, Naritsune (*Engyō* I: 166/I: 257–61//*Kakuichi* I: 155–7, McCullough 107–8); relations between the father, Yasuyori, and his son, Motoyasu (*Engyō* I: 171–5/I: 186/I: 201–2//*Kakuichi* I: 125, McCullough 89); relations between Yasuyori and his mother (*Engyō* I: 172–5/I: 178/I: 194/I: 269//*Kakuichi* I: 129, McCullough 93); and a description of the sorrow of the Naritsune, Yasuyori and Shunkan families, all of whom were sent to Kikai-ga-shima (*Engyō* I: 177//*Kakuichi* I: 111, 124, McCullough 82, 89).

These examples show that the *Engyō* text is deeply orientated towards love between men and women, husbands and wives, and families generally. In contrast, the *Kakuichi* text is more individualistic and even indifferent, although also fond of devoted and modest women. The *Engyō* text emphasises love between a man and a woman or between a husband and a wife while also regarding woman as "the messenger of a country's ruin" and claiming that "if a man had deep compassion for his wife and children, he could not venture to fight". However, these seemingly conflicting elements may not be as contradictory as they first appear. Both positions indicate the same point, namely how important a lover or a wife is for man. Thus, Tabata Yasuko's assertion that a strong bond existed between husbands and their wives in the Kamakura and Muromachi periods is clearly evident in the *Engyō* text (Tabata Yasuko 1987: 17–20, 156).

It is interesting to note that the *Kakuichi* text demonstrates neither candid contempt for women nor a strong bond between men and women. In contrast, the *Engyō* text records both extremes. That is, the latter makes no attempt to conceal apparent and blunt contempt for women while also

88   The Tale of the Heike

strongly emphasising love between men and women and between family members in general. On the whole, we can say that the *Engyō* text openly expresses strong emotion, whereas the *Kakuichi* text is more moderate, or even calm and elegant.

The passage below, which does not appear in the *Kakuichi* text, clearly demonstrates the *Engyō* text's emphasis on the importance of relationships between husbands and wives. In the second year of Juei, Kiso Yoshinaka was suspected of planning to attack Minamoto Yoritomo. In order to prove his loyalty, Yoshinaka sent Yoritomo his 11-year-old heir, Shimizu no Kanja Yoshishige, as a hostage (*Kakuichi* II: 5–6, McCullough 225). With Yoritomo's trust restored, the *Engyō* text continues:

> Yoshinaka returned to Shinano and, gathering the wives of thirty of his favourite men, said to them: "I exchanged the lives of your husbands for the life of Shimizu no Kanja. What do you think?" The wives joined their hands in prayer and said: "We are greatly appreciative. If our husbands were to abandon you in Kyoto or in Kyūshū, and come back to see their wives and children, and if we were to agree to unite our bodies and souls with these husbands (if we unite our mysterious bodies with such husbands) (*otto ni myōtai awaseba*),[21] we could no longer live beneath the sun, nor walk before a shrine." Having said so, they wrote their oaths and departed. Their husbands, upon hearing this, also joined their hands for joy.
>
> (*Engyō* II: 20)

Besides the apparent high value given in the passage to relations between husbands and wives, the phrase "*otto ni myōtai awaseba*" indicates, if implicitly, sexual union and thus openly indicates sexual expression. This is another typical characteristic of the *Engyō* text, a point that will be explored in the following section.

4.5. Indecent *Engyō* text and decent *Kakuichi* text

The *Engyō* text often reveals amorous males gazing upon women in shameful predicaments. These indicators of male pornographic interest are often deleted in the *Kakuichi* text. For instance, the section on "The Burning of Nara" includes a description of monks who were killed in battle. The *Engyō* text says: "Over seven hundred people were killed in battle and the victors carried more than four hundred heads back to the capital. *It is said that among them were the heads of a few nuns*" (*Engyō* I: 562; my italics). In contrast, the *Kakuichi* text writes: "More than a thousand monks were killed in battle. The victors hung a few heads in front of the Hannyaji gate and carried some others back to the capital" (*Kakuichi* I: 320, McCullough 196). It would appear that the *Kakuichi* text intentionally avoids details of what must have been the miserable scene of nuns' heads hanging before the temple gate.

The Tale of the Heike 89

A further example can be seen at the end of the "Tsuzumi Police Lieutenant" section. Following an account of the battle between Retired Emperor Go-Shirakawa and Kiso Yoshinaka, the *Engyō* text makes a comment which is not found in the *Kakuichi* text. The former says: "There are many funny, terrible and miserable happenings. In the cold weather, the soldiers stripped people of their clothes regardless of their ranks, so some *men and women* were left stark naked. It was extremely pitiful" (*Engyō* II: 170; my italics). At the beginning of the "Tsuzumi Police Lieutenant" section both the *Engyō* and the *Kakuichi* texts make reference to the pillaging activities of Kiso Yoshinaka's troops when they occupied Kyoto. However, while the *Kakuichi* text merely notes the manner in which "wayfarers' possessions were seized and the robes stripped from their backs" (*Kakuichi* II: 101, McCullough 275), the *Engyō* text writes: "wayfarers are not safe. Since (the soldiers) stripped them of their clothes, both *men and women* had shameful experiences" (*Engyō* II: 157; my italics). In the *Kakuichi* text, on the other hand, such an image is prudently obscured by using a gender generic term like "wayfarers" and thus omitting clear reference to either men or women.

The contrast between the pornographic or amorous characteristic of the *Engyō* text and the decency of the *Kakuichi* text is further confirmed by incidents such as Higuchi Kanemitsu's sexual abuse of a court lady, which is narrated in detail in the *Engyō* text while deleted in the *Kakuichi* text (*Engyō* II: 224, *Kakuichi* II: 137, McCullough 294–5). There is also the instance of Kiyomori's obscene conduct to the *shirabyōshi*, Hotoke, being vividly narrated in the *Engyō* text while obscured in the *Kakuichi* text (*Engyō* I: 39, *Kakuichi* I: 20, McCullough 32). In addition, it is very instructive in this respect to compare the two passages from the respective texts which deal with Michimori's meeting with his wife at Noritsune's camp quarters following the Heike defeat in the battle of Mikusa and their preparations for Ichi-no-tani. This comparison clearly shows the *Engyō* text's amorous inclinations and the more reserved tenor of the *Kakuichi*. The former citation is from the *Engyō* text and the latter from the *Kakuichi* text:

Michimori put his armour off at Noritsune's camp quarters, called his wife to him and *lay with her* (*fuse tamaheri*). Noritsune looked at them and said several times: "How can you be so unmanly. . . ." *Their meeting had not been planned as a lover's tryst* (*kokoronarazu wakurabano imose no narahi nareba*), and *they had barely had time to exchange words or express affection for each other* (*mada mutsugoto mo tsukizaru ni*). But mindful of Noritsune's words, Michimori sent his wife away under the cover of evening. As it transpired, it was exactly their last meeting. We are overcome with sadness to think of their pathos.

(*Engyō* II: 238; my italics)

Michimori had someone bring his wife to Noritsune's camp quarters so that he might bid her a final farewell. "I was sent to this front because

90   The Tale of the Heike

it was considered dangerous . . . ," Noritsune said in a fury. Michimori may have felt that the rebuke was deserved, for he hastily donned his armor and sent his wife away.

(*Kakuichi* II: 150, McCullough 302–3)

The comparison clearly demonstrates that, while the *Engyō* text chooses candid and direct expressions, such as "lay with her", "Their meeting had not been planned as a lover's tryst", and "they had barely had time to exchange words or express affection for each other", the *Kakuichi* text avoids using such direct expressions. Compared with the *Engyō* text's deep sympathy with the sexually united husband and wife forced to part, the *Kakuichi* text can appear reserved or even puritanical. From this perspective we might recall that, as many commentators such as Mizuhara have noticed and as I have also mentioned, while the section on "The Matter of the Six Paths" in the *Engyō* text suggests that Kenreimon'in had incestuous relations with her brothers (*Engyō* II: 527), the *Kakuichi* text makes no reference to such a possibility (*Kakuichi* II: 405–6, McCullough 436; Mizuhara 1979: 386–8).

To conclude, through a comparison of the *Engyō* and *Kakuichi* texts, this chapter has shown the former text's contradictory features. First, while the *Engyō* text shows great sympathy with people who are insulted and injured, and demonstrates a strong desire for these people to be reborn in the Pure Land, it nonetheless displays blunt contempt for women and for men of humble origin. Second, the *Engyō* text paradoxically features the coexistence of both high praise and severe criticism towards Retired Emperor Go-Shirakawa, that is, towards authority. Third, the *Engyō* text is deeply man–woman/husband–wife/family love orientated, on the one hand, while, on the other hand, it shows a pornographic or amorous interest in women. The *Kakuichi* text, in contrast, eliminates both extremes in favour of an approach that is more individualistic, indifferent, aloof and decent. In addition, this text shows a fondness for modest women who devote themselves to their master/mistress.

Heike scholarship, as I have mentioned, generally tends to evaluate the *Engyō* text as inconsistent, incongruous and lacking serious editorial work, whereas the *Kakuichi* text is regarded as well organised and coherent. Thus, the latter is assessed as having greater literary and artistic value. But there is another, equally plausible evaluation: namely, that each merely adopts a different perspective. For instance, the Oedipus complex is based on the assumption that contradictory desires to respect, adore or admire, and at the same time to hate or even desire to murder, a fatherly object can coexist in one mind. Thus, it should not be surprising to find that similarly ambivalent desires to care, deeply love or sympathise with, while also despising, condemning, bullying or abusing, the weak and the infirm can coexist in a single text. I should like to argue here that in general, as confirmed by the *Engyō* text, the stronger the contempt, the deeper the sympathy towards an object. If either element is eliminated, the other will also disappear. This erasure of extremes has occurred in the case of the *Kakuichi* text. For, as is apparent from this discussion, the opposite of deep love is neither strong hate nor profound contempt. These are the two sides of the same coin opposed to indifference. The process which saw the *Engyō* text transformed into the *Kakuichi* text may well have followed a trajectory of literary and artistic refinement. However, it also traces a shift from both deep love and profound contempt for women, humble men and the weak, and from both stern criticism of and high respect for strong authority, to an attitude of calm and indifferent egalitarianism towards all social ranks.

When there are two mutually inconsistent views, such as "admiration for the strong, beautiful, young, decent and those of high social rank" and "sympathy for the weak, ugly, old, indecent and those of low social rank", *The Tale of Genji* juxtaposes these mainly by means of polyphonic narrative and intertextual comparison. Using these remarkable techniques, *Genji* simultaneously unfolds what appear to be inconsistent views in one text. We may be able to argue that the change from the *Genji*'s intratextual and intertextual multiple viewpoints and the *Engyō* text's juxtaposition of contradiction to the *Kakuichi* text's apparent consistency is comparable to the change from Genshin's antinomy to Hōnen's selection. However, while Hōnen takes sympathy with the weak and discards respect for the strong, the *Kakuichi* text removes both extremes. It is interesting to note that, while in philosophical and religious discourse Genshin's contradictory views are transformed into Hōnen's selection of one of the two views, in fictional literary language the coexistence of contradictory views present in *Genji* and the *Engyō* text is transfigured into the *Kakuichi* text's elimination of both extremes. Once more we see here the difference between monologic and polyphonic narrative. In the former, coexistence of contradiction is regarded as an inconsistency, and the solution is either sublation or selection of one of two possibilities. In the latter, however, the coexistence of contradiction can be regarded as evidence of a fertile text in contrast to the sterility that results from the erasure of either extreme.

5 Sacrifice and revenge, love and war, and a world without violence in *The Eight Dog Chronicles*

5.1. The Confucian aspect of *The Eight Dog Chronicles*

The preceding chapters have examined *The Tale of Genji*, written in the tenth and eleventh centuries, and *The Tale of the Heike*, compiled in the thirteenth to fourteenth centuries. The discussion will now move to the nineteenth century with an analysis of "respect for the strong" and "sympathy with the weak" as these appear in *The Eight Dog Chronicles* (*Nansō Satomi hakkenden*). Author Kyokutei Bakin (1767–1848) composed this romance over a period of more than twenty-seven years from November 1814 to March 1842. The story draws upon the ideologies of Buddhism, Confucianism and Bushidō and aims both to entertain and to enlighten readers. *The Eight Dog Chronicles* was certainly one of the most popular romances in nineteenth-century Tokugawa Japan. In the Meiji period, however, Tsubouchi Shōyō (1859–1935), an influential critic and pioneer of modern Japanese literature, rejected its merits in his groundbreaking treatise entitled *The Essence of the Novel* (*Shōsetsu shinzui*, 1885–6). Peter F. Kornicki has noted that in the short term Bakin's reputation survived Shōyō's criticism. Thus, the author of the *Eight Dog Chronicles* became one of the Tokugawa writers venerated by scholars in the years before the Asia-Pacific War (Kornicki 1981: 463–4). However, although he was held in considerable esteem, even in prewar Japan Bakin's reputation failed to reach the heights of other Tokugawa literary figures such as Saikaku (1642–93), Chikamatsu (1653–1724) or Bashō (1644–94). Following the Asia-Pacific War, his works did not receive as much critical or popular attention as they had in earlier times, owing at least partially to a revival of the influence of Shōyō's negative critical assessment. Since the 1980s, however, both Bakin and *The Eight Dog Chronicles* have been re-evaluated in Japan, and there has been revived interest in his works, many of which have been issued in new editions.[1] Academic studies in English, however, remain limited. We have only the partial translations of *The Eight Dog Chronicles* made in 1955 and 2002 by Donald Keene and Chris Drake respectively, Leon M. Zolbrod's studies from the 1960s, and some comments in literary histories.[2] Besides exploring the strong–weak issue, this chapter will go some way towards redressing the relative absence of English-language commentary on this text.

The following discussion is based on the assumption that there are at least three different aspects of *The Eight Dog Chronicles*. These are premodern Confucian, modern anti-Confucian and anti-modern postmodern. The Confucian aspect can be seen in qualities such as loyalty between ruler and subject, faithfulness between friends, filial piety between father and son, precedence of the older brother over the younger brother, and the distinction between husband and wife. The focus of the modern aspect, however, shifts to concepts such as romantic love and violent conflict with others. In contrast again, the anti-modern postmodern aspect highlights a utopian egalitarian world without violence.[3]

It should be noted that the discussion that follows accords equal status to each of the Confucian Tokugawa premodern, post-Meiji Restoration modern and anti-modern postmodern aspects, privileging none of the three over any of the others. For example, the modernist interpretation, from its own perspective, severely criticised Confucian elements in the text and called for the liberation of the individual from this hierarchical system. However, from a different viewpoint, the postmodernist interpretation gave a critical reading of modernist claims by arguing for a subversion of the power structures inherent in the work. In this discussion, however, I shall refrain from reading against each or any of these interpretations, preferring instead to make a neutral reading of *The Eight Dog Chronicles*. In this regard, I owe much to Herman Ooms's study of Tokugawa ideology. Pointing out the need for the scholar as far as possible to make an attempt to distance himself or herself from the social and ideological context of his or her era, Ooms writes: "If the historian uses present-day concepts such as modernization or scientific rationality to explicate the texts to his readers, he cannot help but lose the significance the texts had in their own time" (Ooms 1998: 11).

The focus of my neutral reading of the three different aspects of the narrative will, of course, be the strong–weak issue. Specifically, I shall argue that, while the Confucian aspect confines the strong–weak power struggle within the frame of family relations in the form of sacrifice and revenge, the modernist disseminates the strong–weak power relation outside the family sphere to the binary of individual/society or self/others. In contrast to these two ideologies, a postmodernist reading of the narrative seeks to realise a total erasure of the power systems of egalitarian society. In the final analysis, however, I shall raise some questions about the concept of postmodernism from the point of view of this new setting.

The Confucian aspect of the strong–weak power relations of *The Eight Dog Chronicles* is evident in the tragedy associated with sacrifice and revenge. Tragedy in Japanese literature, in both Confucian and modern texts, has generally been narrated through the conflict faced by ordinary people between human emotional desires and moral obligations. As Donald Keene has noted, this contrasts with European tragedy, which features strong heroes defeated by fate (Keene (trans.) 1961: 1–3; Keene 1976: 253–63). The conflict between loyalty, faithfulness, filial piety and respect for elder brothers,

94 The Eight Dog Chronicles

on the one hand, and husband–wife affection or male–female love, on the other, is a prevalent storyline in many Japanese works of tragedy. Bearing this in mind, I shall examine how the discourses of sacrifice and revenge have been used to construct a typical Confucian tragedy in *The Eight Dog Chronicles*.

The beginning of *The Eight Dog Chronicles* is based on the historical "battle of Yūki Castle" which took place in 1440 in the Yūki region in present-day Ibaraki Prefecture. In an unsuccessful rebellion led by Ashikaga Mochiuji against the Muromachi shogunate, the head of the Yūki family, Yūki Ujitomo, sided with the rebels and thus fought against the shogun's deputy, Uesugi Norizane. The Satomi family, the protagonists of *The Eight Dog Chronicles*, also sided with the rebels and were eventually defeated in the battle at Yūki Castle. The narrative opens with a conversation during the battle between the head of the family, Satomi Suemoto, and his eldest son, Yoshizane. Suemoto insists on helping Yoshizane escape from the castle to ensure the family's continuity. However, Yoshizane, filled with love for the older man and also cognisant of his obligation in terms of filial piety, wants to fight to the death alongside his father. In spite of this, Yoshizane is forced to depart from the castle by two retainers assigned to him by his father (I 18–19).[4] This is the first sacrifice in the story, with Suemoto choosing to stay to die in battle, and Yoshizane sacrificing his father for the sake of the family. Later we learn that in the same battle a very similar sacrifice has been made involving the head of the Ōtsuka (later Inuzuka) family, Ōtsuka Shōsaku, and his son Bansaku (I 256–65). Later, Bansaku will also kill himself to help his son, Shino, one of the eight heroes of the story (I 336). In each case, the fathers, Suemoto, Shōsaku and Bansaku, sacrifice themselves to give their sons strength and to ensure the continuity of their families. Strong reader sympathy is elicited for these elderly and declining men who give their lives for the sake of their families.

The storyline of *The Eight Dog Chronicles* continues with Yoshizane, supported by the two retainers assigned by his father, escaping the battlefield and defeating the evil lord Yamashita Sadakane at his two castles in Nansō. Yoshizane thus becomes the lord of Nansō. Respected by the local populace, he begets a daughter, Fusehime, and a son, Yoshinari. Some years later, famine strikes Yoshizane's fief, providing the neighbouring evil lord, Anzai Kagetsura, with a chance to attack. Surrounded by enemies, and believing that he is about to die, Yoshizane jokingly tells his dog, Yatsufusa, that if he, the dog, is able to kill the evil Kagetsura he will be rewarded with Yoshizane's daughter, Fusehime. That night, Yatsufusa brings Kagetsura's severed head to his master. After peace is restored, Yatsufusa requests to marry Fusehime, whereupon Yoshizane tries to kill the dog. Fusehime, however, seeks to resolve the conflict Yoshizane has imposed upon himself by offering to live with Yatsufusa as if she were his wife – thus allowing her father to keep his promise and demonstrating her own filial piety. Yatsufusa and Fusehime thus go to live together on Mount Toyama (Tomi-san). In this way Fusehime sacrifices her own worldly life through a sense of filial piety and a desire to help her father.

All four cases of sacrifice mentioned above involve strong–weak power-structure issues. In order to maintain the family, the weaker party sacrifices itself for the stronger party – declining fathers sacrifice themselves for their rising sons, while a weak daughter sacrifices herself for her strong father. Gender issues are also involved. For, in a patriarchal society, declining fathers are required to hand over their position to their sons, not to their daughters. Therefore, while daughters can be sacrificed, sons must survive. In each case the socially weak individual is sacrificed for the strong in order to strengthen the group.

Later, on Mount Toyama (Tomi-san), in spite of not having had sexual relations with the dog, Yatsufusa, Fusehime appears to be pregnant. As she is expressing her shame at her figure, her father, Yoshizane, and his retainers arrive to help her. Yatsufusa is shot and killed, but one of the bullets accidentally injures Fusehime. After recovering consciousness, she proves her own chastity by committing *seppuku*. As she does, eight jewels from a rosary fly out of her abdomen, each inscribed with one of eight Chinese characters: *jin* (compassion), *gi* (righteousness), *rei* (propriety), *chi* (wisdom), *chū* (loyalty to one's master), *shin* (faithfulness, especially to one's friends), *kō* (filial piety to one's parents) and *tei* (respect for one's elder brothers). When the eight heroes appear later in the story, each has one of these jewels. These eight combine forces to help the Satomi family.

The first hero is Shino, whose father sacrificed himself in order to save his son. Following his father's death, Shino was raised by his aunt, Kamezasa, and her husband, Hikiroku. This couple have a foster daughter, Hamaji, who is in love with Shino. At first, the older couple consents to the engagement of Shino and Hamaji. However, when the deputy lord, Hikami Kyūroku, expresses an interest in Hamaji, Kamezasa and Hikiroku decide to send Shino away in order to marry the girl to a spouse with greater social advantage. Although Hamaji hates Kyūroku, she is prepared to sacrifice herself for her foster parents' sake; and, while Shino does not openly disclose his emotions, he also loves Hamaji and knows the reason he is being sent away from home. In a well-known scene, Shino rejects Hamaji's wish to go with him and sacrifices their love for the benefit of her foster parents. His sense of filial piety forces him to abandon Hamaji, and their parting scene is narrated as a tragedy (II 81–7; Keene 1955: 423–8; Shirane (ed.) 2002: 904–9). Although present-day readers should be careful not overly to despise Kyūroku, the repellent man of power, or to idealise the young and pure love of Hamaji and Shino unnecessarily, it is clear that the narrative leads the reader to sympathise with Hamaji and to reject Kyūroku.

This sacrifice is slightly different from the four previously described, each of which involved father–son or father–daughter relations, and a weaker person being sacrificed for a stronger in order to guarantee the survival of the family. In contrast, the case of Shino and Hamaji saw the love of a man and a woman sacrificed in the name of filial piety for the benefit of the

96   The Eight Dog Chronicles

couple's foster parents. In Confucian society, the loyalty felt by retainers for their masters, the faithfulness of friend for friend, children's filial feelings for their parents, and younger brothers' respect for their elder brothers are all considered morally admirable sentiments. On the other hand, the bond between a husband and a wife or between lovers is suspect.[5]

One explanation for Shino's refusal to follow his desire to remain with Hamaji is that it would be selfish to do so and is thus morally unacceptable. Hamaji, too, understands that the pair must separate and that she must remain at home. To do otherwise would be to be motivated by a deplorable selfishness. For this couple to be together would be an immoral expression of self-centred longing, whereas to follow their step-parents' wishes would be an admirable expression of filial piety. They are in this way caught up in the conflict between selfish desire and filial piety. For both of them, the partner (Shino for Hamaji, and Hamaji for Shino) is an insider, while their foster parents are outsiders. The sacrifice of Hamaji for Shino is therefore the sacrifice of an insider for the benefit of an outsider, without which element the story would not be a tragedy.

The strong identification felt between lovers and/or married couples is a recurring motif in Tokugawa literature, as demonstrated by the many love-suicides which feature in the writing of this era. As we have seen in Chapter 4, Tabata Yasuko reports that in the Kamakura and Muromachi periods a strong identification was evident between husbands and wives, and it is reasonable to assume that this tendency continued into the Tokugawa period (Tabata Yasuko 1987: 17–20, 156). Yet this does not mean that lovers or a husband and a wife have identical status, or are represented on an equal basis; rather it shows that a woman belongs to a man as part of his property. This is clear from the fact that, while the sacrifice of a man's wife for his parents (especially for his father) is morally admirable, the sacrifice of a woman's husband for her parents (especially for her mother) is not accept-able.[6] This fits Hélène Cixous' assertion that woman has always functioned "within" the discourse of man (Cixous 1980: 257). For a man, a woman is a part of his self; whereas, for a woman, her self is a part of a man. Therefore, to caress a woman is a sort of narcissistic self-love for a man; while to follow a man is, for a woman, a kind of feeling of belongingness which brings about a self-expansion of consciousness.

Later Hamaji is kidnapped by another admirer, the masterless samurai Aboshi Samojirō. Hamaji does not give her heart to Samojirō, and finally dies at his hand. Sacrificed for the benefit of her foster parents, Hamaji's fate resembles that of Fusehime's earlier in the narrative. In addition, although each defends her chastity, both women are sacrificed to fulfil the sexual desire of a beast (dog) or a loathsome man (Kyūroku and Samojirō). The difference lies in the roles of Kanamari Daisuke and Inuzuka Shino, the respective men attracted to Fusehime and Hamaji. While the would-be lover, Daisuke, tries to help Fusehime, Shino does not help Hamaji. Therefore, in the latter case, both the couple's love and Hamaji's life are sacrificed. Upon dying, Hamaji says that she values the reputation of her future husband, Shino, above her own life (II 151). The conduct of Shino and Hamaji would have been highly praiseworthy in the Confucian ethic, while at the same time eliciting the reader's deep emotional sympathy.

Elsewhere in *The Eight Dog Chronicles* this point of the necessity of wifely sacrifice for the sake of a husband's parents is narrated with even more force in the story of Inumura Daikaku and his wife, Hinakinu. In this anecdote, Daikaku sits idly by while his parents force his wife to commit suicide. Hinakinu is required to disembowel herself to provide medicine to help cure Daikaku's father (it is actually not Daikaku's real father but a monster wildcat with the ability to change shape and assume human form). Here, again, Daikaku's understanding of the demands of filial piety makes it impossible for him to act to save his wife. Of course, this scene fails to evoke the present-day reader's sympathy, since to demand the life of a pregnant woman and her unborn child to cure the woman's father-in-law is totally unacceptable in terms of the current moral system. There are a number of points that need to be clarified here. First, while the demands of filial piety in the Tokugawa period were extremely high, to an extent difficult for the present-day reader to imagine, the bonds between husband and wife at this time were also very strong. Thus, the tragedy of the story is achieved, from Daikaku's point of view, by the juxtaposition of the pious desire to cure his father with the pain of the sacrifice of his wife. Since, as I have mentioned, one's spouse or lover is one's "inside", whereas one's parents are "outside", to let his wife kill herself in order to help his father is a form of self-sacrifice for Daikaku; it is synonymous with extinguishing the most precious and vulnerable part of his self in order to help a stronger member of his family. For Hinakinu, to sacrifice herself means not only to help her father-in-law but also to help her husband fulfil his obligation.

Furthermore, since she is part of him, in helping her husband she also fulfils her own mission. Before her death, Hinakinu declares that she does not regret dying, for it is her great honour to perform such a distinguished service for her husband (IV 85). For this reason, she readily invites the sympathy of the Confucian reader.

Another, similar example of self-sacrifice in *The Eight Dog Chronicles* is the story of Yamabayashi Fusahachi and his wife, Nui. Fusahachi kills both himself and Nui, partly in atonement for his grandfather's sin (showing filial piety) and partly to help the heroes of the story (displaying loyalty, faithfulness or brotherly love). Shino, who is a wanted man, resembles Fusahachi. Fusahachi therefore decides to commit suicide in the hope that the authorities will mistake his dead body for that of Shino, who has, moreover, been stricken by tetanus. The decision to kill himself and his wife is also fuelled by Fusahachi's desire to help cure Shino, for it was believed that a mixture of the blood of a young man and a young woman could cure the disease (II 294). In this case, man and wife are sacrificed in order to help the man's friend, who is venerable, outstanding and superior.

98   The Eight Dog Chronicles

As a final example of this kind of sacrifice, I shall introduce a variation on that theme as seen in the story of the twin brothers Jūjō Rikijirō and Shakuhachirō. These twins are killed in battle while trying to avenge their master's death and also to help the story's heroes, who are being pursued by the authorities. The narrative gives a highly sympathetic account of the return home of the dead spirits of the young men in order to visit their wives, Hikute and Hitoyo, and their mother, Otone. The story presents loyalty to one's master and the desire to help admirable heroes as qualities worthy of the sacrifice of both the self and valued members of the family such as a wife or a mother (III 144).

Each of these cases indicates that love between a man and a woman, whether husband and wife or son and mother, is to be sacrificed for the higher ideal of loyalty to one's master, faithfulness or respect to one's superior friends, and/or filial piety to one's father. Masters, outstanding friends and strong fathers are positioned as superiors, in contrast to lovers, wives and mothers, who are weaker in terms of their position in the Confucian scheme of values. The weaker are always sacrificed for the stronger, despite the fact that the tragic hero has a deep emotional wish to be with or to help the weak. Related to this, it is interesting to note that Fusahachi, Rikijirō and Shakuhachirō, all male figures who sacrifice themselves for their superior friends, have no father. Fusahachi's father has been dead for two years, while Rikijirō and Shakuhachirō are estranged from their father, Kaniwa Yasuhei (alias Obayuki Yoshirō). For these young men, superior heroes who reside in the symbolic order replace their fathers. These superior heroes are objects of longing as strong "outside" people.

This is the typical trope of tragedy in *The Eight Dog Chronicles*. The tragic model presented has at least two axes – inside/outside and weak/strong. Generally speaking, this tragedy resides in the sacrifice of the relatively weaker "inside" people for the benefit of the relatively stronger "outside" people. As a consequence, the sacrifice by a man of his lover, wife, or mother for the benefit of his master, father, or outstanding friends involves discarding a closer weaker person in order to help the superior, more distant stronger other. In fact, the very role of the eight heroes in *The Eight Dog Chronicles* is patiently to endure the sacrifice of weak persons close to them, and to placate and carry out revenge for the spirits of these people who have been sacrificed to help the strong. While the former serves for the progress of the whole family, the latter compensates the unfairness caused by the former. The former requires the reader's sympathy, whereas the latter relieves the reader's dissatisfaction brought on by the former.

Scholarly commentary generally considers sacrifice to play a role in stemming a rising tide of violence and redirecting this into legitimate channels. In order to avoid a vicious circle of reciprocal violence, two antagonistic parties in a society select a third party as scapegoat towards whom the desire for violence is redirected and eventually extinguished. In this way the crisis of violence passes.[7] In order to make this mechanism work effectively, the object of the sacrifice should be selected from either a third party or from the periphery of each group. In the story of *The Eight Dog Chronicles*, however, the party to be sacrificed is skilfully selected from the close family members or friends of the tale's heroes. Thus, unlike the model of sacrifice deployed to avoid a violent confrontation between the principal opposing parties, sacrifice in this story is used to create an opportunity to evoke a strong desire for revenge. This is one of the main factors that drives the narrative and holds the attention of the reader.

I shall now turn to the theme of revenge for the Confucian sacrificed in *The Eight Dog Chronicles*.[8] Revenge is, together with sacrifice, one of the two major motifs repeatedly invoked in the narrative, and there are two major revenge stories which drive the main plot. One is the case of Inusaka Keno, the son of Aihara Tanenori. In order to further their own promotion, two samurai retainers of the Chiba family, Makuwari Tsunetake and Komiyama Yoritsura, conspire against Tanenori. After making false charges, they assassinate Tanenori and, furthermore, force his son, Yumenosuke, to commit suicide. The two retainers also execute Tanenori's wife, Inaki, and daughter, Tamakura. Tanenori's concubine, Tatsukuri, later gives birth to Tanenori's son, Inusaka Keno, one of the eight heroes of *The Eight Dog Chronicles* (III 275–89).

Keno has long wished to take revenge for his family's death (III 323). His wish is fulfilled on two occasions. First, at Makuwari Tsunetake's arbour, Taigyūrō, Keno beheads Tsunetake and kills his son, Kurayago. He also kills Tsunetake's wife, Tomaki, and daughter, Suzuko (III 323–6). The deaths of Makuwari Tsunetake, his wife Tomaki, their son Kurayago and daughter Suzuko are apparently deemed to correspond with the deaths of Keno's father, Aihara Tanenori, his wife Inaki, their son Yumenosuke, and daughter Tamakura. Later Keno also succeeds in killing Komiyama Yoritsura. Upon the death of Yoritsura, Keno addresses his dead family members, informing them of his successful revenge, and praying for their peaceful repose (V 217–18). This clearly shows that one of the purposes of revenge in *The Eight Dog Chronicles* is to placate the anger of one's deceased family. Revenge is an action performed to appease defeated and vengeful spirits of the weak.

The second major revenge story is that of Inuyama Dōsetsu, a retainer of the Toshima family, who seeks to revenge the deaths of both his father and his master on the shogun's deputy, Ōgigayatsu Sadamasa. Following a battle in the Nerima region, the Toshima family is defeated by the families of the shogun's two deputies, the Yamanouchis and the Ōgigayatsus (II 34, 144). The Toshima retainers include Dōsetsu's family, as well as the families of Obayuki Yoshirō (Kaniwa Yasuhei), his wife Otone, their sons Jūjō Rikijirō and Shakuhachirō, and also the sons' wives Hikute and Hitoyo (III 112–15). The family of Ochiayu Aritane are also Toshima retainers (V 59). Dōsetsu's urgent wish is to revenge his dead family and master on Ōgigayatsu Sadamasa. On one occasion, Dōsetsu succeeds in approaching Sadamasa at

Shirai. However, his attempt to assassinate the latter ends in failure (III 94–6). Sadamasa again has a narrow escape from Dōsetsu at Isarako (V 231–6). Finally, at the battle between the Satomi family and the shogun's two deputies, Ōgigayatsu Sadamasa and Yamanouchi Akitada, Dōsetsu frantically pursues Sadamasa but again fails to kill him.

Why do Dōsetsu's revenge attempts end in failure? Dōsetsu's revenge differs from that of Keno. Both Makuwari Tsunetake and Komiyama Yoritsura, the objects of Keno's revenge, are depicted as evil characters who falsely accuse the faithful retainer, Aihara Tanenori, and then murder his family purely for self-promotion. Dōsetsu's family and the family of his master, however, are defeated by the families of the shogun's deputies in legitimate battle. While both these deputies, Ōgigayatsu Sadamasa and Yamanouchi Akitada, are portrayed as incompetent and untalented masters, neither is completely evil or sly or morally depraved. This surely explains why Keno's act of revenge is sanctioned, whereas Dōsetsu's is not.

A slightly different kind of revenge deserving special attention is the case of revenge carried out against Nitayama Shingo. During a skirmish with Shino, Sōsuke, Rikijirō and Shakuhachirō at the Totakawa River, Nitayama Shingo's retainers shoot and kill Rikijirō and Shakuhachirō. After beheading the pair, Shingo falsely announces that he has the heads of Shino and Sōsuke in order to claim a better reward (III 176). In a later battle with Sadamasa at Isarako, Dōsetsu captures and executes Nitayama Shingo, now Sadamasa's retainer. Upon beheading Shingo, Dōsetsu declares that, while it was permissible to kill Rikijirō and Shakuhachirō upon the order of the lord, it was a craven act to claim falsely that the heads were those of Shino and Sōsuke. Thus, Dōsetsu executes Shingo not only to appease Rikijirō's and Shakuhachirō's resentment but also to carry out the punishment of Heaven against Shingo's dishonesty (V 271).

A similar case involving the substitution of captured heads is that involving Mita no Gyoranji, Nedu no Yachūji and Anaguri Sensaku, all of whom are retainers of Ōgigayatsu Sadamasa. Following Sadamasa's defeat at Isarako, the heads of more than twenty of his dead retainers are put on public display. Gyoranji, Yachūji and Sensaku try to hide the shame of their master, Sadamasa, by throwing the retainers' heads into the sea and replacing them with the heads of the villains Obanai and Funamushi (V 286–7). Later, at the command of Sadamasa, they capture and torture Kawagoi Takatsugu, and then attempt to kill Ochiayu Aritane (VIII 342–56). Upon attacking Aritane's mansion, they find that his family has already fled. Instead, therefore, they kill innocent neighbouring farmers and, after setting fire to several of the bodies, make the claim that these are the bodies of the Aritane family (VIII 358–9). Thus, they twice engage in deception about the identity of dead bodies. When Inuyama Dōsetsu captures Gyoranji, Yachūji and Sensaku, he hands them over to the survivors of the innocent victims of the trio, the people of the Toshima clan. These survivors conduct one of the most graphically brutal vendettas in the story. Before beheading the

The Eight Dog Chronicles   101

villains, they chop off their hands and legs, stab them in the chest, disembowel them and, finally, cannibalise some parts of them (X 72).

Both in this case and in the case of Nitayama Shingo, there are two factors which explain the cruel manner in which the miscreants are killed. First, they abuse captured heads and, second, they kill many innocent people. Thus, revenge is here regarded as Heaven's retribution when the mortal authorities fail to exact punishment. Upon reading a story in which evil characters are cruelly killed, readers would be satisfied that such punishment represented a fair penalty.

Although the above demonstrates that we cannot neglect Heaven's punishment as an aspect in the case of revenge, this does not automatically require us to downplay the need to appease the mortification of the weak people. Keno's act of revenge is sanctioned, while Dōsetsu's is not – this is surely because, besides the moral justification explained above, while the weak and innocent members of Tanenori's family were, as clearly narrated, murdered mercilessly and brutally, the Dōsetsu family was merely killed (legitimately) in the battle. It should not be overlooked that, although the vengeance can be sanctioned only on the condition of moral justification, a major role of revenge in this story is to appease the vengeful spirits of the weak.

In addition to giving insights into the varying degrees of revenge penalty, *The Eight Dog Chronicles* also suggests an order of revenge priority. This priority is apparent, for example, when Inusaka Keno places his duty to avenge his father's death above his duty towards brother or friend. Inukawa Sōsuke explains Keno's action by saying that

> parents come first, and then brothers. Wife and children follow brothers. And finally, after wife and children, come grandchildren and other descendants. When deciding one's obligation among the competing demands of filial piety, respect for elder brothers and the affection of a husband for a wife, there is a clear order of precedence. Since filial piety must not be overlooked, reverence towards one's parents must be placed above respect for elder brothers, which is also more important than affection between husbands and wives. Filial piety is the source of the myriad of other conducts and must always be observed.
>
> (IV 423).[9]

Inumura Daikaku observes that he would take revenge even on a friend if it were for the sake of a blood relative (IV 73). Kawakoi Moriyuki also declares that filial piety has precedence, then loyalty to one's master, and finally faithfulness to one's friends (V 149). Thus, the priority order in matters of revenge is: parents, brothers, master, and then friends.

In the discussion on sacrifice, we noted that the wife and children occupy the domain of the self. Drawing on this point, we can now construct a diagrammatic image of revenge and sacrifice, as in Figure 5.1.

102 The Eight Dog Chronicles

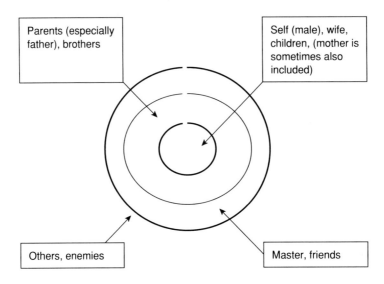

Figure 5.1

In the innermost sphere at the site of the male self[10] are the wife and children. Father and brothers occupy the next band, followed by master and friends. Beyond the master and friends are others or enemies. The significance of a group's position in the diagram differs depending on whether the context is one of sacrifice or of revenge. For example, harm to an inner member by an outer member requires an act of revenge. The exceptions are the self, wife and children, who are objects of sacrifice rather than of revenge. It is for this reason that the story obscures any notion of revenge for either Hamaji or Hinakinu. Thus, Aboshi Samojirō is killed not by Shino (Hamaji's husband-to-be) but by Dōsetsu (Hamaji's blood brother); similarly, Daikaku's father, a monster wildcat who has assumed the shape of a man, is accidentally killed by Hinakinu herself, not by Daikaku. The story is skilfully constructed so that neither Shino nor Daikaku is permitted to take revenge for his wife. Therefore, the tropes of sacrifice and revenge can be summarised as follows: while required to sacrifice weaker/inner members for stronger/outer members up to the limit of master/friends (the outer bold circle), one must take revenge on the stronger/outer members for the sake of weaker/inner members to the limit of parents and brothers (the inner bold circle). Inspired by Confucian interpretations of sacrifice and revenge, readers would have sympathised with the former (sacrifice) and felt satisfaction at the latter (revenge). These are the elements of the typical Confucian-inspired plot as it appears in *The Eight Dog Chronicles*. An understanding of the Confucian logic of the storyline must be preceded by an acceptance of a strict distinction between the strong and the weak, as well as between each family group and their others.

5.2. The modernist aspect of *The Eight Dog Chronicles*

As mentioned above, and as has often been pointed out in the past, critical modernist readings of Bakin's *The Eight Dog Chronicles* began when Tsubouchi Shōyō launched a realist criticism of the work at the beginning of the Meiji period. By criticising *The Eight Dog Chronicles* from the standpoint of realism, Shōyō freed both himself and his readers from the power exerted by one of Confucian literature's highest achievements. He pioneered this iconoclastic reading in order to create a space for the birth of a new, modern, democratic literature. However, as Kimura Ki and others have noted, although Shōyō was critical of the didactic aspect of *The Eight Dog Chronicles* and insisted on the need for a realistic description of the characters' psychology, he did not criticise the *kanzen chōaku* (encouraging virtue and chastising vice) principles of Confucian moral education *per se*.[11] In fact, he argues that, if we regard *The Eight Dog Chronicles* as a moral education book, the work should be highly valued as something rare in both Western and Eastern countries (Tsubouchi 1977, Bekkan, volume 3: 44).[12] In other words, it is not Bakin's message to which Shōyō objects, but rather the manner in which the former overtly advocates Confucian moral precepts encapsulated in the expression "encouraging virtue and chastising vice".[13] Accordingly, Shōyō criticises the didactic elements of *The Eight Dog Chronicles*, insisting on the need for a realistic description of the characters' psychology. In urging less didacticism and a more real and faithful depiction of human psychology, however, Shōyō's criticism identifies the cause of the modern reader's distaste for the Confucian aspects of Bakin's *Eight Dog Chronicles*.[14] Concerning this point, there are two issues we must take into account.

First, as discussed by Kimura Ki, although Shōyō's criticism of Bakin and *The Eight Dog Chronicles* is not specifically directed at the latter's Confucianism, it should be understood as part of the general anti-Confucian climate which was vigorously initiated by Fukuzawa Yukichi in early-modern Japan (Kimura Ki 1982: 83, 86; Tanizawa 1971: 242). As we have observed in Chapter 2, in his *An Encouragement of Learning* (*Gakumon no susume*, 1872–6) and *An Outline of a Theory of Civilization* (*Bunmeiron no gairyaku*, 1875) Yukichi points out the defects of Confucianism. To repeat our argument, though Yukichi is commonly revered as the early-modern champion of notions of individual freedom, independence and egalitarianism in Japan, he had a conditional interest in these concepts, focusing more closely instead on competition in capitalist society and the independence of Japan as a nation-state. Yukichi introduces notions of human equality and rights as the starting-point in the competition for entry to the ruling strata of society, a competition which ultimately results in social inequality. And in essence, for most of his life, Yukichi proclaimed the Enlightenment message that equality, liberty and individualism are necessary for wealth and power. Yukichi's writings, however, were widely welcomed by Japanese people in

104   The Eight Dog Chronicles

the Meiji period as a bible teaching freedom and equality. His material greatly encouraged individual independence and a sense of egalitarianism, both of which had until then been occluded by Confucianism.

It was in this anti-Confucian climate that, in *The Essence of the Novel*, published in 1885–6, Shōyō criticised the didactic aspects of *The Eight Dog Chronicles*. Though Shōyō did not criticise Confucian morality as such, his ideas were misinterpreted by many who saw his criticism as a wholesale condemnation of Confucianism. In 1897, for example, Takayama Chogyū published an article in which he praised Shōyō's criticism of Bakin, arguing that Shōyō had abolished the idea, prominent in Bakin's novels, of "encouraging virtue and chastising vice".[15] Chogyū's argument well shows that, although Shōyō criticised only the didactic aspect of *The Eight Dog Chronicles* and not Confucian ethics themselves, his work was regarded as anti-Confucian by early-modern Japan's literary commentators. It is ironic that Confucian Shōyō's anti-didacticism was prejudicially misinterpreted as anti-Confucianism in the space opened up by Fukuzawa Yukichi's attack on that traditional way of thought.

Criticisms of Bakin and his work as examples of Confucian hypocritical authoritarianism were discernible to some extent from the time of Shōyō and Yukichi until the late 1970s and even beyond. As might be expected, commentary of this nature is most prevalent among modernist critics active after the China–Japan and Pacific Wars. For instance, in a 1949 essay, Odagiri Hideo draws an analogy between the pressure placed by the authorities on writers in Bakin's time and the pressure placed on writers by the militarist authorities in the years leading up to the war. Focusing particularly on the Kansei Reform (1787–93), Odagiri argues that writers such as Santō Kyōden (1761–1816) and Bakin were forced by the Tokugawa government to change their genre from the sensual *sharebon*[16] or *kibyōshi*[17] to the didactic *yomihon*.[18] He argues that this was similar to the process whereby in the China–Japan and Pacific Wars (1937–45) writers of popular literature were forced by the military government to write militaristic novels. Odagiri writes:

> Instead of the khaki military uniform or people's wartime uniform [of the China–Japan and Pacific Wars], the *yomihon* writer wore a samurai suit on which were printed the terms "loyalty, filial piety, compassion and righteousness." Moreover, in place of the slogan "sound and healthy amusement" [which appeared during the wars of the Shōwa era], the writer from Tokugawa times carried a placard which read "encouraging virtue and chastising vice."
>
> (Odagiri 1974: 35)

In this analogy, the left-wing Odagiri imputes the Confucian Bakin with having the same relationship with the Tokugawa authorities as the relationship that writers who supported Japanese imperialism had with the Shōwa militarist government before and during the Second World War. Informed by postwar democracy, Odagiri seeks to censure not only the prewar and wartime collaboration of his own era but also what he believes is a feudalistic authoritarianism in Bakin and his work. He thus adds an extra layer of condemnation to the purely modernist critiques which commenced with Shōyō in the early Meiji period.

Other postwar writers would also be critical of Bakin's allegedly authoritarian attitude. For example, in a 1976 essay, Sugiura Minpei tells us that, although Bakin had the documents in question in his possession, the latter rejected a request by Rangaku scholar Watanabe Kazan (1793–1841) to see material concerning the Russian landing in Japan which occurred at the time. Sugiura also refers to Bakin's comments that it was fitting that Kazan be imprisoned on the occasion of the publication of *Bansha no goku* (*Imprisonment of the Companions of Barbarian Studies*, 1839) since this punishment was necessary to chastise servants who interfered with the policies of their masters. Sugiura argues that this blindly authoritarian attitude underlies both Bakin's life and his literary work. The critic concludes that, since Bakin advocated the idea of "encouraging virtue and chastising vice", in addition to didactic loyalty, filial piety and chastity, it is no wonder that his books were regarded as the literary educational staple of the samurai bureaucrat (Sugiura 1976: 317–18).

Criticism of this kind is made from the position of a modernist anti-authoritarian opposed to the absolute nature of feudal authority. Bakin's willing submission to the Tokugawa feudal government reminded people in the period after the Second World War of those writers and artists who advocated and blindly followed the authoritarian imperial government before and during the war. From the viewpoint of our discussion, however, it is particularly important to distinguish between authoritarianism and anti-egalitarianism. Supporters of war can be either authoritarian or egalitarian. The former blindly follow an authority which is belligerent by nature. However, as we have observed in Chapter 2, the desire to support the weak and thus create an egalitarian society also often leads to the emergence of a very warlike society which seeks to attack another allegedly unfair society (enemy). Bakin, as we shall see later, is in a sense authoritarian, but not anti-egalitarian. In fact, he respects authority only as far as it is based on an egalitarian ethic which helps the socially powerless.

The condemnation of Bakin by modern critics, erroneously derived from Shōyō's realistic critique of didacticism in *The Eight Dog Chronicles*, has not been confined to claims of support for Confucian authoritarianism. However, before investigating these further issues we need to question the meaning of the term "realistic". "Reality" can be interpreted differently according to the ideology prevailing in a society. Shōyō put forward the idea that, rather than illustrating the didactic message of "encouraging virtue and chastising vice", the novel should be concerned with depicting *ninjō*. Declaring that *ninjō* refers to the human passions (*jōyoku*), the so-called One Hundred and Eight

106   The Eight Dog Chronicles

Lusts, he argued that, since human beings are creatures of passion, there are few men who have been without either evil or lustful desires. Shōyō's particular concern was that each of the eight heroes in Bakin's *Eight Dog Chronicles* seems to lack these evil or lustful passions (Tsubouchi 1977, Bekkan volume 3: 42).[19] Following its initiation by Shōyō in this discussion, the attempt to depict the negative side of humanity more objectively, frankly and graphically caught the imagination of writers and their reading public. Thus, it developed that one of the main themes of modern Japanese literature became the depiction of the evil, selfish, lustful and immoral aspects of human desire. Naturalist literature and the I-novel are particularly orientated around this interest, insisting that one of the aims of literature is to configure the evil side of human nature as faithfully as possible.

The concept of self-identity, ego (*jiga*), or, more broadly, individuality was one of the key concepts of the early-modern Japanese literary scene. This notion of self-identity was also related to the new understanding of the evil side of humanity. Based on an analysis of the work of a range of scholars, Mark Williams presents a series of factors which gave rise to the notion of Japanese selfhood in the early Meiji era. These include the emergence of a literary style derived from the "unification of written and spoken language" (*genbun itchi*), the social and political reforms implemented by the new Meiji oligarchy following centuries of suppression under neo-Confucian orthodoxy, and the introduction of Christianity (Williams 1999: 4–14).[20] Here, I wish to focus on the anti-Confucian aspect of the Japanese notion of the self. It is important to be aware that, although Western influences played a significant role, the modern literary Japanese "I" or Japanese individuality was not constructed simply through following imported Euro-American ideas of modern self-identity. These notions also developed through attempts to create a distance between the Japanese feudal ideology of fiefdom and family and ideas of the new modern times. In Confucian ethics, self-centredness was regarded as disruptive of family harmony. Therefore, the recognition of the positive or beneficial aspects of Euro-American ideas of self required a rejection of Confucian ethics which viewed the selfish side of humanity negatively. As a result, Confucian morality was now regarded as hypocritical. This permitted an interpretation of realism as the sincere recognition of the ugly elements of one's own humanity, such as selfishness or erotic desire. This recognition had, until then, been suppressed by Confucian ethics. Hence, Shōyō's realistic criticism that Bakin's characters only represent the positive aspects of humanity and the rejection of the Confucian refusal to acknowledge the legitimacy of the evil side of humanity (anti-Confucianism) are closely interrelated.

Tsuda Sōkichi was one of a number of scholars who took up this realistic criticism of Bakin and who rejected the moral paradigm presented in *The Eight Dog Chronicles*. In his *An Inquiry into the Japanese Mind as Mirrored in Literature* (1916–21), Tsuda compares Bakin unfavourably with Chikamatsu Monzaemon. He argues that Chikamatsu's characters are vigorously depicted

The Eight Dog Chronicles   107

as experiencing an agony which results from a conflict between their own private wishes or natural feelings of love, on the one hand, and a public sense of honour or duty, on the other. This agony culminates in their giving up the private for the public. Bakin's characters, according to Tsuda, however, are all mere puppets moving from the outset under a fixed set of moral ideas without experiencing any such psychological complication. Tsuda concludes his argument by claiming that, from the moral point of view, the work of Bakin is undeniably far below that of Chikamatsu.[21] A similar revaluation was made six decades later by Katō Shūichi in his *A History of Japanese Literature* (original 1980). Katō comments on Bakin's novels as follows:

> The values that underpin these novels [Bakin's *Eight Dog Chronicles* and *The Crescent Moon* (*Chinsetsu yumihari zuki*)] are the Buddhist notion of *Karma* and the Confucian injunction to "reward the good and chastise evil." The good in this case is the virtues of filial piety and loyalty. Men must be courageous and women chaste. Evil, the lack of the basic virtues, involves treachery, flattery, deception, the lust for inordinate power, cowardice, cruelty, wiliness and promiscuity. The good characters are absolutely good, the evil characters extremely evil, and no characters appear with a mixture of both qualities. Nor are there any scenes in which it is difficult to distinguish between the two.
>
> Bakin's sense of value – at least as it appears in his novels – seems to have involved an extreme simplification of humanity and a belief in accommodation with the dominant ethos. There are none of the finely observed descriptions of emotional and psychological nuances that [Tamenaga] Shunsui achieved, albeit within the small world of the licensed quarters.
>
> (Katō 1983: 55–6)

It is thus apparent that Shōyō's insistence on depicting the evil side of human desire more realistically produced a tendency towards a rejection of family-orientated Confucian virtues and a concomitant preference for depicting the evil side of the individual self. These dual tendencies resulted in criticism of Bakin's naïvely virtuous characters and also of the authoritarianism the critics believed his novels displayed. In urging a more realistic and faithful depiction of human evil and selfish desires, and a less didactic moral teaching, Shōyō's criticism inadvertently resulted in Bakin's *Eight Dog Chronicles* being labelled as Confucian hypocritical authoritarianism. As Matsuda Osamu noted, and as Odagiri's comments cited earlier confirm, Bakin was stigmatised as an Establishment reactionary, a writer patronised by the government. He was thus regarded as a representative of the feudal system that the modernist fought to overcome.[22] It is useful to note that the very features which modernism sought to emphasise in its rejection of Confucianism – namely the depiction of selfish and erotic desire and anti-authoritarianism – can be deemed two of the major characteristics of modern Japanese literature. Given that

108   The Eight Dog Chronicles

literature inevitably reflects the contemporary society, it is clear that these elements were already critical features of the society of modern Japan. It is likely that these are two features that Japan shares with other modernist cultures, in the sense that they urge competition with others in order to break down the old system and progress towards a new ideal.

In spite of these modernist criticisms of Bakin and his work, however, *The Eight Dog Chronicles* actually does depict selfish and erotic desire and anti-authoritarianism.[23] We shall now examine representations of these modernist features in the text. First, let us look at the modern form of romantic love featured in the narrative, beginning with Hikiroku and Kamezasa. Kamezasa is a young woman who fails to sympathise with either her father or her elder brother, both of whom are besieged in Yūki castle. Neither does she take care of her stepmother (I 278). She thus lacks filial piety and respect for her elder brothers. When she reaches adolescence, she becomes fascinated with making herself up and styling her hair, and indulges in a love-affair with Hikiroku. It is significant that Kamezasa's love for Hikiroku is so strong that she can sacrifice her consanguine family. Thus, while it is true that the love of this pair is caricatured as that of troublemakers who cause difficulties for Shino and Hamaji, it should also be noted that their relationship is described in a manner lacking any regret for the sacrifice of the consanguine family ideology of filial piety and respect for elder brothers. According to Confucian ideology, any desire to sacrifice family should be condemned as repellent and selfish. It is, however, precisely the type of sacrifice that modernists choose to praise.

Two other examples of this modern form of love would be the illicit love-relations between Nabiki and Awayuki Nashirō, and also between Okoze and Dojōji (IV 168–9; V 126, VII 82). After his wife's death, Yorogi Mukusaku marries his daughter's wet-nurse, Nabiki. Later Nabiki falls in love with a villainous samurai vassal, Nashirō, who eventually kills Mukusaku. Ishikameya Jidanda suffers a similar fate to that of Mukusaku. After his wife's death, Jidanda marries his servant, Okoze. Later she falls in love with her husband's henchman, Dojōji. Importantly, both women were servants who married their masters and who later betrayed their husbands. Nabiki betrays her husband as an expression of her love for Nashirō while Okoze does the same on account of her love for Dojōji.

The early form of this kind of marriage between master and servant can be found in Bakin's *The Tale of Tsuneyo Which Encourages Virtue* (*Kanzen Tsuneyo monogatari*, 1806). In this narrative, Tamaki, the second wife of Fujiwara Masatsune who is also Masatsune's son's former wet-nurse, conspires to kill her husband's son. This is a typical story of the ill-treatment of a stepchild and of the household raider.[24] In this early story, the marriage of a master and his servant is merely depicted as a catalyst for the mistreatment of a child and treachery in the household. But the examples from *The Eight Dog Chronicles* present not only the servant who, upon marriage to her master, is transformed into a wicked stepmother, household raider and

The Eight Dog Chronicles 109

unfaithful wife; they also provide passionate details of the lovers' illicit relationship. In the earlier tale, Mukusaku and Jidanda are the masters as well as the husbands of Nabiki and Okoze. The lovers, Nashirō and Dojōji, however, are both men outside the family relations of these women. In this sense, Nabiki's and Okoze's illicit love parallels that of Kamezasa's in that each woman rejects an inside superior in preference for an outside stranger. Thus, they are the exact opposites of women such as Hamaji, Otone, Hikute, Hitoyo, Nui and Hinakinu, each of whom is faithful to her husband and father-in-law. Of these women, Hamaji and Hinakinu have stepbrother–stepsister relationships with Shino and Daikaku. In this sense, there is a vital distinction between Nabiki/Nashirō, Okoze/Dojōji and Kamezasa/Hikiroku, on the one hand, and between Hamaji/Shino and Hinakinu/Daikaku, on the other. The former are relations across the family boundary, while the latter are relations within a family.

This illicit love appears as a typical theme in a number of Ihara Saikaku's novels and Chikamatsu Monzaemon's dramas. For instance, Saikaku's *Five Women Who Loved Love* (*Kōshoku gonin onna*, 1686) depicts how a cooper's wife is suddenly seized with the desire to make love with a man who is no more than an acquaintance and how this passion finally destroys the peace of her happy married life. The novel also tells of the illicit love between Osan and her almanac-maker husband's employee, Moemon. Jihei, the hero of Chikamatsu's *Love Suicides at Amijima*, is torn between his affection for his wife, Osan, and his passion for the prostitute, Koharu. Since Osan is Jihei's cousin, this is again a typical conflict between family members and outsiders. The protagonists of Chikamatsu and Saikaku desperately long for a new life with strange others, leaving their happy, calm and comfortable families. Modernist critical standards based on an affiliation with erotic desire and anti-authoritarianism greatly value these illicit loves and their inherent power to overcome the exclusiveness of the Confucian ethic. In contrast, the familiar affection between relatives which Confucian society valued so highly was regarded by modernists as hypocritical, boring and lacking in tension.

Now we move on to examine the modernist anti-authoritarian aspects of *The Eight Dog Chronicles*. First, anti-authoritarianism in *The Eight Dog Chronicles* is found in the fact that, with the occasional exception, the good characters in the novel are from the lower social classes or from defeated families. They are far removed from positions of authority. For instance, Satomi Suemoto and his son Yoshizane are from a family defeated in the battle of Yūki Castle, as are Inuzuka Bansaku and his son Shino. Likewise, Inuyama Dōsetsu is from the family defeated in the battle of Nerima. Kanamari Hachirō, his son Daisuke, Inue Shinbei and Inuta Kobungo are all from families defeated by the evil power-broker Yamashita Sadakane. Inukai Genhachi and Inukawa Sōsuke are from poor families, while Inusaka Keno is a son of Aihara Tanenori's concubine. Inumura Daikaku's father was killed by a monster wildcat.

110   The Eight Dog Chronicles

In contrast to these heroes from the lower social classes or from defeated families, many of the villains are authority figures. The deputy lord, Hikami Kyūroku, and his retainer, Nurude Gobaiji, are both depicted as evil (II 58). Lord Ashikaga Nariuji, his regent Yokohori Arimura and one of his head samurai, Niioriho Atsumitsu, are the antagonists who attempt to catch Shino and Genhachi (II 201). Hikami Shahei (a younger brother of Kyūroku), his retainer, Isakawa Iohachi, and deputy lord, Yoborota Machinoshin, are all evil figures in positions of authority (III 38–9). Chiba family's retainer, Makuwari Tsunetake, too, is depicted as an evil man (III 258). These unprincipled leaders, however, are clearly rejected in Bakin's view, which is almost always focused on the weak and the poor. "To side with the weak and crush the strong" and "to deliver the [common] people from agony" are set phrases repeatedly used throughout the narrative (I 188, III 65, V 263, X 62). In this sense *The Eight Dog Chronicles* is a story in which powerless people from the lower social classes must fight against strong people who hold authority. While at first the latter cruelly oppress the former, as the narrative progresses the former rise up against and defeat the latter.

Against these anti-authoritarian aspects, authoritarian features are also found in *The Eight Dog Chronicles*, in that the eight heroes are totally obedient, loyal and faithful to their master, Satomi Yoshinari. It is apparent, therefore, that the Confucian structure depicted in *The Eight Dog Chronicles* advocates, first, siding with the weak by crushing evil authorities who sacrifice the weak and the powerless, and, second, loyally following a good authority able to deliver the people from suffering. As mentioned previously, Bakin is author-itarian only as far as this is defined as an egalitarian ethic which helps the socially powerless. Thus, the problem of the Confucian ethic of authoritar-ianism from the modernist viewpoint in this story is that it is based upon established concepts of good and evil and also presupposes a fixed family structure consisting of children, self (male), wife, brothers, parents, masters and enemy. It clearly teaches who should be respected, who should be sacrificed and who must be revenged. The sympathy of readers familiar with this formula would be activated upon being presented with a character required to suppress his own emotion in order to obey this teaching.

In contrast, modern ideology repudiates this predetermined structure. It favours autonomously judging what is good and what is evil in order to create something new. Accordingly, in *The Eight Dog Chronicles*, what Confucians regard as an established and fixed ethic, the viability of which is never in any doubt, modernists criticise as authoritarianism. In order to support the emergence of the concept of individuality, we have seen that modern ideology further emphasises the importance of those outside the family in the form of romantic illicit love between others. It also values the story that weak people from the lower social classes finally defeat strong people who hold authority. In the relation to our strong–weak issue, we can point out that, in contrast to the Confucian aspect of sacrifice and revenge power relation within the confines of the family, the modernist aspect of *The*

Eight Dog Chronicles lies in the romantic love of individuals and their resistance to established authority.

However, separate from the above-mentioned tension between Confucian and modernist ideologies, the narrative also suggests a different problem regarding Bakin's support for the weak and for egalitarianism. The following section will investigate this problem.

5.3. The postmodernist aspect of *The Eight Dog Chronicles*

Before investigating how Bakin's support for the weak and for egalitarianism is supported in the postmodern aspect of *The Eight Dog Chronicles*, it is necessary to clarify the structure of the narrative. *The Eight Dog Chronicles* can be roughly divided into two unequal parts.[25] Although the entire story consists of nine volumes, the first eight of these occupy about two-fifths, while the ninth volume alone covers about three-fifths of the narrative. This unevenness has long attracted critical attention. Following the death of Fusehime, the first section of *The Eight Dog Chronicles* introduces the eight heroes, who are mysteriously the sons of Fusehime and the grandsons of General Satomi Yoshizane. After undergoing many adventures and overcoming various difficulties, the eight heroes finally assemble to restore the Satomi family to its former glory. These events are related from the beginning of the work to section 131 of volume 9. At the end of section 131, all eight heroes join before General Yoshinari, Yoshizane's son, and the narrative is brought to a happy ending.

However, for more than a third of the work's whole length, the story relates the battle between the Satomi family and the shogun's deputies. Bakin explains that this battle was the original idea for the story (VIII 222–3). He also mentions that, since "nine" is the last one-digit odd number, it is also a good number for ending the story (VI 5–6). Thus, the long story added following the denouement in section 131 could not be placed in a new volume since it was considered undesirable to add a further volume in terms of the significance of the number nine. It is for this reason that the narrative in this section was expanded beyond its original limits without making the necessary structural adjustments in terms of adding an extra volume. Yet, in addition to the difficulties created by the addition of such a large amount of material so late in the plot, the plot itself is also problematic. Many early critics claimed that, in contrast to the first half of the novel, which is full of exciting and at times grotesque scenes, the latter half is uneventful and boring (Konishi 1992, 5: 228).

The postmodern feature of *The Eight Dog Chronicles* is closely related to this two-part structure. We have seen that Confucian issues of strong–weak expressed as sacrifice and revenge, or the modern power struggle evident in romantic love and anti-authoritarian conflict, feature significantly in the first half of *The Eight Dog Chronicles*. In contrast to this, a new paradigm that is, to some extent, related to anti-modern or postmodern egalitarianism is

112   The Eight Dog Chronicles

introduced in the latter half. This is a utopian ideology symbolised by the Confucian virtue *jin* (compassion), as represented by the final hero, Inue Shinbei. To repeat our analysis of Itō Jinsai's and Ogyū Sorai's concepts of *jin* in Chapter 2, while Jinsai interprets *jin* as "the virtue of compassion and love", Sorai defines *jin* as the virtue of the leader who brings peace and the great virtue of the sages to the people.[26] The notion of *jin* in *The Eight Dog Chronicles* is well explained by Fusehime. She tells Shinbei that

> among the eight [good] conducts and five virtues, Confucius thought that the one that is not easily accessible is *jin*, because its virtue was originally different from that of *heaven*. *Jin* is the name given to the [principle that governs] man, while *heaven* is the name given to the [principle that governs] nature. . . . Avoid destroying life and train the power of empathy and compassion for others: this will suffice to attain it.
>
> (VI 29)

This definition of *jin* is closer to that of Jinsai than to that of Sorai, for it advocates a "horizontal" ethic rather than one which discriminates between "high" and "low" or between ruler and subject.[27] *The Eight Dog Chronicles* also mentions that the concept of *jin* is similar to unsophisticated naïvety (V 131). Not to punish one who surrenders is also a characteristic of *jin* (V 269). The dominant ideology of the latter half of *The Eight Dog Chronicles* is underpinned by this sense of *jin*, which urges people to have compassion even for their enemies. For instance, Yoshinari, the head of the Satomi family, tells his soldiers that the most distinguished way to behave in the war with the shogun's deputies is not to kill the enemy but to take the enemy general prisoner. If they offend against this order, Yoshinari continues, they will be punished (IX 82). In addition, Shinbei provides the enemy with a special medicine that can revitalise the dead, so that even those who are mistakenly killed might now be revived.

Thus, although the shogun's deputies, Ōgigayatsu Sadamasa and Yamanouchi Akitada, are completely trounced following their attack on the Satomi family, they are not executed. Akitada escapes to Numata castle (X 77). When Sadamasa is cornered by Kominato Katamune, one of the samurai leaders under the command of Inusaka Keno, he cuts off his own hair and presents it to Katamune, who generously permits Sadamasa to go free (X 18). Altogether twelve generals under the command of the shogun's deputies are taken hostage. However, they are treated as guests in the Satomi castle and subsequently released (X 106).

This characteristic of *jin* is actually well prepared in the novel beforehand. For example, although the villain Hikita Motofuji is executed the second time he is defeated (VII 154), the first time he is assisted by Shinbei (VI 120–2). Furthermore, after defeating the Yūki family's evil retainers and a number of evil monks, Sōsuke, Kobungo, Genhachi and Shino do not execute the hostages, who include Neoi Motoyori, Katakunashi Tsunekado, Tokuyō and

Kensaku (VII 241–3). The villainous monks Tokuyō and Kensaku later appear in the story of Shinbei's killing a tiger in Kyoto. They hold Princess Fubuki hostage, are attacked by the tiger (VIII 216) and finally executed by the authorities (VIII 310). It can thus be said that, as a rule, villains are forgiven the first time, but punished for a second offence.

In order to make the ideology of *jin* work, Bakin seems to have made further careful preparation. First, the role of sacrifice, so abundant and crucial in the first half, becomes gradually less significant in the latter half of the novel. As we have seen, sacrifice presupposes a hierarchical order of master, superior friend, father, elder brother, wife and self. As we have also seen, according to Confucian ethics, virtuous conduct requires the sacrifice of one's wife for one's parents, but never vice versa. The absence of sacrifice in the second half of the text therefore indicates a new impartial and equal status of the characters who were ranked previously in a hierarchy.

One clear example of how this ban on sacrifice works can be seen in the story of Higaki (Ochiayu) Aritane. Like the tragic figures in the first half, Aritane venerates the eight heroes, but he sacrifices neither himself nor his wife for them. In the first half, for instance, Fusahachi kills himself and his wife, and Rikijirō and Shakuhachirō sacrifice themselves and their happy lives with their families in order to help the heroes they adore. One of the factors which drives the plot in the first half of the story is vengeance for the sacrificial death of these various family members. But Aritane does not follow the pattern set by his predecessors. A significant incident occurs in the battle with Ōgigayatsu Sadamasa's army when, because he has a family, Aritane is ordered by Inuyama Dōsetsu not to join in the fighting, but to stay in his boat and wait for the return of the other men (V 187). Later, Aritane discovers that Sadamasa's retainers, Mita no Gyoranji, Nedu no Yachūji and Anaguri Sensaku, are about to attack him because he helped the eight heroes. Nevertheless, rather than risk his life fighting, he follows the advice of his wife, Omoto, and runs away, together with his family and the people of his village (VIII 351, IX 44). This is very different from the behaviour of the tragic figures in the first half of the story.

Second, in the latter half of the story, following the absence of sacrifice, the motive of revenge is also drastically downplayed. In the first half there are many revenge incidents. As I have noted, the Confucian notion dictates that we should avenge persons, according to a revenge priority order of parents, brothers, master and friends. Therefore, the insignificance of revenge in the latter half of *The Eight Dog Chronicles* indicates a shift from the ideological order of "filial piety, respect for elder brothers and then others (master and friends)" to that of "universal love".[28] This means that the ideology that is shared only among one's family and household in the first half of the story is extended as a universal rule to others, even enemies, in the latter half. The most significant example of this is Ōgigayatsu Sadamasa's vassal, Kawagoi Takatsugu. Some of the eight heroes are responsible for his father's suicide, and his master Sadamasa is about to be killed by Dōsetsu. But Takatsugu respects the eight

114   The Eight Dog Chronicles

heroes and avenges neither his father's death nor his master's shame (V 250). He eventually becomes a friend of the Satomi family. In other words, the ideological priority order – father, brother, master, friend and others – is, in this instance, in the process of being replaced by impartial universal love.

The appearance in the story of the father-and-son pair Kawagoi Moriyuki and Takatsugu seems, in itself, to deviate from the revenge plot. Ōgigayatsu Sadamasa, Takatsugu's master, is the target of Dōsetsu's revenge; and Sadamasa's retainer, Komiyama Yoritsura, is the target of Keno's revenge. If Dōsetsu and Keno took their revenge together on the same occasion, the dramatic effect would be increased. However, Bakin declines to orchestrate such a possibility. In fact, it is likely that he deliberately developed the plot in a different direction. In addition to the previously discussed less-supportable motive of Dōsetsu's revenge, this different direction is also taken to avoid a clear distinction between enemies and friends. Even among the enemy there should be good persons, such as Kawagoi Moriyuki and his son Takatsugu. In fact, as we have seen, neither is Ōgigayatsu Sadamasa exactly an evil character although he is a principal enemy figure. While revenge, such as that pursued by Keno and Dōsetsu, might drive the plot in the first half, this element cannot be found in the second half. As I have mentioned earlier, there are certainly examples of revenge present in the latter half of the story. These include Inuzuka Shino's killing of Yokohori Arimura and Nihioriho Motoyuki, in addition to the cruel deaths of Mita no Gyoranji, Nedu no Yachūji and Anaguri Sensaku at the hands of the members of the Toshima clan. But, in terms of significance with respect to driving the plot, there is no comparison between these incidents and the revenge incidents in the first half of the narrative.

No significant illicit erotic love-story features in the latter half of the narrative. Furthermore, while the battle between the Satomi clan and the shogun's deputies, which occupies much of this second half, may appear to be an anti-authoritarian battle, it is actually neither a desperate fight by the weak against strong authority nor a fight to overturn established authority or to create a new ideology. It is rather a fight based on the concept of *jin* between the strong and right Satomi family and the weak and bad shogun's deputies.

It can thus convincingly be said that, from the Confucian, modernist and postmodernist perspectives on the issue of the strong–weak, the ideology underlying the narrative changes from sacrifice, revenge, illicit love and anti-authoritarianism in the first half to *jin* in the changed context of the latter half. In the first half, the sacrifice of the weak and the strong hero's revenge realise the Confucian reader's satisfaction, while illicit love and anti-authoritarian conflict open the modernist romantic space. In the latter half, however, sacrifice, revenge, romantic love and anti-authoritarianism are replaced at the outset by impartial egalitarianism represented by the concept of *jin*. Thus, it now seems clear that Bakin attempted to portray *jin* as a concept that could replace the ideologies of sacrifice and revenge, and romantic love and conflict.

The Eight Dog Chronicles 115

In some ways, this new context, which values universal love above familial love (prohibiting revenge), impartial kindness over hierarchical ranking (obviating sacrifice), and the disappearance of erotic love and anti-authoritarian conflict, resembles an anti-modern (postmodern) ideology. Though Confucianism is parallel to modernism in the sense that both are constructed on a matrix of power, they are different in their domains. As we have seen, Confucian ideology confines itself to the consanguine male-centred family and household. Master/retainer, parents/children and elder/younger brothers are all power relations within the family and household. Modernist ideology subverts this confinement and values the romantic lover over parents or siblings. It allies the self with those outside the consanguine family (sweetheart/wife/husband) and values the newly formed conjugal family more highly than the consanguine family. Since the enemy–friend relation and the competition implied by the pairing remain in modern society, modernists eventually either fight or love at the level of the individual, and also of the nation-state. But the ideology of *jin* in the latter half of *The Eight Dog Chronicles* goes further in that it subverts not only the consanguine and conjugal families but also the distinction between friend and enemy. In this way it strives for a state of impartial and indiscriminate kindness.

Three questions can be raised concerning the new setting governed by the concept of *jin* as depicted in the latter half of *The Eight Dog Chronicles*. First, as Koyano Atsushi points out (Koyano 1990: 208–11, 226, 230, 238, 266), and as we have confirmed above, in Bakin's fair and egalitarian society there is a lack of eros, romance and/or adventure, all of which are the product of power structures. This is the reason why modernists, who are used to striving for erotic and romantic adventure on a matrix of differentiation, are inevitably bored by a perfectly fair and egalitarian postmodern society. In this regard, it might be possible to say that the first half of *The Eight Dog Chronicles* corresponds to the *Engyō* text of *The Tale of the Heike*, in the sense that both texts show strong emotion between sacrifice and revenge, between love and conflict, or between sympathy and contempt. The latter half of the narrative, on the other hand, resembles the *Kakuichi* text in the sense that both texts show indifferent, aloof and decent egalitarianism. Although the egalitarianism of the latter part of the *Eight Dog Chronicles* might be considered to resemble an ideal anti-modern (postmodern) society, most critics comment on the tedium of this section of the narrative. It is therefore hard to say that the fair and egalitarian setting created by Bakin succeeds in appealing to the reader.

The second problem in Bakin's egalitarian setting is that the complete egalitarian society realised by the concept of *jin* results in a monopolisation and, eventually, a sort of paralysis of the value system by the beliefs of the average people.[29] It is important, however, to preserve or rather produce elements "outside" the bounds of the cultural confinement of a single, homogenous group. This is because a society inevitably becomes stagnant if

116   The Eight Dog Chronicles

a single value system prevails, thus preventing the creation of new values. One of the flaws in the latter half of *The Eight Dog Chronicles* is that Bakin seems to have erased the possibility of producing a new value system.

The third difficulty arises from the fact that avoiding violence by means of non-violence is a project that finds little theoretical support. Walter Benjamin, for example, states that a legal contract, such as that which operates between the shogun's deputies and the Satomi family, can never be negotiated through a purely non-violent resolution of conflict. For, he argues, the contract confers on each party the right to resort to violence in some form, should one or the other break the agreement. Benjamin further remarks that not only the outcome but also the origin of every contract points towards violence. Even if this penalty does not involve direct physical violence, the violent origin of the contract ensures that some penalty will be incurred for violation of the conditions of the agreement (Benjamin 1996: 243–4). This is surprisingly similar to the situation discussed by Thomas Hobbes and John Locke and their assumptions that the "state of nature" is necessarily hostile. The second half of *The Eight Dog Chronicles* is set against a background of conflict between the shogun's deputies and the Satomi family. However, rather than non-violence as an expression of *jin*, it is the enormous imbalance of power between the shogun's deputies and the Satomi family that prevents a direct and violent confrontation. Concerning this point, Satō Miyuki argues that, rather than being an ideal of non-violence, the suppression of the pursuit of revenge and the conflict that accompanies such a strategy in the latter half of *The Eight Dog Chronicles* and its replacement by the concept of *jin* is, in fact, an indication of the Satomi family's monopoly of violence (Satō Miyuki 1988: 103).

As we have seen in Chapter 2, the modern nation-state was mostly brought about by violent revolution and born by means of accumulating this violence and concentrating it in the newly born government of nation-state. Likewise, the Satomi family kingdom was also realised by a monopoly of violence that prohibited others from using violent means. This monopoly was concealed by the concept of *jin*, which here is no longer "compassion" but the "generosity" of power-given authority. Thus, rather than solving the problem of violence, this model in fact relies on violence for its existence. For instance, in *The Tale of the Heike*, or rather in the historical event of the battle between the Heike and the Genji, both families attempt to obliterate their enemy, so that the respective enemies can never seek revenge. This, too, is an attempt to monopolise legitimate physical violence. However, if we compare the Heike and Genji families with the Satomi family in *The Eight Dog Chronicles*, we find a distinct difference in the way of achieving a monopoly on legitimate physical violence. The earlier Heike–Genji strategy of obliterating the enemy and governing by a reign of violent terror has been transformed to the application of a merciful and generous non-violence with an apparent egalitarianism. However, this egalitarianism is, in fact, grounded in an enormous imbalance of power.

It is likely that a number of factors operated in the emergence of such a possibility. First, the political stability of the Tokugawa regime from the early seventeenth century to the mid-nineteenth century paved the way for the non-violent solution of political problems, a solution which depended on the great imbalance of power between the Tokugawa shogun and other daimyōs. Second, as we have pointed out in Chapter 2, as a result of what might be termed a "perversion" in education, ideological unification increasingly became a feature of society, since, in addition to aristocrats, scholars and samurai, merchants and farmers also began to acquire learning in the Tokugawa period (Hall (ed.) 1991: 715–25; Dore 1984: 1–3, 14–32). Third, early-seventeenth-century Japan saw the beginning of the Tokugawa government policy of approval for licensed quarters. This move helped to castrate male sexual desire, which is innately directed towards outside others (strangers). As I have mentioned in Chapter 1, and shall soon explain again in Chapter 6, since male sexual desire is in a sense closely related to a desire for violence to outside others, the licensed quarters play a key role in rendering male desire inwardly consumable. Each of these factors led to a monopoly of legitimate violence by means of the putatively egalitarian concept of *jin*.

If we refer here again to Max Weber's definition that "the state is the form of human community that (successfully) lays claim to the *monopoly of legitimate physical violence* within a particular territory" (Weber 2004: 33; Weber's italics),[30] the victory of the Satomi family heralds the birth of the nation-state, not simply by the monopoly of violence, but by camouflaging this with the concept of *jin*. As we have seen in Chapter 2, the equality and the freedom realised by violence in a conflict situation were confined to the nation-state, could not go beyond its boundary, and were exploited, so to speak, for the purpose of competition between like states. We are obliged, at the risk of our lives, to fight for the nation-state because this is the entity that bestows freedom and equality on us.

As we have also observed in Chapter 2, egalitarianism of this nature can thus be used effectively by the authorities to unite people in one society to fight against another society. Even if its people are not treated equally by the authorities, once the moral value of egalitarianism is established in a society, individuals are then inclined to pay more attention to the injustice caused by other societies than to injustices within their own society. This may result in a very belligerent society, as in the case of the Satomi family in *The Eight Dog Chronicles*. Shinoda Jun'ichi, in a different context, argues that Mount Toyama (Tomi-san), where the eight heroes were born, represents Mount Fuji, and that the world of *The Eight Dog Chronicles* represents the united Japan (Shinoda 2004: 424). By treating all enemies in the Kantō region as a family formed through the monopolisation of legitimate violence under the cloak of *jin*, the latter half of *The Eight Dog Chronicles* actually represents the appearance of the idea of Japan as a nation-state. In the concept of Japan the nation, all individuals should be treated equally, with the ideologically weak aided by the authorities as compensation for the divisions of social class.

118   The Eight Dog Chronicles

This is exactly the situation that Fukuzawa Yukichi and the Japanese authorities attempted to realise after the Meiji Restoration, imported from Western thinkers of the seventeenth to nineteenth centuries. In the new Meiji society all the four ranks – samurai, farmer, artisan and merchant – were treated equally, albeit superficially. Furthermore, the whole society was then encouraged to fight with other societies which treated Japan unequally (Fukuzawa 1981b: 62–3, 78–9, 90–2). Importantly, it is precisely the concept of generous *jin* (*isshi dō jin*: to treat everybody equally with *jin*) that later justified Japan's colonisation of Korea.

As we have seen in our discussions on the versions of egalitarianism proposed by Hōnen and Yukichi, Bakin's concept of "equality" is not the humanistic variety of equality based on a sort of agnosticism posited on an assumption of the need for collaboration and cooperation, and that thereby argues against the capacity to measure the contribution made by the individual to society. Rather, it is the equality of the members of the nation-state, which was born by overthrowing the unequal aristocratic and feudal class society of the past. This equality ultimately works to preserve the modern nation-state by means of conflict with other like states. In this sense, we might say that *The Eight Dog Chronicles* helped pave the way to unifying the people of Japan as a belligerent nation.

We have attempted to unfold three different ideologies of *The Eight Dog Chronicles*, namely the premodern (Confucian), modern (anti-Confucian) and anti-modern (postmodern). In the premodern Confucian aspect we have identified the strong–weak power relation in the form of sacrifice and revenge as major plot elements which drive the story. At the same time we have noted that behind the Confucian ideology lie the problems of both a suffocating fixed family structure and a stagnant predetermined concept of good and evil. In the anti-Confucian modernist ideology we have examined the principal modernist features of the tale, namely power struggle between self and others in terms of illicit love or erotic desire and the anti-authoritarian struggle for the purpose of progress. We have also seen discriminatory and merciless fighting in this context. Finally, in the anti-modernist or postmodern ideology, we have discussed the notion of egalitarian fairness which underpins the concept of *jin*. We have furthermore noted problems associated with this concept, including a lack of eros, romance and adventurous fighting, and the pervasion of a single value system. Most importantly, we have explained how the egalitarian concept of *jin* can actually be perverted to represent what is, in fact, a monopoly of violence which ultimately results in the confinement of egalitarianism and an ensuing aggression against other discriminative societies. It remains to be seen how attractive the postmodern reader will find fiction based on an egalitarian fairness intended to overcome or even circumvent the vicious circle of sacrifice and revenge and the power struggle between self and others.

6 Dancing girl, geisha, mistress and wife in Kawabata Yasunari's stories: *The Dancing Girl of Izu, Snow Country, Thousand Cranes* and *The Sound of the Mountain*

6.1. Femininity created by the male gaze

In this chapter I shall examine four stories by Kawabata Yasunari, with a focus on the women who appear in these works and the issue of the strong and the weak. The four stories are *The Dancing Girl of Izu* (1926), *Snow Country* (1935–47; book published in 1948), *Thousand Cranes* (1949–51; book published in 1952) and *The Sound of the Mountain* (1949–54). Early Kawabata scholarship was largely the province of male commentators. Thus, in marketing material for Imamura Junko's 1988 book, *A Study of Kawabata Yasunari* (*Kawabata Yasunari kenkyū*), Hasegawa Izumi noted that "To date the study of Kawabata has been developed from a male perspective and by male pens. [Imamura's] book is the first monument built by a woman's hand."[1] Imamura's book began what became an extended discussion of Kawabata's material by women critics, a number of whom adopted a strongly critical feminist position. In the following year, 1989, for example, two essays on Kawabata's work, one by Komashaku Kimi and the other by Tajima Yōko, appeared in the feminist journal *Espace des femmes* (*Josei kūkan*) (Komashaku 1989; Tajima Yōko 1989). Two years later, in 1991, Saegusa Kazuko published a book in which she pilloried Kawabata's representation of women characters (Saegusa 1991). In the following year, 1992, a revised version of Tajima Yōko's earlier *Espace des femmes* essay appeared as a book chapter (Tajima Yōko 1992: 149–79).

Influenced by these scholars, Komori Yōichi also noted that it is obvious that an aggressive male gaze which voyeuristically objectifies and reifies female characters and their bodies is embedded in many places throughout Kawabata's stories (Kawabata et al. 2000: 90). However, Nakayama Masahiko's narrative study, which distinguishes between the voice of the narrator and the voices of the characters in Kawabata's work, and a follow-up study by Katsuhara Haruki (Nakayama 1984; Katsuhara 1999) are useful reminders that the voice of the protagonist is not always that of the narrator. Following these studies, in this chapter I should like to focus attention on

120   *Kawabata Yasunari*

the relationship between the male gaze and the position of the weak female characters in these narratives.

Laura Mulvey's feminist film studies interpretation of "male gaze" is based upon the binary of gender imbalance – the strong male who views and the weak woman who is viewed. The determining male gaze projects its fantasy on to an accordingly styled female figure. This position is supported by the fact that the traditional "exhibitionist" role of women has them simultaneously viewed and displayed. Their appearance is thus coded for strong visual and erotic impact connoting *to-be-looked-at-ness* (Mulvey 1999: 62–3). As I have stated in Chapter 1, we can see here the modernist ideology of progress based on power struggle. Modern progress is basically acquired by according the stronger the privilege of abusing the weaker. As discussed in my previous book, if we examine sexual desire, it becomes apparent that a power struggle occurs when we unite with strangers. We have a desire to do violence as well as to communicate and sexually unite, not with our family members, but with strangers outside the family. For heterosexuals such as Kawabata's male characters, strangers are classified as members of the opposite sex. In essence, as Georges Bataille states, "the domain of eroticism is the domain of violence, of violation" (Bataille 1986: 16; cited in Murakami Fuminobu 2005: 65). On the other hand, however, it is also true that in reality, besides the binary of the powerful gazing male and the weak gazed-upon woman, we can logically have the pairing of a strong woman and a weak man, or a man and a woman who are equal. There is also the possibility of a generous, longing, or tender gaze. Thus, I would begin by distinguishing two aspects of love: power-driven masculine love seen in the arrogant gaze; and calm and tender spiritual or romantic love seen in the generous, longing and tender romantic gaze. As the discussion proceeds, it will become apparent that these two aspects are, in fact, interdependent.

One of the critic's major tasks is to analyse literary works from the past using a contemporary perspective and thereby to reveal and elaborate upon elements previously occluded by the hidden ideologies operating at the time in which the works were created. Through this process, critics develop their own new ideologies. We have already examined the manner in which Tsubouchi Shōyō's criticism of the didactic aspect of *The Eight Dog Chronicles* from the perspective of realism was instrumental, albeit coincidentally, in a modernist critique of Confucian ideology. In its confrontations with male-centred stories, feminist critical practice has similarly revealed the male ideology inherent in much literary production. The importance of these critiques should be fully acknowledged. However, we should be careful to avoid, as Shōyō did, moving indiscriminately from one extreme to another. We should also concede that what Kawabata attempted is, as I understand it, not to establish a new gender-free egalitarian society, but to find and create beauty in romantic love-relations as these operate between men and women in the modern male-centred society. This he did in much the same manner as Bakin attempted to create a form of beauty that would attract people living in Confucian society. Therefore, as well as criticising the discriminative ideology hidden in a literary work, or revealing the reciprocal complicit relation between discriminatory ideologies and literary production, it is also incumbent upon the critic to objectify both Kawabata's work and modern society. Thus, in the same way in which we placed *The Eight Dog Chronicles* in Confucian society and neutrally examined the devices that made it so attractive to people living under the Confucian system, in this chapter I shall locate Kawabata and his stories in the modern male-centred culture, not because I subscribe to that ideology, but in order to examine the stories from that perspective. We shall thus be able to examine the creation of female beauty in male society in addition to the nature and significance of relations between the "strong" male and the "weak" female characters in this writer's material.

I should like to begin by trying to identify the feminine beauty attributed to the heroines of four stories: Kaoru (the dancing girl) in *The Dancing Girl of Izu*, Komako (a geisha) in *Snow Country*, Mrs Ota and her daughter Fumiko (a mistress and her daughter) in *Thousand Cranes*, and Kikuko (the wife) in *The Sound of the Mountain*. Thus, we shall consider how Kawabata locates feminine attraction in Kaoru, Komako, Mrs Ota, Fumiko and Kikuko, and how the feminine features of these characters attract the male character and reader. Japanese literature of the modern period has any number of strong women characters, including those created by Higuchi Ichiyō and Yosano Akiko from the Meiji period, proletariat writers such as Hirabayashi Taiko and Sata Ineko, and, as will be mentioned later, the strong women of Nagai Kafu's novels. In Kawabata's stories, nevertheless, many women accord with traditional feminine virtues and are thus depicted as shy, innocent, pure, childish, tidy, methodical, warm, soft, gentle, delicate, sentimental, submissive and obedient.[2] The purpose of this discussion is to probe the significance of these attributes in terms of the relationships depicted between the strong and the weak.

The shyness of female characters in these four stories is typically encapsulated in their propensity to blush. Kaoru in *The Dancing Girl of Izu*, for instance, blushes in her first conversation with the protagonist high-school student (J: II 300; E: 9–10).[3] When the student asks her about her island home, Oshima, she does not directly answer him. Instead, she talks to the young woman beside her in a way that ensures that the student will hear the answer. When he asks a second question, Kaoru again blushes and nods very slightly. She cannot converse directly with the male student because of her shyness. In a culture like that of Japan, in which direct eye contact is regarded as showing a strong confidence and an iron will, or sometimes even bad manners, the avoidance of direct speech indicates the humility required of the lower classes. Since women in 1920s Japan generally did not have access to education above the basic level, they were regarded as socially lesser than men. They were therefore required to desist from speaking directly to men and to display a shy and modest demeanour even when opportunity for conversation with a man arose.

122 *Kawabata Yasunari*

On the day of their first meeting, Kaoru brings tea up to the student's room at the inn where both are staying. Here, again, her shyness is remarkable. As she comes to him, blushing and with her hand trembling, the tea cup almost drops from its saucer. Although she tries to set it down sharply in an effort to steady the cup, she succeeds only in spilling the tea. As an old woman observing this scene notes, this girl has come to a dangerous age (J: II 301; E: 10). Her shyness indicates that Kaoru is now old enough to start thinking about the opposite sex and that she has a crush on the student from Tokyo whom she regards as a strong, socially superior and protective figure. In these scenes both the blush and her shyness indicate the desire of a weak female character to attract and be protected by a strong male character.

Komako, one of the young women featured in *Snow Country*, is also portrayed as easily blushing bright red. Her shyness is such that she often loses her composure and must hide her face in her hands (J: X 18, 21f, 35, 36, 43, 44, 59, 91, 100, 104, 117; E: 16, 20, 21, 39, 40, 51f, 70, 114, 124, 130, 144). A typical scene occurs when Shimamura returns from taking a walk. As she notices him, a blush covers Komako's throat. Nonetheless, with a grave expression on her face, her eyes remain fixed upon Shimamura (J: X 43; E: 50–1). For shyness to attract the opposite stronger sex, it must be sensual. Thus, it is natural that Komako's shyness arouses Shimamura's male voyeuristic desire, as in the following:

> She smiled quietly, as though dazzled by a bright light. Perhaps, as she smiled, she thought of "then" [a reference to the couple's making love], and Shimamura's words gradually colored her whole body. When she bowed her head, a little stiffly, he could see that even her back under her kimono was flushed a deep red.
>
> (J: X 35; E: 39)

This passage gives a typical example of an instance in which Komako's feminine reserve is used to awaken Shimamura's male sexual and sensual desire.

Fumiko in *Thousand Cranes* also blushes. When Mrs Ota first meets the male protagonist, Kikuji, at Chikako's tea ceremony, she urges Fumiko, her daughter, to be quick with her greetings to Kikuji. Fumiko then blushes. She cannot make eye contact with Kikuji and, instead, looks at the floor (J: XII 20; E: 16). Fumiko's mother, Mrs Ota, also blushes (J: XII 20, 27; E: 17, 24). Later, when Fumiko becomes aware of the relationship between her mother and Kikuji, she visits him and requests that he not see her mother again. "Don't telephone her," she commands, nonetheless blushing as she speaks. She raises her head and looks at Kikuji, as if in an effort to master the shyness. But, as the shyness deepens, the blush spreads to her long, white throat (J: XII 39; E: 37). On the day after the seventh-day memorial services following her mother's suicide, Kikuji visits Fumiko. During their conversation, Fumiko's face indicates her shame, and a blush spreads from the unpowdered cheeks over the white throat (J: XII 75–6; E: 74). When

Fumiko hesitantly talks about her mother's sexuality to Kikuji, she again blushes (J: XII 81; E: 79). Like Komako's shyness with respect to Shimamura, Fumiko's blush is repeatedly used to arouse Kikuji's sensual desire (J: XII 117, 138; E: 113, 133).

Like Kaoru, Komako and Fumiko, Kikuko in *The Sound of the Mountain* also blushes. This she does when praised (J: II 277; E: 36); when asked about her pregnancy (J: XII 339; E: 93); when seen by Shingo, her father-in-law, without make-up (J: XII 384–5; E: 133); and when observing Shingo's delight at her present of an electric razor (J: XII 464; E: 203). She generally blushes if praised or if someone comments on her sexuality, including her pregnancy (J: XII 269, 280, 412, 431, 481, 512, 540; E: 28, 38–9, 159, 175, 219–20, 250, 275).

Besides being shy, Kaoru (*The Dancing Girl of Izu*) is portrayed as pure, innocent and childish. A typical occasion upon which Kaoru's childishness is revealed is the famous scene in which the protagonist student, while bathing, catches a glimpse of Kaoru running naked across the road from the bath house. Seeing the girl, he laughs happily and thinks: "She's a child – a child who can run out naked in broad daylight, overcome with joy at finding me, and standing tall on her tiptoes" (J: II 304–5; E: 14).[4] Kaoru's childishness is repeatedly depicted throughout the story. She says frankly that the student is nice and that she likes being with someone so nice. Her open way of speaking and youthful, honest way of saying exactly what comes to her enables the student, too, to think of himself as frankly "nice" (J: II 317–18; E: 27).

Like the pure and childish Kaoru, Komako (*Snow Country*) is also described as childlike (J: X 21; E: 20). However, the specific features emphasised in her case are cleanness and freshness, rather than childishness (J: X 18, 23, 28, 30, 41, 56, 61, 92, 122; E: 18, 23, 31, 32, 48, 66, 73, 115, 150). She is also tidy and methodical, and even feels obliged to fold up her dirty clothes (J: X 55; E 66). She insists that the mattresses are square with one another and that the bedsheets are folded correctly. Her need to be clean and neat is so strong that she spends the whole day tidying up (J: X 82; E: 102).

Mrs Ota (*Thousand Cranes*) is often described as being soft (*yawarakai*) and gentle (*yasashii*), while both Mrs Ota and Fumiko have rounded faces (J: XII 35, 41; E: 33, 38). Kikuji has the illusion that this softness and gentleness lightens his own suffering (J: XII 58–9; E: 56–7). In Kikuji's arms, Mrs Ota is as soft as a small child (J: XII 64; E: 62). Fumiko also receives Kikuji softly (J: XII 70; E: 68). With their warmness (J: XII 29, 31f, 72, 137; E: 27, 29f, 70, 133), softness (J: XII 35, 74; E: 33, 72) and gentleness (J: XII 80f, 104; E: 78, 79, 100), both Mrs Ota and Fumiko, in addition to a Shino water-jar said to represent them, are depicted in this story as typically feminine characters.

In *The Sound of the Mountain*, Kikuko's feminine beauty is portrayed in her delicate figure (*hossori*) (J: XII 256; E: 16) and her white skin. She is also childlike (J: XII 256, 354, 384; E: 16, 105, 133) and easily moved to tears. When Shingo expresses concern about Shuichi's extramarital relations with Kinu, suggesting that Kikuko and Shuichi should live away from Shingo and Yasuko, there are tears in Kikuko's large eyes (J: XII 393; E: 140). When Kikuko puts a Noh mask to her face, Shingo says: "Kikuko. You thought if you were to leave Shuichi you might give tea lessons." Kikuko answers by saying "I think I'd prefer to stay on with you here and give lessons". During this conversation, tears are flowing down Kikuko's face and on to her throat (J: XII 414; E: 160). Her tears also feature in other scenes (J: XII 398, 537; E: 145, 273), including when she aborts Shuichi's child (J: XII 421, 431; E: 167, 175). Kawabata uses tears in this story skilfully to represent the feminine character. Given that the presence of tears indicates a problem which cannot be solved and for which help must therefore be sought, they indicate the dependence of the weak on the strong. Like shyness, tears are a sign of a socially weak female character who wishes to be helped by a strong male character. The strong, in contrast, are required to overcome shyness and choke back tears.

The next attributes which attract the male characters are obedience and devotion. Kaoru's obedient character is visible in her bowing and kneeling (J: II 307, 312; E: 17, 21). At the tea house, she turns over the cushion on which she has been sitting and pushes it politely towards the student. When he fumbles for tobacco, she hands him an ashtray (J: II 295–6; E: 4). She often arranges the student's clogs so that he can step into them with ease (J: II 313, 319; E: 22, 28). Kaoru's obedient character is particularly evident when the group of travellers takes a shortcut over a mountaintop. In spite of the incline, the student's pace is brisk, and most of the party fall behind. Kaoru, however, tucks her skirts high and follows with tiny steps. She is mindful, too, always to remain a couple of yards behind the student, neither trying to come nearer nor letting herself fall farther back. Sometimes, when the student speaks to her, she stops and answers with a startled little smile. On these occasions he pauses, with the hope that she will come up and walk beside him. She always waits, however, until he starts out again and follows the same two yards behind. When they come to the summit, she bends down to dust the skirt of his kimono, falling to one knee when the student draws back in surprise (J: II 315; E: 24). She thus demonstrates the politeness, obedience and good behaviour expected of a woman.

In *Snow Country*, Komako's obedient and submissive character is evident in the scene in which she rearranges clothing thrown to the floor by Shimamura (J: X 40; E: 46). This tendency is also suggested in her propensity for housework. When Shimamura returns from taking a bath at the inn where Komako works, he finds her industriously cleaning his room, a kerchief draped artistically over her head. She stirs up the charcoal with a practised hand, and polishes the legs of the table and the edge of his brazier almost too carefully. When ash drops from Shimamura's cigarette, Komako gathers this in a handkerchief and then brings an ashtray (J: X 55; E: 65).

Towards the end of the war, when Fumiko was a girl, she did her very best for her mother's lover, Kikuji's father. She bought him chicken and fish, and was determined to help him even when risks were involved. Thus, she would venture out into the countryside for rice, even during the air raids (J: XII 28; E: 25). If there was an air-raid warning, in spite of the danger, Fumiko always insisted on seeing Kikuji's father home (J: XII 28; E: 26).

Kikuko is also obedient. As a housewife, she sees to supplying a brimming cup of tea to her father-in-law, Shingo, each morning when he rises and each evening when he comes home (J: XII 269, 385; E: 28, 134). She lays out his change of clothes and prepares his meal. She also prepares the hot-water bottle from which Shingo takes warmth while he sleeps in the winter (J: XII 378; E: 126). In addition, Kikuko nurses Shuichi's hangover (J: XII 384; E: 133). Kawabata's skilful manipulation of honorific language by each of the women protagonists in these four stories underlines their respect for the male characters. The shy, innocent, childish, pure, tidy, methodical, warm, soft, gentle, delicate, sentimental, obedient and submissive characteristics displayed by Kaoru, Komako, Fumiko and Kikuko amalgamate to comprise a form of beauty created by the strong male gaze. Kawabata specifically sees feminine beauty in these pure and submissive favourable-for-male characteristics which he gives to those women who decline to challenge the male-centred system.

However, the women in Kawabata's stories do not merely submit themselves to the existing order. They also attempt to rise up in the class-based society featured in these novels. We have noted that Kaoru is depicted as clever, enthusiastic and hardworking. With her solemn face (*ririshii kao*) (J: II 296; E: 4), she has strong willpower and a desire to learn, as evidenced by the fact that she is surprisingly good at checkers (J: II 310; E: 19). While playing this game with the student, she becomes so engrossed that she forgets herself and leans intently over the board (J: II 310; E: 19). She also likes books and looks up at the student with a serious expression of concentration while he reads her a piece from a storyteller's collection. Her eyes are bright and unblinking (J: II 311–12; E: 19). As we have seen, moreover, when the student goes up to the mountaintop, Kaoru alone follows him. This last point in itself shows her strong will and physical power (J: II 314; E: 23).

Komako knows more about Kabuki actors and styles than Shimamura does (J: X 20; E: 19). She has carefully catalogued every novel and short story she has read since the age of 15 or 16, and has a greater knowledge of new novelists than Shimamura (J: X 36–7; E: 41–2). She is also extremely good at the samisen. Listening to her play, Shimamura is overcome with a feeling that borders on reverence (J: X 59; E: 71). Though Komako claims to lack willpower (J: X 86; E: 106), on other occasions she is described as being both strong and stubborn (J: X 39, 69, 71; E: 44–5, 83, 87), and as a person with strong self-control (J: X 33; E: 35). The reader is clearly told that she is not a bad girl (J: X 86; E: 107), and the fact that she has become a geisha to help pay the doctor's bill for her music teacher's son is considered

126 *Kawabata Yasunari*

by Shimamura proof that she is "completely in earnest" (J: X 95; E: 117–18). Komako's serious attitudes are also noted elsewhere in the narrative (J: X 17, 43; E: 15, 51).

In these stories by Kawabata, all of the women are diligent workers, and their income is a very important element in setting the direction of the narrative. In *The Dancing Girl of Izu*, Kaoru works hard and is frequently depicted playing her drum. The protagonist student, on the other hand, shows little interest in work. We have seen that Komako in *Snow Country* must work as a geisha to help pay the doctor's bill for her music teacher's son (J: X 95; E: 117–18). While she is on duty, so to speak, we are impressed by her commitment, evident in comments such as "Well, back to work. . . . Business is waiting" or "Back to work. I'm all business. Business, business" (J: X 103, 107; E: 128, 133). The detailed description of the calculation of a geisha's income gives a clear indication of the circumstances of women in paid work (J: X 86; E: 107–8). This image of the working woman is expanded upon by the portrayal of the Russian woman peddler (J: X 73; E: 90). In addition, women at work are also the focus of a long description of the production of the Chijimi grass-linen of the snow country which is described as the handwork of mountain maidens through the long, snow-bound winters (J: X 122–4; E: 150–3).

In *Thousand Cranes*, although only mentioned incidentally, Fumiko enters the employment of a wool wholesaler in Kanda (J: XII 150; E: 146); Chikako works hard as a teacher of the tea ceremony. In *The Sound of the Mountain*, Shuichi's mistress, Kinu, is describeded as working at a tailor's shop, while her room-mate, a woman referred to only as Miss Ikeda, does tutoring. Kinu is described as a skilful worker who reads all sorts of American magazines about sewing. She also picks up the gist of French with a dictionary (J: XII 371, 492; E: 120, 230). At the close of the story, Fusako asks her father, Shingo, to open a little shop for her. Hearing this, Kikuko says that if Fusako is prepared to do this she, Kikuko, would also like to help (J: XII 539–40; E: 275).

These features, such as seriousness, intelligence, enthusiasm, desire to learn, capacity for hard work, strong willpower, stubborn determination and willingness to work, show a desire for self-improvement, if not to compete with others and to rise in social class. There is little evidence of a wish obediently to follow the existing order. To some extent, at least, part of the attraction of these women, and the reason the reader finds them desirable, relates to the beauty inherent in improving oneself and achieving an aim. Thus, the beauty of Kaoru, Komako, Fumiko and Kikuko lies not only in their obedience but also in their desire to challenge. This is in spite of the fact that their challenging spirits are carefully concealed behind a submissive demeanour and never become strong enough to threaten the male position in society. However, the important point is that, in addition to obedience, Kawabata's fictional beauties are simultaneously marked by a desire to challenge.

Kawabata Yasunari 127

If the weak challenge the strong, it will result in the latter ambushing the former and a power struggle ensuing. Were the weak to be insulted or injured by the strong, even if the former are obedient, the result would be discrimination, abuse or bullying. Were the strong challenged by the weak, regardless of any wish by the former to protect and help the latter, the result would be blasphemy, defiance or rebellion. The romantic ideal occurs when the weak obediently respect, serve and help the strong, and the strong take care of and protect the weak. In this book I have used the term "romance" to indicate such a relation. Of course, in *The Dancing Girl of Izu*, *Snow Country*, *Thousand Cranes* and *The Sound of the Mountain* the relations between the heroes and the heroines involve neither power struggle, nor discrimination, nor rebellion. Therefore, on the surface at least, we can define each of these works as a romance. The male characters in each work are all, even if only superficially, kind and helpful towards the submissive and obedient female characters, whose putative weakness carefully conceals their challenging spirits.

It is useful to note that, if the male characters show kindness towards the weaker women in these stories, then the women themselves, including Kaoru, Komako, Fumiko and Kikuko, also behave kindly to the weak. This is evident from Kaoru's petting her family's puppy on the head (J: II 309; E: 18), her handing out pennies to and playing with the inn children, as well as her also petting an unknown dog (J: II 319–20; E: 28–9). Komako plays happily in the *kotatsu* until noon with the 2-year-old daughter of the innkeeper, at which time they go together for a bath (J: X 62; E: 75). Though children do not appear in *Thousand Cranes*, in its sequel, *Plover on the Waves* (*Nami chidori*), Fumiko shows her interest in some children in Kyūshū in a letter she writes to Kikuji (J: XII 199, 207). Kikuko also takes care of Fusako's two girls and treats kindly a dog, Teru (J: XII 278, 322; E: 38, 77). It is likely that Kaoru, Komako, Fumiko and Kikuko look at these children and dogs in the same manner as the student, Shimamura, Kikuji and Shingo look at Kaoru, Komako, Fumiko and Kikuko respectively. That is, these female protagonists are shy and obedient to their superiors (male protagonists) and generous and kind to their inferiors (children and dogs). Each character mentioned, therefore, faithfully follows the required social class formation. The narrative thus leads the reader to align himself or herself with Kaoru, Komako, Fumiko and Kikuko, and to recognise the four women as beautiful.

Besides Kaoru, Komako, Fumiko and Kikuko, another kind of woman, Yoko, appears in *Snow Country*. Her significance is depicted as follows:

Now that he [Shimamura] knew Yoko was in the house, he felt strangely reluctant to call Komako. He was conscious of an emptiness that made him see Komako's life as beautiful but wasted, even though he himself was the object of her love; and yet the woman's existence, her straining to live, came touching him like naked skin. He pitied her, and he pitied himself.

128　*Kawabata Yasunari*

He was sure that Yoko's eyes, for all their innocence, could send a probing light to the heart of these matters, and he somehow felt drawn to her too.

(J: X 102–3; E: 127–8)

Here Yoko is presented as a symbol of the innocent woman. But, in spite of considerable overlap, Yoko's innocence features a subtle difference when compared to that of other female protagonists in Kawabata's stories, who are depicted as evoking the male characters' sexual desire for conquest in a power-struggle matrix. While the name Komako ("horse child") indicates an animal sexual desire, the name Yoko ("leaf child") shows the vegetative life without sexual desire. Yoko never blushes, though she sometimes cries. In this woman who is without sexual desire and who does not rely upon men, Kawabata sees "a probing light to the heart of these matters".

On one occasion, Komako says: "After all, it is only women who are able really to love." Shimamura murmurs: "In the world as it is." Komako replies: "As it always has been. You didn't know that?" (J: X 104–5; E: 130–1). Shimamura is presumably thinking here about the fact that Yoko can live without the sort of love which, as Komako has observed, gives women a weakened position. In order to create an egalitarian new society which transcends the current one, then, we must look for a new beauty which is neither the beauty of the kind and caring strong nor the reverence of the weak. Thus, Shimamura thinks that to run off with Yoko to Tokyo, as if eloping, would be in the nature of an intense apology to Komako, and a penance for himself (J: X 109; E: 136). It is both an apology to Komako and a penance for Shimamura because he has deprived Komako of the possibility to live, like Yoko, without the need to be burdened with the love required of women in a male-centred society. However, in this story, Yoko is destined to die. In the final scene, as Komako struggles forward holding the unconscious Yoko to her breast, we read that it is "as if she bore her *sacrifice*, or her *punishment*". Komako cries: "This girl is *insane*. She's *insane*" (J: X 140; E: 175; my italics). If Yoko is in a sense an alter ego of Komako, Yoko's death must be a *sacrifice*, because it indicates that, by loving Shimamura, Komako must sacrifice the possibility of living, like Yoko, without the need to love. Yoko's death is, moreover, Komako's *punishment*, for the act of love must be punished from the humanistic viewpoint of egalitarianism. For women to live without feeling love in the context of modernity and its characteristic power struggle doubtless leads to *insanity*.[5]

In the Kawabata stories discussed here, there is one more female figure who, like Yoko, never blushes. She is Yukiko in *Thousand Cranes*. Although she is characterised by an obedient shyness in the sequel, *Plover on the Waves* (J: XII 156, 164, 230, 236), she does not blush in the earlier work. In the tea ceremony depicted in the opening pages of *Thousand Cranes*, Yukiko stands aside deferentially to let Kikuji pass, but she does not blush (J: XII 15; E: 11). When Chikako suggests marriage between Yukiko and Kikuji, Yukiko becomes shyly uncomfortable but she does not blush: "A sort of primeval shyness came over her. The shyness was a surprise to Kikuji. It flowed to him like the warmth of her body" (J: XII 56; E: 54). Kikuji's surprise indicates that he presumes Yukiko not to be shy, and that her shyness indicates a wish to marry him herself. He feels her shyness like the warmth of her body, because it contains the wish to be helped by Kikuji. It is interesting to note that, though Kikuji is sexually attracted to Fumiko and her mother, Mrs Ota, both of whom easily blush, he is unable to desire sexually or have sexual relations with Yukiko, who is not shy, even after their marriage in *Plover on the Waves*.

6.2. Open/hidden discrimination against femininity: *The Dancing Girl of Izu*

As discussed in the previous section, each of the male protagonists in *The Dancing Girl of Izu*, *Snow Country*, *Thousand Cranes* and *The Sound of the Mountain*, at least superficially, shows kindness towards and tries to help the weaker women protagonists. In *The Dancing Girl of Izu* the non-discriminatory attitude of the protagonist student is well contrasted with society's discrimination against the itinerant performers. When the student asks the old woman who runs a tea house at the mouth of Amagi Pass where the dancers will stay for the night, she answers:

> "There's no way to tell where people like that are going to stay, is there, young man? Wherever they can attract an audience, that's where they stay. It doesn't matter where it might be. I don't think the likes of them would have a place already planned."
>
> (J: II 298; E: 6)

When the student invites Eikichi, one of the performers, to his room at an inn where he is staying, the inn manager's wife points out that it is a waste of good food to invite such people in for meals (J: II 310; E: 19–20). Reference is made to a sign occasionally seen outside various villages which reads: "Beggars and itinerant entertainers – KEEP OUT" (J: II 318; E: 27).[6] The performing women themselves engage in self-discrimination. This is evident, for example, from comments they make when they see the student go to drink from a spring where they have been waiting for his descent from a mountain path. "You'd think", they say, "it was too dirty after us women" (J: II 316; E: 25). Later, when the student calls at their lodging-house, the women invite him to join them in eating communally from a pot of chicken stew. Nevertheless, an old woman from the group observes that, since they have used their chopsticks to eat from the pot, the meal is now unclean (J: II 319; E: 29).

While the dancers in *The Dancing Girl of Izu* are discriminated against both by others and by themselves, the student perceives himself as a man free from

130 *Kawabata Yasunari*

this discrimination. He does not join the old tea-house woman in her contempt (J: II 298; E: 7). He invites Eikichi to his room, dismissing the inn manager's wife's comment that it is a waste of good food to feed such a person, visits the dancers' inn, and is prepared to stay with the dancers in their cheap lodgings (J: II 302; E: 11). We have seen that when Kaoru bends down after climbing a mountain road to dust off the skirt of his kimono, as women of the time often did for men, he draws back surprised (J: II 315; E: 24). The student himself relates: "My common goodwill – which neither was mere curiosity nor bore any trace of contempt for them, *as if I forgot about their status as itinerant entertainers* – seemed to have touched their hearts" (J: II 313; E: 21–2. The italics are mine; I amended Holman's translation, referring to the original). Being touched by the student's goodwill, Kaoru and Chiyoko observe: "He's a nice person." "You're right. He seems like a nice person." "He really *is* nice. It's good to have such a nice person around" (J: II 317–18; E: 27; italics in the original). Previous commentary on *The Dancing Girl of Izu* generally interpreted the basic theme of the narrative as the narrator/protagonist's "liberation from his 'orphan psychology'".[7] Hatori Tetsuya, who regards the story as sweet, romantic, innocent and beautiful, is a representative of this view (Hatori 1993: 159–246). There are, in fact, two possibilities presented by this interpretation. The first is simply that the narrator/protagonist's orphan psychology is liberated by his encounter with the innocent Kaoru and the other itinerant performers. The second is more complex and suggests that any masculine sexual desire or discriminative superiority consciousness and arrogance which the student may have felt has been purified by his encounter with the innocent Kaoru and the itinerant performers. Any negative attributes have thereby been transformed into pure kindness which has neither curiosity, nor condescension, nor a sense of superiority. It is through this process that liberation from his orphan psychology occurs.

Against this reading, Hara Zen and Ueda Wataru present a critical view of the student and problematise the young man's self-defined kindness (Hara 1999; Ueda 1991). The "beautiful romance" element of the narrative upon which Hatori focuses is easy to find on the surface of the story. However, Hara and Ueda highlight what they both regard as the student's selfish, masculine, narcissistic and arrogant gaze, and his accompanying desire and subjectivity. For example, to the contempt of the old tea-house woman, the student thinks that if the women dancers are prepared to spend the night with anyone who will pay them, then he would be happy to have the dancing girl spend the night in his room (J: II 298; E: 7). This wish is extremely ambiguous and open to different interpretations, namely that it is either arrogant male desire or a pure wish to protect the girl. Hasegawa Izumi insists on the former, whereas Morimoto Osamu argues the latter (Hasegawa Izumi 1991: 221, 253, 259–60; Morimoto 1990: 31–65). But what is important for our discussion is not so much deciding which of these two positions is correct as the fact that the young man's desire can be interpreted in two ways. That is, the student's desire can be read as the arrogant masculine gaze that views the female figure as an object of male desire grounded in hidden discrimination, or as the romantic male gaze which finds in relations between men and women a beautiful pure love without discrimination accompanied by male willingness to help the weak.[8] It is this possibility of a double reading that I wish to explore further.

As many critics have observed, the student's latently discriminatory attitude towards the itinerant performers is demonstrated in the scene in which he tosses money from the first floor of the inn down to Eikichi, telling the latter to use the money to buy persimmons or something (J: II 302; E: 11). Citing this, together with the fact that the young man overpays the old tea-house woman at Amagi Pass, Ueda Wataru argues that the student's generosity with money demonstrates that he does, in fact, discriminate against the lower social classes (Ueda 1991: 482–95). For, as Ogino Anna points out with respect to the italicised section in the passage cited above, far from revealing a lack of consciousness regarding social class, the student's words, "*as if I forgot about their status as itinerant entertainers*", clearly reveal a very strong class awareness (Ogino 1991: 120).

If we read this story acknowledging the operation of the arrogant masculine gaze which regards the female figure as an object of male desire grounded in hidden discrimination, we become aware of the narrative being skilfully, clearly and intentionally unfolded so that it reveals the double standard of the protagonist student. We have already noted that the protagonist student's observation of Kaoru running naked across the road from the bath house functions to satisfy his male voyeuristic desire, in addition to showing Kaoru's childish innocence. Furthermore, throughout the story, the reader witnesses the student's insincerity towards the itinerant performers. For instance, when he must go back to Tokyo for financial reasons, the young man lies and tells the dancers he must return to school (J: II 319; E: 28). Ultimately, he also lies to Kaoru and parts from her without any promise to meet again. This must hurt her deeply.

As Roy Starrs noted, the dancers repeatedly invite the student to their home on the island of Oshima. The student relates: "Before I knew it, they had decided that I should accompany them to their place on Oshima. . . . Moreover, I was to help out during New Year holidays when they performed at the port in Habu" (J: II 313; E: 22). When the group sights Oshima from the road outside Yugano, Kaoru urges: "Please do come" (J: II 314; E: 23). The old woman repeats this invitation before the student goes back to Tokyo, saying: "Well, then, during the winter vacation, we'll all come out to meet your boat. Just let us know what day you'll arrive. We'll be waiting. Now don't try staying at an inn or anything. We'll meet you at the boat" (J: II 320; E: 29). There is no record of an answer from the student on any of these occasions (Starrs 1998: 57–9). Had there been a response, it would not have been necessary to repeat the invitation so many times. The student is also asked to attend the memorial service in Shimoda commemorating the

132 *Kawabata Yasunari*

forty-ninth day of death of the baby of one of the women. But, again, he declines (J: II 308, 319–20; E: 17, 29). To participate in the memorial service for a dead child or to stay at the home of someone is to become part of the family or close circle of friends. However, the student's failure to reply leads to the group realising that he will not be a long-term friend. Roy Starrs has pointed out that this is one of the reasons why the old woman will not permit Kaoru to attend a movie with the student. Had he replied and indicated his willingness to accept their invitation, the group would have trusted Kaoru to him on a movie outing. Unaware of this, the young man finds the old woman's refusal very strange (J: II 320; E: 29).

The student's decision to distance himself from the itinerant performers by not answering their invitation must also be one of the reasons why only Eikichi and Kaoru come to see him off at the dock. As they part, Eikichi says once more: "They said they'll be waiting for you this winter, so please do come." Once more, there is no response recorded from the student. Eikichi then gives him some cigarettes, persimmons and a mouthwash called "Kaoru" as souvenirs (J: II 321; E: 30). As Hara Zen noticed, it was persimmons that the student told Eikichi to buy when he threw money down to the performer (Hara 1999: 51–85). We can interpret this gift of persimmons as Eikichi's attempt to clear the debt and as an indication that the two are not intimate friends. But the student, once more, is oblivious to the significance of Eikichi's behaviour. As Ueda Wataru remarked and Hara Zen confirmed, Eikichi comes to see him off wearing black formal clothes, obviously for the forty-ninth day's service for the dead baby. But this, too, is misunderstood by the obtuse young man, who thinks: "Apparently, he had dressed formally to send me off" (J: II 321; E: 30; Ueda 1991: 489; Hara 1999: 72). As Hara argues, this misunderstanding is crucially important since it clearly reveals that the student is what Wayne C. Booth refers to as an unreliable narrator/protagonist, that is, a narrator who misinterprets the events that occur around him. It also gives the reader a clear indication of the young man's self-centred narcissistic and subjective prejudices.[9]

If we accept this reading, then one reason for Kaoru's coming to bid farewell the student is that she hopes he will promise to come to see the group once more in Oshima before he leaves for Tokyo. But he has no notion of her wishing such a thing. When he tries to make smalltalk with Kaoru, she says nothing, and merely stares down at the water pouring from a drainpipe into the sea. Kaoru's demeanour might be sorrow at parting from the student, and this is certainly the student's interpretation. However, we need to consider the use of the expression "*yosoyososhii*" (to keep him at arm's length), "as though she might even be angry", and the fact that Kaoru does not respond to the student's words but instead merely nods repeatedly even before the student finishes speaking (J: II 320–2; E: 30–1). Focusing on these elements raises the possibility that she is dissatisfied with the student, or perhaps even really angry at him, because he does not promise to visit Oshima. When he gets on the launch, she keeps her mouth tightly closed, staring at the same spot. The narrator student writes: "she tried to say good-bye but gave up and merely nodded one last time" (J: II 323; E: 32). The student clearly assumes that she is overcome at parting, but we might also interpret her reticence as a refusal to bid farewell to someone unfaithful. However, while the reader understands her silent resistance to the student, the young man himself, an unreliable narrator/protagonist, is totally unaware of this possibility (J: II 321; E: 31).

In contrast to the unhappy Kaoru, who, depending on how we read the narrative, is possibly actually quite angry, the student looks very happy in the last scene. This is the result of his being able to satisfy his romantic expectations without being soiled by sexual contact with the girl. Thus, he could part leaving no seeds of future trouble. Instead he fulfils the unsatisfied desire of physical contact by warming himself against a boy beside him in the boat (J: II 324; E: 33). As Ueda Wataru noticed, he can feel easy with the boy, the son of a factory-owner preparing to enter school. That is, the boy is both rich and intelligent (Ueda 1991: 486).

Before he boards the boat, a man he has never met before asks the student to accompany an old woman and her three grandchildren to Tokyo. The man says that the old woman's son, who was working in the silver mines at Rendaiji, and his wife both died in the influenza epidemic (J: II 322; E: 31). Later, on the boat, he contentedly muses: "It was utterly natural that I should accompany the old woman to Ueno Station early the next morning and buy her a ticket to Mito" (J: II 323–4; E: 33). The reader might wonder how he can buy someone a ticket, since he has no more money to travel. Furthermore, the silver mine at Rendaiji was known as Kawadu mine and was a site of Korean forced labour in the 1940s, a practice which possibly began as early as the late 1920s.[10] Here, the hint of discrimination and the student's irresponsible and narcissistic response well correspond with a similar remark made by the student at the beginning of the story in the Amagi Pass tea house. On the earlier occasion, the young man wonders why the old woman's husband, who suffers from palsy and whose whole body is almost paralysed, does not move down to a lower level in the house (J: II 297; E: 5–6). Although only palsy is mentioned, with his pale body swollen like the corpse of a drowned man and the petrified yellow pupils of his languishing eyes (J: II 296–7; E: 5), the old man's symptoms indicate that he may well be afflicted with the type of disease which incited a discriminative fear of contagion.[11] Given that the narrative begins and ends with references to two possible objects of discrimination – namely the old man of the tea house and the old woman on the boat – we can convincingly argue that Kaoru's story, too, is tinged with a discriminatory element.

The story of *The Dancing Girl of Izu* thus permits two contradictory readings. One is the story of a beautiful and innocent pure romance between a student and a dancing girl while the other tells of a selfish and arrogant student who discriminates against a dancing girl as he gazes at her with voyeuristic masculine sexual desire. Let me repeat and confirm here that

134   *Kawabata Yasunari*

Morimoto Osamu interprets the student's wish to have the dancing girl stay in his room as a pure desire to protect her, whereas Hasegawa Izumi sees this as masculine sexual desire. While Hatori Tetsuya interprets the story as a beautiful and innocent pure romance, both Ueda Wataru and Hara Zen consider the student's attitude to be one of narcissistic arrogance.

Beauty is often appropriated in a manner that serves to affirm an ideology. That is, we often use aesthetic judgement as one of the standards which reflect an ideological position. Thus, to find beauty in ugliness or ugliness in beauty indicates the subversion of a prevailing ideology and the birth of a new ideology. In this sense, Morimoto's and Hatori's readings clearly show their own male gaze cast from outside to inside the story. Though Hatori refers to feminist criticism of Kawabata, he ultimately sees the story as a beautiful romance. This is in spite of the fact that it is possible to interpret the narrative as the tale of a student's arrogant and mercilessly self-centred egotism. Certainly, the readings given by Hasegawa, Hara and Ueda reveal a critical perspective imbedded in the story which objectifies the selfishness and arrogance of the student. This is juxtaposed against the miserable sorrow of Kaoru, the object of the student's male desire. The critical gaze imbedded in the story to which Hasegawa, Hara and Ueda refer shows the perspective of the weak, a perspective which extends beyond the female to other marginalised elements in the story, and simultaneously criticises the strong, whether this be masculine power or not. The narrative is constructed in such a way that, once the reader acquires the critical viewpoint of the itinerant performers, particularly that of Kaoru, he/she can easily find the ugly face of the student. Thus, the narrative is, like *The Tale of Genji*, constituted by a duplicate structure which permits the simultaneous expression of both the male gaze and a critical gaze which objectifies the male gaze and masculine desire.

Ueda and Hara, after revealing the selfish and narcissistic attributes of the student, attempt to solve the inconsistency between the student as a nice person in the superficial story foregrounded by Morimoto and Hatori and the student as a discriminatory person at the deeper level of the story as they read it. Ueda suggests dividing the protagonist/narrator into two figures. These are the protagonist/narrator who narrates the story at the time of the incidents related and the protagonist/narrator who retrospectively narrates the story at a later time. While Hara Zen supports this suggestion, Ueda apparently shows a lack of conviction for his own argument; and, indeed, there are difficulties associated with clearly dividing the protagonist/narrator into two temporal "selves" (Ueda 1991: 493–4; Hara 1999: 80–1). Moreover, any attempt contradictorily to compromise the two different views temporally results in a monologic narrative of the type referred to in the discussion given in Chapters 2 and 3 of earlier philosophical and religious writing. Therefore, rather than forcing a temporal compromise that is likely to be inconsistent with the narrative, it is more convincing to note that the story is neither one of beautiful romantic love nor merely of the discriminative masculine male gaze revealed by a self-referential perspective. Rather, *Dancing Girl of Izu* features a double-fold structure which expresses the viewpoint of the double standard of both positions. Important for our discussion is not which is the correct interpretation, but the fact that the student's desire can be interpreted both as a romantic male gaze which views male–female relations as a beautiful pure love and, simultaneously, as an arrogant masculine gaze which views the female figure as an object of male desire grounded in hidden discrimination.[12] Rather than seeking a compromise for the apparent inconsistencies in the student, it would be better to presume that two ideologies operate upon this young man. The story, after all, creates a beautiful romantic love on one level, while at the same time casting a critical light by revealing the unreliable, irresponsible protagonist's narcissism. In this sense, the story's structure is doubly multilayered. First, there is a double structure between society's discrimination against the itinerant performers and the hero's ostensible anti-discrimination towards them. Second, there is a double structure between arrogant masculine discrimination and romantic love in the protagonist student's own mind.

One more point which I would like to highlight here is the mutual relation between the above-mentioned discrimination against the women featured in these novels and the deep male love shown towards them. Ueda Wataru points out that "apparently one of the reasons why 'I' [the student] feels sympathetic affection for the dancing girl is his emotional pity and sorrow which arise from a discriminatory consciousness" (Ueda 1991: 485). We can thus argue that pity and sorrow, on the one hand, and discrimination, on the other, simultaneously appear in the emotions shown by the student towards Kaoru in a way that makes it difficult to distinguish between them. That is to say, the discriminatory consciousness or discriminatory arrogant male desire and romantic male love for the female not only coexist in the student's mind but are also, in fact, mutually dependent on each other. In other words, the axis of discrimination and egalitarianism and that of masculine sexual desire and male romantic love are inextricably entangled. When these two axes intersect chaotically in this way, the contradictory desires of discriminatory arrogant male masculine consciousness against the weak female *and* anti-discriminative male romantic love for the female become reciprocally necessary. That is, in order to love the dancing girl romantically, it is necessary for the student to discriminate against her. For power imbalance is at the heart of romantic love. This is precisely the point we observed in the *Engyō* text of *The Tale of the Heike*.

6.3. Open/hidden discrimination against femininity:
Snow Country

The same general argument that applies to *The Dancing Girl of Izu* can be used to interpret relations between women and men in *Snow Country*. This narrative clearly highlights the social discrimination experienced by women.

136　*Kawabata Yasunari*

An old notice pasted on a wall beside the road reads: "Pay for field hands. Ninety sen a day, meals included. Women forty per cent less" (J: X 98; E: 121). This detail seems to be purposely incorporated into the narrative in order to show that work done by women counts for only 60 per cent of that of men. The story of a geisha, Kikuyu, also demonstrates women's financially weak position compared to that of men. Kikuyu has a patron build a restaurant for her, and then, when she is ready to move in, finds someone she wants to marry. But this man eventually runs off and abandons her, leaving her with nothing (J: X 78; E: 97). The description of Komako's two lodgings, one an attic used previously to house silkworms, the other a second-floor room like a fox's or badger's lair, shows both the difficulties of her life and the difficulties generally for women who are discriminated against by society (J: X 45, 116; E: 53, 143).

In the context of the difficulties experienced by women in a male-centred society, Shimamura clearly adopts an anti-discriminatory attitude to Komako. He loves Komako, comes to see her, and wishes to make her happy. But, in the same way that the student in *The Dancing Girl of Izu* is simultaneously discriminatory yet anti-discriminatory, though Shimamura does not discriminate ostensibly against Komako, he treats her irresponsibly and unfairly. During the 199 days which elapse between his first and second visits, Shimamura neither writes to Komako nor comes to see her, failing even to send her the dance instructions he promised (J: X 17, 35; E: 15, 40). He tells himself that, no matter how long he stays with Komako, he can do nothing for her (J: X 65; E: 79). When Yoko says, "Be good to Komako," Shimamura again answers, "But I can do nothing for her" (J: X 108; E: 135) – words he repeats later in the narrative (J: X 112; E: 138). Compared with Komako's financial difficulty, and with her vital intensity (J: X 71; E: 86), Shimamura appears as an idler who has inherited his money (J: X 26, 89, 104; E: 27, 112, 130). He is criticised by Komako for being financially secure (J: X 66; E: 80–1). "You have plenty of money," she says, "and you're not much of a person" (J: X 82–3; E: 102). After his second visit to the snow country, Shimamura again breaks his promise to return the following February. The irresponsible arrogant character which leads to his toying with the feelings of a woman is apparent from the outset of the narrative when the reader discovers that Shimamura is the kind of man who satisfies his sexual desire by buying a geisha (J: X 20; E: 20).

His insistence on parting from Komako leaving no seeds of future trouble marks him, in fact, as worse than the student in *The Dancing Girl of Izu*. First, while the student makes no promises, Shimamura does make promises which he then breaks. Second, while the student's wish to avoid leaving the seeds of future trouble is merely vaguely hinted at in that story when no reply is recorded to the several invitations extended by the performers, there is no such room for doubt in *Snow Country*. Here the reader is clearly told that Shimamura dislikes the drawn-out complications arising from an affair with a woman like Komako, whose position is so ambiguous (J: X 23; E: 23–4).

Looking at these issues from within the male characters' viewpoint, it is now clear that Shimamura in *Snow Country*, unlike the student in *The Dancing Girl of Izu*, committed crimes knowing his actions to be criminal. In contrast to the student, who as an unreliable narrator is seemingly unconscious of his own discriminatory behaviour, Shimamura is well aware of his selfishness. However, it is exactly because of this that we can say that he has a self-referential critical gaze. It is not that he is unaware of what he does; rather, his crime is that he has no intention of solving his own problems. The *Snow Country* narrative is constructed in such a way that a careful reading reveals the ugly selfish face of Shimamura being acknowledged by himself. This is a case of the strong male character being criticised from what is, in effect, the position of the weaker female. Thus, as is the case in *The Dancing Girl of Izu*, in *Snow Country* we find the duplicate structure of a discriminatory arrogant male gaze coupled with an opposing critical gaze.

From a patriarchal humanistic moral viewpoint, according to which men are responsible for supporting families with women and children, and women are dependent on men, we can argue that, if the student in *The Dancing Girl of Izu* really loves Kaoru and wants to help her, he should not tell lies, should participate in the commemoration service and should promise to visit Oshima. Likewise, if Shimamura really loves Komako and is committed to solving her various difficulties, he should divorce his wife and marry Komako. Since the student is young and unmarried, we can simply blame his behaviour on immature irresponsibility, frivolity and flippancy. In the case of Shimamura, however, there are a wife and children to consider. The balance of power between wife (Shimamura's wife) and mistress (Komako) in *Snow Country* is ambiguous. We have seen in the previous chapter how in *The Eight Dog Chronicles* male–female or husband–wife love is sacrificed for the higher ideal of loyalty to one's master, faithfulness or respect to one's superior friends and/or filial piety to one's parents. Masters (loyalty), fathers (filial piety) and outstanding friends (faithfulness or respect for elder brothers) are located as superiors, in contrast to lovers, wives and mothers, who represent the weak. In Confucian society dominated by the consanguine family, the parent–child relationship is strong and stable, while relationships between lovers or husbands and wives are weak and fragile. In this situation, at least Bakin finds beauty in the sacrifice by a man of his wife or lover for the benefit of his parents or master, that is, the sacrifice of the weak inside for the benefit of the strong outside. In modern society, in which the conjugal family dominates, however, the husband–wife relation is strong and stable, while the relationship between illicit lovers is weak and fragile. In this context, at least, Kawabata finds beauty in sacrificing the man's extramarital lover for the benefit of his wife.

Thus, we can presume that in *Snow Country* the reason why Shimamura does not divorce his wife and marry Komako is not only his awareness that this will result in financial difficulty for his wife and children but also that he realises that it would mean the loss of his love for Komako. For his love

138 *Kawabata Yasunari*

is formed on the basis of romantic longing and discrimination. The point is therefore not that the love of Shimamura and Komako is so strong that they cannot help loving each other illicitly. If this were the case, their difficulties could be solved by divorcing and remarrying. The reason Shimamura does not intend to take this action is that he knows well that his love is based on the illicit. Like some of Chikamatsu's and Saikaku's works and, as we have seen, like the first half of Bakin's *Eight Dog Chronicles*, this is precisely the genuine nature of "romantic" love in the modern age. Shimamura calls this reality a sort of nostalgic remorse and feels as though he were waiting tranquilly for some undefined revenge (J: X 99; E: 123). This revenge is inevitable given his sacrifice of the weak.

Shimamura says to Komako: "You are a good girl." It is likely that these comments are in praise of her liveliness and vitality. However, Komako mistakes his meaning as referring to her body, and she slips from the room scarlet with anger. She believes she has been reified and gazed at voyeuristically, and that it is her body that Shimamura loves. Shimamura cannot bring himself to follow, because he thinks that she has good reason to feel hurt (J: X 119–20, 134; E: 146–8, 166–7). Until that point, he has required her to give everything she has to an illicit relationship without any reward. The reason that Komako is a good girl for Shimamura is that she satisfies Shimamura's desire to love a marginalised woman from a lower social class without the need to offer her the least assistance. This again shows the multiple implications of sexuality. In the same way that the student in *The Dancing Girl of Izu* needs to discriminate against Kaoru in order to feel love for her, Shimamura can love Komako only when she is discriminated against and in a miserable situation. She fulfils Shimamura's sexual desire without demanding to secure her social position by marriage. On the contrary, she satisfies herself with her low social position. This is exactly the reason that she is a good girl for Shimamura and precisely why he permits himself to hurt her.

Saegusa Kazuko argues that, in Kawabata's work, male characters who occupy positions of high social status injure and humiliate women from the lower social classes. She further suggests that, in spite of the fact that he recognises the wrongdoing involved, the author aggressively insists that this exactly is the nature of art (Saegusa 1991: 98). Saegusa regards Kawabata's approach as arrogant. However, arrogance is merely one of the many attributes characteristic of Kawabata's male protagonists. As we have seen in the two stories discussed, and as we shall soon see in *Thousand Cranes* and *The Sound of the Mountain*, the ugly face of the male protagonist is depicted so as to be apparent to the careful reader. That is, embedded in the narrative is a criticism of the male from the viewpoint of the weaker female character, or the masculine gazing male's self-referential viewpoint. In other words, the stories feature a critical gaze which objectifies male arrogance. Further, it is implied that, as we have seen in the previous section, the male–female or the strong–weak relation is inherent as a necessary component of romantic love. If we consider that the discursive basis of love resides in the affection inherent in parental love, brotherly/sisterly love, a teacher's love, God's love and heterosexual love, close consideration reveals the fact that each of these kinds of love is based on an unequal, uneven power relationship. Children know well that they cannot live without their parents. Parents also know well that their children are wholly dependent on them. That is why children desperately love their parents, and parents give their children limitless love. Though there are surely many other aspects of this relationship, I believe that the uneven power balance is one of the core ingredients of parent–child love. And, in the same way that relations between God and humans is based upon an imbalance of power, heterosexual love between a man and a woman, too, is based on an uneven power relation. So Kawabata's often-mentioned wish to unify with the mother he lost as a child is a desire for a return not only to the happy original unity of existence in the womb, but also to the origin of a love which resides in an imbalance of power and upon which romantic love-relations are also based. If we accept that romantic love is formed on the basis of this distinction between the strong and the weak, then we must also concede that what Kawabata presents is not just the arrogant male persona but pure romantic love. Thus, extending Saegusa Kazuko's criticism, we can argue that when the male characters in Kawabata's narratives discriminate, humiliate and abuse the female characters in the full knowledge that this is an evil deed, then the reader is being aggressively presented with exactly the basis of *romantic love*. If equal status were realised between Kawabata's men and women, romance, as well as discriminatory violence, would surely disappear. We still have no knowledge of the beauty of romantic love between equals. This remains to be found.

The characteristics of *Snow Country* can be usefully contrasted with Nagai Kafū's *Geisha in Rivalry* – a novel also dealing with the world of geisha and published in 1916–17, about twenty years before *Snow Country*. This story is based on the modernist understanding as defined in Chapter 1. As the narrator's commentary makes clear, the text concerns itself with the manner in which human vitality is transformed in modern civil society into the strenuous pursuit of riches, honour and pleasure – fame, wealth and women (J: 82; E: 88).[13] This narrative also demonstrates the social discrimination experienced by women, as demonstrated by the comment by newspaper novelist Nanso to the effect that "women and small men (humble men) are hard to manage" (J: 115; E: 124).

The story tells of a three-way love-affair between Yoshioka, a businessman, Segawa, a Kabuki actor who has countless admirers, and Komayo, a geisha. At the beginning of the story, the reader learns that, in addition to supporting his formal wife, Yoshioka has been keeping the geisha, Rikiji, for about three years. However, he then meets Komayo, the first geisha he ever knew, after a break of seven years. The pair take up together once more, and their new affair unfolds as the story develops.

In a society which discriminates against weak and lowly ranked women, Kawabata's male characters feel kindness for and a desire to assist these weaker

140   *Kawabata Yasunari*

women while simultaneously being compelled to discriminate against, abuse and bully them. By looking at women so treated, the strong men of Kawabata's narratives feel sympathy, sadness and pity, and find beauty therein. In the same discrimination-based society, however, Kafū's male protagonist, Yoshioka, tries to buy Komayo her freedom. This is something that Shimamura never attempts to do for Komako. Yoshioka's offer comes with the condition that she must forever be faithful to him, although there is no guarantee that his love for Komayo will be undying. Faced with this ultimatum, Komayo cannot decide whether to devote herself to Yoshioka's love, or to love the very attractive Segawa and risk losing the security offered by being Yoshioka's mistress. This is because she also has a financial patron, the ugly but constant Chomondo, who is unperturbed by her desire for relations with other men. Chomondo is a rich antique-dealer likened to a sea monster who uses Komayo as a tool of his special pleasure to torment and sexually embarrass women in urgent need of money. As Stephen Snyder has argued, Kafū's demimonde is not simply a place where men use women for their own ends. Women, too, have internalised the rules of the contest, and therefore compete with intelligence and energy for the mastery of the object (the most desirable lover, the wealthiest patron, or the most appealing man) (Snyder 2000: 71). In contrast to Kafū's *Geisha in Rivalry*, in which all major characters compete to satisfy their desire for money, fame and sex, Kawabata's *Snow Country* emphasises "waste of effort" (*torō*) (J: X 37, 60, 102; E: 41, 72, 127).[14] While Kafū criticises the competitive effort valorised by the modernist project, Kawabata has Shimamura and Komako seek beauty through a waste of effort. Komako's effort to love Shimamura achieves no personal gain. Shimamura, as we have seen, tries neither to buy Komako her freedom nor to marry her. As discussed in Chapter 2, Hōnen, Jinsai and Tōkoku also resist development and progress by rejecting endeavour and effort. By so doing, they ultimately refuse to make egalitarianism a means to evolution, keeping it rather as a final goal. Likewise, while Kafū's characters compete to satisfy their modernist desires by making love a means to achieve another goal, Shimamura and Komako reject the reification and appropriation of the idea of love for other purposes. Like Hōnen, Jinsai and Tōkoku in Japan, and Marx and Rawls in Western culture, by purifying the concept of egalitarianism, they also purify the concept of love. This is in spite of the fact that their love, like purified egalitarianism, results in nothing but stagnation.

Kawabata's stories are organised around the precept that the more women are despised, discriminated against and abused, the more the protagonist men, as well as male readers, will love them. The material analysed in this chapter provides insights into the process by which the strong and high-social-status male characters – superficially at least – feel kindness towards or the desire to help the weak and lower-social-class women discriminated against by society. But, deep in their minds, these men are simultaneously discriminating, abusing and bullying the weak, thus causing injury and humiliation. Looking at the injured weak, however, the strong feel sympathy and love. The source of the sadness, pity and romantic love in Kawabata's novels lies in the conflict between, on the one hand, a desire to improve the lot of the weak and, on the other, a desire to discriminate against, abuse and bully them. Were an egalitarian relationship to be established between the weak and the strong, particularly between women and men, or if love became a means of realising this, then the beauty of purely romantic love would disappear. In order to keep this alive we must, like the characters in Kawabata's stories, concede to the imperative of discrimination, deny making love a means merely to achieve a goal, and thus refuse to make an effort to change society. This is very different from the egalitarianism which necessitates fighting together as a group with others from outside as advocated by Saichō, Bakin and Fukuzawa Yukichi, or from the ideal of absolute egalitarianism promoted by Hōnen, Jinsai and Tōkoku. In fact, the ideal underlying Kawabata's narratives involves a process that reverses the development which occurred between the *Engyō* and *Kakuichi* texts of *The Tale of the Heike*, and from the first to second part of *The Eight Dog Chronicles*. In both of those works we saw the disappearance of love and hate, and the emergence of egalitarianism. In Kawabata, egalitarianism must be suppressed in order to allow romantic love to flourish. He rejects endeavour and effort as a means of promoting egalitarian society or satisfying one's desires. By so doing, he ultimately refuses to make love a means to realise an egalitarian society, keeping it rather as a final goal.

Besides the critical gaze representing the perspective of the weak and the notion that romantic love presupposes discrimination, we can find another viewpoint in Kawabata's stories. It is, as in *The Tale of Genji*, the perspective of the ugly. In the final section of this chapter, I shall examine *Thousand Cranes* and *The Sound of the Mountain*, focusing not only on the male gaze and its critical counterpoint, but also on how the ugly are portrayed.

6.4. The perspective of ugly women: *Thousand Cranes* and *The Sound of the Mountain*

Discrimination against women in *Thousand Cranes* is also found in the bullying of Mrs Ota, mistress of the protagonist and former mistress of the protagonist's father, and her daughter, Fumiko, by Chikako, the woman who preceded Mrs Ota in the protagonist's father's bed. After the death of Mr Ota, Kikuji's father's companion in the pursuit of tea, the latter was drawn to Mr Ota's widow. When his then mistress, Chikako, caught wind of this secret, she shadowed Kikuji's father and frequently went to threaten Mrs Ota, berating the widow even in front of Kikuji and his mother (J: XII 18; E: 14). In spite of Chikako's obvious bullying of Mrs Ota and Fumiko, Kikuji loves this mother and her daughter. In fact, drawing on the ideas discussed in the previous section, we should expect that the more Chikako discriminates

142 *Kawabata Yasunari*

against the pair, the more Kikuji will love them. This is because his love, like that of the protagonists of *The Dancing Girl of Izu* and *Snow Country*, is enhanced by society's discrimination.

The relationship between discrimination and romantic love within the protagonist's/narrator's consciousness depicted in *The Dancing Girl of Izu* and *Snow Country* appears also in *Thousand Cranes*. Although superficially Kikuji does not support Chikako's behaviour, and loves the two women, on another level he also discriminates against and despises Mrs Ota and Fumiko. On one occasion, having met Mrs Ota and Fumiko, his father's mistress and her daughter and therefore symbols of pollution, he avoids looking at Yukiko, his fiancée-to-be and a metaphor for pureness reminiscent of Yoko in *Snow Country* (J: XII 21; E: 18). That is, he does not want to defile Yukiko's beauty and purity with an image of Mrs Ota and Fumiko. Later he thinks that it would have been better if he had met Yukiko without Chikako, Mrs Ota and his father's ghost. To see his fiancée in the presence of this trio seems to be an insult to Yukiko (J: XII 26; E: 23). He does not wish to marry Fumiko, though he considers marriage to Yukiko, and actually does marry her in the sequel, *Plover on the Waves*. Saegusa Kazuko has referred to the discriminatory ethos underlying the scene in which, after having slept with Mrs Ota, Kikuji responds thus: "Giving his body to the wave, he even felt a satisfaction as of drowsing off in triumph, the conqueror whose feet were being washed by a slave" (J: XII 31; E: 29; Saegusa 1991: 106). Sexual relations for Kikuji are a confirmation of triumph and conquest. Furthermore, when Chikako, Fumiko and Kikuji drink tea, Chikako makes every remark an insult to Fumiko. But Kikuji does not seem disposed to protect Fumiko from Chikako's venom. Noting this fact, Kikuji thinks himself odd (J: II 115; E: 111). Thus, the reader can clearly detect Kikuji's discriminative attitude towards Mrs Ota and Fumiko. In contrast, he does not show any apparent discriminative consciousness towards Yukiko. But, precisely because he discriminates against his father's mistress and her daughter, Kikuji conceives romantic desire for them. Conversely, since he does not discriminate against Yukiko, he cannot make love to her. Looking at the Shino tea bowl, the rim of which is faintly brown, as if stained by Mrs Ota's lipstick, Kikuji simultaneously feels a nauseating sense of "uncleanness" and an overpowering "fascination" (J: XII 108; E: 104). These two – "uncleanness" and "fascination" or, expressed in terms of the concepts discussed above, "discrimination (uncleanness)" and "deep romantic love (fascination)" – are almost inevitably related and exactly constitute feminine attraction in Kawabata's story.

Kikuji's latent male masculine attitude is also evident in his desire to do violence. Lying with Mrs Ota in an inn, Kikuji comes at her as if to bite her (J: XII 36; E: 34). Elsewhere, when Mrs Ota visits Kikuji, he grasps her with both hands between the throat and collarbone, as if to strangle her. Later, Mrs Ota says: "You were about to strangle me. Why didn't you?" (J: XII 64–5; E: 62–3). When Kikuji is with Fumiko, he asks himself: "What could one do to make her resist?" (J: XII 80; E: 79). Here, again, it should be noticed that Kikuji's desire to do violence clearly registers in the narrator's/protagonist's own consciousness and is openly perceived – at least by Mrs Ota. This is evidence of yet another view of the critical gaze which objectifies the desire of the strong to do violence towards the weak. But, besides this objectification of the ugliness of male masculinity, another perspective is also revealed in this story. It is the perspective of the ugly woman.[15]

There is a notoriously ugly woman in *Thousand Cranes*, namely the bullying Chikako, who first appears in the story in a very impressive manner. The former mistress of his father, Chikako invites Kikuji to a tea ceremony she will conduct. The invitation brings back memories from Kikuji's childhood, and he recalls that, when he was 8 or 9, he was taken by his father to visit Chikako. Upon arrival, the pair found Chikako cutting the hair on a purple-black birthmark, as large as the palm of the hand, which covered half the left breast and ran down into the hollow of her breastbone (J: XII 9; E: 4). Kikuji was obsessed with the idea that any child who sucked at this breast, with its birthmark and hair, must become a monster (J: XII 12; E: 8). From this introduction, Chikako is portrayed by the narrator/protagonist, Kikuji, as a typical evil character, antagonistic to all around her. As we have seen, Chikako represents society's discrimination against Kikuji's father's mistress and her daughter, with whom Kikuji and the reader tend to sympathise. In this instance, the reader is expected to sympathise with Mrs Ota and Kikuji's father's illicit relationship rather than with the relationship between Kikuji's father and mother. This is because, as I have mentioned, the former is weaker than the latter. Chikako's discriminative attitude and anti-heroine persona, which sides with Kikuji's mother, is used as a catalyst to activate Kikuji's love and the reader's sympathy for Mrs Ota and Fumiko. However, if we carefully examine Chikako, we notice that the narrative also reveals her tenderness and even constructs a scene in which she might be regarded as beautiful.

On one occasion, having remembered that it is the anniversary of the day when Kikuji's father held his tea ceremony, Chikako is so restless she can hardly contain herself. She bursts into Kikuji's house, begins to clean his father's tea room and does some cooking in the kitchen. She then phones Kikuji at his office and tells him to bring friends for a tea party. When he refuses, she invites Yukiko to come instead. Kikuji is repulsed by her aggressive entry into the house, her commandeering of the kitchen and, especially, her summoning of Yukiko. He is convinced that she is planning something untoward and asks himself:

> "Did she [Chikako] mean to use the Inamura girl [Yukiko] as bait to draw him near again? Was he again to become entangled with her? . . . Has she sensed the weakness, and was she hastening to take advantage of it? . . . Had she meant from the start to call the girl?"
>
> (J: XII 46–7; E: 44–5)

144 *Kawabata Yasunari*

If we read this story from Kikuji's perspective, we, too, recoil from Chikako. But Kikuji's supposition is flawed. Chikako could not have originally intended to contact Yukiko, since this would not have occurred if Kikuji had accepted Chikako's first invitation to bring friends. This mistaken supposition reveals that, like the student in *The Dancing Girl of Izu*, Kikuji is also an unreliable narrator/protagonist. Chikako's restlessness is exacerbated by the fact, which she later discloses, that Kikuji's father's cottage is full of memories (J: XII 105; E: 101). This shows that she still deeply loves Kikuji's father, and that her wish to care for Kikuji is, therefore, likely to be genuine. The incident demonstrates that, like the student in *The Dancing Girl of Izu* who misunderstands Kaoru, Kikuji almost always misunderstands Chikako's real intention.

It is also hinted in the text that Chikako is not, in fact, a malicious character. Although it is not apparent to either Kikuji or the less attentive reader, sincere and careful scrutiny of the narrative reveals a gentle side to Chikako's nature. For instance, regarding Chikako's bullying of Mrs Ota, there is a suggestion that the former was forced to play the role of villain by Kikuji's father (J: XII 101; E: 97). Though this suggestion is not specifically confirmed, it is possible that, rather than being the result of either jealousy or of the intention to side with Kikuji's mother, Chikako's jealousy is, in fact, ordered by Kikuji's father. If this is the case, it demonstrates Kikuji's father's arrogant selfishness, rather than Chikako's ill intentions. Although Kikuji loathes the feeling of being manipulated by Chikako, it is made clear in the narrative that love for his father and the desire to be of service to her dead lover's family are the reasons behind her attempts to arrange a marriage for the son (J: XII 124; E: 120).

At the beginning of the "Double Star" chapter, when the sky is still bright at eight-thirty at night, Kikuji lies on the veranda after dinner watching caged fireflies brought in by the maid. Chikako enters and kneels in the corridor at Kikuji's feet. Feeling a little uncomfortable watching the fireflies while talking to Chikako in the evening dark, Kikuji momentarily thinks of turning on the lights. However, he decides that to do so would be a nuisance. Chikako, though she mentioned the dark as she came in, makes no move to get up, in spite of the fact that it is her habit to be of service. Kikuji wonders if her ardour in serving him has dimmed or perhaps she is getting old (J: XII 126; E: 123). But, in this *Genji*-like situation,[16] she is likely to be imagining herself talking with Kikuji's father, looking at his figure through his son's back in the dark room. This is the reason she does not want to turn on the light. The narrative tells us that Mrs Ota cannot make a distinction between Kikuji's father and Kikuji himself (J: XII 29, 64–5; E: 27, 62–3). If this is the case, why should the same principle not apply to Chikako? Chikako advises Kikuji to sell his father's tea collection and to start a new life. She says that it makes her a little sad to give up the work she was able to do when Kikuji's father was alive. She, too, tries to pull herself together and start a new life (J: XII 125–7; E: 122–3). Kikuji thinks that

Chikako's aim is only to take over his father's collection and earn money. But the reader by now realises that this is the last thing she wants to do.

The story is structured in such a way that, once we realise that Kikuji is unreliable, and once we find beauty, tenderness and sincerity in Chikako, we shall simultaneously find the ugly face of Kikuji, something that the careless reader can easily overlook. But, as we have seen, Kikuji's ugliness is clearly indicated in that he discriminates against Mrs Ota and Fumiko, in that he openly talks about and hates Chikako's birthmark and her ugliness, and in that he conceals a desire to do violence. The revelation of the ugly face of Kikuji and the beauty of Chikako yet again provides a critical viewpoint which operates against and thus exposes the male-centred ideology.

The Sound of the Mountain also contains three perspectives – the male masculine gaze/romantic male love for the female, the self-referential critical gaze and sympathy with the ugly woman. First, male discrimination against women is evident in the behaviour of Kikuko's husband, Shuichi. Shuichi has an extramarital affair with Kinu, and even gets the money to pay for an abortion for Kikuko from Kinu (J: XII 453; E: 194).[17] Shingo, Shuichi's father, seems to be very good to Kikuko. But, as a matter of fact, he gives no pocket money to Kikuko and has only recently bought her an electric appliance as a gift (J: XII 462, 465; E: 201, 204). The miserable situation of women is also depicted in the story in the form of Shingo's awareness: Shingo realises that there is no solution at all for a woman whose marriage has failed (J: XII 344; E: 97), and thinks it ironic that Kikuko the injured party in her marriage is also Kikuko the absolver (J: XII 381; E: 129). He is struck by a newspaper article which reports the case of an old couple who committed suicide together, leaving only the husband's note that a wife's self-identity is lost in her husband (J: XII 399; E: 145–6). The understanding that the more the male character discriminates and abuses the female character, the more the former loves the latter is also depicted in this story. The narrator/protagonist, Shingo, comments that in the presence of Shuichi's cruelty and moral paralysis (discrimination) – indeed, because of them – Kikuko has awakened as a woman (the object of romantic love) (J: XII 355; E: 105). Shuichi claims to be dissatisfied with Kikuko because she is a child. Shingo senses that Shuichi has referred to her immature body (J: XII 353–4; E: 104–5). But it is also the case that, by calling Kikuko a child, Shuichi has referred to her Yoko-and-Yukiko-like "pureness" or "cleanness". If "uncleanness" is a source of "fascination", as it is to Kikuji in *Thousand Cranes*, Kikuko cannot fascinate Shuichi's sexual desire, because, in the same way that Yukiko is too pure for Kikuji, Kikuko is not unclean.

Like Kikuji in *Thousand Cranes*, Shingo and Shuichi also have the desire to do violence to the weak. Violence to women is narrated in this story more clearly than in *Thousand Cranes*. Shuichi becomes violent and orders Kinu to sing; after hearing about the relationship between Shuichi and Kinu, Shingo is irritated and, at a business dinner in a geisha house that night, clutches violently at a geisha's shoulder; when Kinu is pregnant and decides to give

146 *Kawabata Yasunari*

birth to the baby, Shuichi beats her, stamps on her, kicks her and drags her down the stairs to try to get her to a doctor for an abortion; Shingo also asks himself impatiently if violence of some description might not prevent Kinu from having her child (J: XII 316, 370, 373, 496, 508; E: 72, 119, 122, 234, 247).

In the story Shingo is depicted as a man with a typical arrogant male gaze in whose figure the masculine ideology is fully developed. For instance, Shingo's male gaze is evident in the fact that he openly pays voyeuristic attention to the female body (J: XII 252; E: 12). He mentions his secretary Eiko's small breasts and often refers to his daughter Fusako's fertile breasts (J: XII 265, 279, 281, 292, 375, 386; E: 24, 39, 41, 50, 123, 134). He is obsessed with appearances and repeatedly mentions a yearning for the young and a loathing for the ugly and the old (J: XII 326, 327, 436; E: 81, 82, 179). He is repelled by the sight of the aged flesh of his wife, Yasuko, with whom he has lived for so long (J: XII 246; E: 6), and refers repeatedly to the ugliness of Yasuko and Fusako (J: XII 246, 265, 302, 386, 403; E: 5, 24, 60, 134, 150). Like Shimamura in *Snow Country*, he is also the kind of man who amuses himself with geisha (J: XII 249, 373, 473, 498; E: 9, 121, 212).

However, it is clear that, in the process of the narrative, Shingo gradually comes to realise his own ugliness. Shingo feels sorry that for some time he has been giving Kikuko nothing resembling an allowance. He regrets this and thinks that, if he had shown her more sympathy, she would not have been forced to submit to the indignity of having the money for her abortion come from her husband's mistress (J: XII 462; E: 201–2). At Yasuko's direction, Shingo buys a vacuum cleaner for Kikuko (J: XII 465–6; E: 204). Furthermore, Shingo feels responsibility for Fusako's unhappy marriage. He also thinks that it is not impossible to call himself the murderer, by remote control from a distance, of the woman who committed suicide with Fusako's husband, as well as of Kikuko's dead child (J: XII 480; E: 219). Shingo feels no tenderness at the footsteps of his grandchild and comments that there is no doubt that he is wanting in affection (J: XII 343; E: 96). Having mentioned Fusako's ugliness, Shingo feels inescapable guilt, thinking that, if he and Yasuko had paid more attention to Fusako, they might have been given a pretty grandchild (J: XII 409; E: 156). Realising that he is searching for the image of Yasuko's beautiful sister even in his grandchildren, he regards himself with distaste (J: XII 436; E: 179). Shingo feels in Shuichi's extramarital affair with Kinu a frightening paralysis of the soul, cruelty and ugly decay (J: XII 354–5, 454, 487; E: 105, 195, 225). But it seems to him that he is caught in the same filthy slough, and he is overcome by a dark terror (J: XII 454; E: 195). In other words, he notices the cruelty and decay of male masculinity which applies to himself as much as to his son. As Sakata Chizuko argues, the narrative reveals a cruel man lacking tenderness, and Shingo has a keen sense of awakening that he himself is abnormal (Sakata 1992: 189–90). Thus, like Shimamura in *Snow Country*, it is obvious that Shingo, too, fixes a self-referential critical gaze on his own actions.

Like the student in *The Dancing Girl of Izu* and Kikuji in *Thousand Cranes*, Shingo also misunderstands Kikuko. The process of the story superficially unfolds the delicate relation between Shingo and Kikuko, the wife of his son, Shuichi. Deep in his heart, Shingo conceives sexual desire for Kikuko, which she appears on the surface to reciprocate. But close reading reveals hints in many places that the one for whom Kikuko conceives romantic longing is not Shingo but his son and her husband, Shuichi. For instance, when Shuichi comes home early, Kikuko's exhilaration makes her face glow with pleasure in a manner that does not occur when Shingo comes home early (J: XII 282; E: 41–2; Kobayashi Hiroko 1999: 216–17). Kikuko touches her cheeks with rouge, and seems unusually bright and lively, when she goes to see Shuichi, who has gone fishing (J: XII 514; E: 252). While Shingo keeps both his treatment of Kikuko's nosebleed and their visit to the Shinjuku Garden a secret, there are hints that Kikuko unhesitatingly relates both incidents to Shuichi (J: XII 367, 459; E: 117, 198; Tsuruta 1985: 41–5). In Shinjuku Garden, where Shingo feels so restless sitting on a bench beside Kikuko that he almost immediately stands up, Kikuko looks at him, puzzled (J: XII 450–1; E: 192). This suggests that, while Shingo may have a guilty conscience at sitting on a bench in the park with Kikuko, Kikuko has no such concern. When Kikuko phones Shingo at his office, he happily assumes that she phoned only him, when she had, in fact, phoned Shuichi first (J: XII 518; E: 255; Tsuruta 1985: 45).

In the "Fish in Autumn" chapter, when Shingo asks Kikuko if she intends to leave Shuichi, Kikuko says solemnly: "If I were to, I'd be able to look after you as I pleased." Shingo answers, "Your misfortune," to which Kikuko responds: "It's no misfortune when you're doing something you want to do." Interpreting this comment as a tentative expression of affection, Shingo feels a certain danger (J: XII 536; E: 272). But, as Sakata Chizuko argues, rather than indicating any reciprocation of Shingo's romantic desire, Kikuko's comments are more likely to indicate an intention to serve the ageing Shingo's personal needs after he is confined to bed (Sakata 1992: 197). Instead of romantic love, it is much more likely that Kikuko feels a daughterly love towards Shingo. Nevertheless, the argument I have presented here suggests that we need to be careful about concluding absolutely that Kikuko's feelings for Shingo are completely removed from her romantic love. This is because both daughterly love and romantic love for a male are indistinguishable by origin in the sense that both are based on the power imbalance between the strong and the weak. It is therefore very difficult to separate the two.

Finally, let me point out that the narrative does not neglect the tenderness of the ugly woman which is concealed in the heart of Yasuko. Although Yasuko snored when she was 15 or 16, this stopped when she married, demonstrating her sense of modesty in Shingo's presence (J: XII 246; E: 6). Yasuko does not give cold drinks to Shingo in consideration of his weak digestion (J: XII 269; E: 28); when they are in bed together, Yasuko reaches for Shingo's

148 *Kawabata Yasunari*

hand, and gently touches it, or touches his pillow gently (J: XII 284, 506–7; E: 43, 245), evidence of an innate tenderness. Kobayashi Hiroko refers to these actions as indicators of the womanliness of the middle-aged Yasuko, something she claims is neglected by both Shingo and the narrator. She argues that this womanliness is only depicted negatively in the story through a prejudice based on gender (Kobayashi Hiroko 1999: 207–15). But the description of her tenderness referred to above, and which Kobayashi herself also notes, clearly proves that Yasuko's femininity is not totally neglected.

Furthermore, there is an important story of Yasuko hidden in the narrative. In the "A Dream of Islands" chapter, one of Shingo's old friends, Suzumoto, brings Shingo two Noh masks – *kasshiki* and *jido*. The *jido* mask is a symbol of eternal youth. When Eiko and Kikuko try the mask, it strikes Shingo as so beautiful that he wants to cry out in surprise. Later, as he brings his face towards it from above, the mask comes to life, and Shingo is on the point of kissing it (J: XII 328–31, 334; E: 83–6, 88). In contrast to the *jido* mask, the *kasshiki* mask reminds Shingo of someone he knows (J: XII 329, E: 84). Later, when Shingo sees puppies playing in the garden, he has a sense of seeing exactly such a scene before. Thinking for a moment, he realises that the puppies remind him of a Sotatsu ink painting. Abruptly he recalls the *kasshiki* mask, musing: "Sotatsu and the mask-maker were of the same period. Sotatsu painted what would today be called a mongrel puppy" (J: XII 336–7; E: 91). This remark indicates that the *kasshiki* mask is related to the common people, as Sotatsu's dog is to the mongrel puppy. The *kasshiki* is a masculine mask, and the eyebrows are those of a man. When Shingo asks Yasuko which she likes, she takes the *kasshiki* mask without hesitation, saying that it is livelier (J: XII 333; E: 87). Shingo then hangs this mask on the wall, and puts the *jido* mask far back in the drawer, like some esoteric object (J: XII 337; E: 91). Painted on the *kasshiki* mask is a gingko-shape hairstyle. The mask also has dimples (J: XII 329; E: 83). Later Shingo and Yasuko talk about Yasuko's hairstyle. Shingo suggests she cut her hair off and make a tea whisk out of it. Yasuko thinks he means for her have short hair pulled back like a tea whisk. But Shingo answers: "I don't mean hair tied up to the back. I mean hair cut off down" (J: XII 427–8; E: 172. I changed Seidensticker's translation, referring to the original). The meaning of Shingo's last answer is not clear. However, if we read it as referring to a hairstyle which is somehow similar to the gingko-shaped hair of the mask, then this indicates that the one most resembling the *kasshiki* mask is Yasuko. Judging from the conversation regarding Yasuko's hairstyle, Shingo seems to have already noticed this. If the *jido* mask represents Kikuko, and the *kasshiki* mask Yasuko, it indicates that Shingo gives Yasuko a position of considerable importance. The *kasshiki* mask is less fascinating than the *jido* mask, and Shingo at first does not notice whom it resembles. However, once the comparison between Yasuko and the mask has been established, Yasuko's significance to Shingo is clear from the fact that this mask is the work of a master and it is this mask that he chooses to display on the wall.[18]

Let me conclude the chapter here. We have seen that the feminine beauty created by the male gaze in Kawabata's stories is characterised as shy, innocent, childish, pure, tidy, methodical, warm, soft, gentle, delicate and sentimental. These are values expected in women as the subordinate gender. In Kawabata's stories, weak women who display beauty of this nature are obediently respectful as they serve and help the strong male. In turn, the strong male, at least superficially, tries to take care of and protect these weaker women. This relationship constitutes "romantic love". However, the women in Kawabata's stories are not merely submissive to the existing order. They also attempt to raise themselves socially, though this occurs within a limit that does not threaten the male-centred class society.

The stories dealt with in this chapter depict the contrast between society's discrimination against women and the male protagonist's superficial non-discriminatory attitude towards women. Simultaneously, however, the protagonist's hidden discrimination against woman is also revealed. Therefore, the narrative is constructed not by a single-fold structure, but by a double standard which allows (at least) two different readings. There is, first, the reading which unfolds a beautiful tale of love and romance, and which relies upon the protagonist's superficial narrative. Second, the narrative also clearly features the perspective of the weak criticising the strong through the use of strategies which reveal the narrator's unreliability and self-referential gaze critical of the protagonists, in addition to the viewpoint of women conventionally dismissed as ugly. Consideration of these readings demonstrates that a discriminatory consciousness or discriminatory arrogant male desire and a deep romantic male love for the female coexist within the protagonist. In this sense, Kawabata's stories are narrated with the realisation that a strong male discriminatory consciousness against the weaker female, and male romantic love for the female are reciprocally dependent. Thus, in order to experience romantic love for the weaker female characters, it is necessary for the protagonist to discriminate against them. That is, in Kawabata's stories, the more women are despised, discriminated against and abused, the more both the protagonist men and the male-orientated reader will love them. Emotions such as sadness and pity reside in the conflict between, on the one hand, the desire to discriminate against, abuse and bully, and, on the other, a deep romantic love. Once an egalitarian relationship between men and women is realised, the beauty of this kind of romantic love can no longer exist. In order to keep romantic love alive, the characters in Kawabata's stories must endure sadness.

7 Conclusion

This book analysed the notions of "respect for the strong" and "sympathy for the weak" as they appear in selected works of Japanese narrative. Let me repeat and confirm the result of our discussion. We examined three premodern literary works – *The Tale of Genji*, *The Tale of the Heike* and *The Eight Dog Chronicles* – in addition to four twentieth-century stories by Kawabata Yasunari. As preparation for this analysis, we referred to the philosophical, religious and political writings of Saichō, Tokuitsu, Genshin, Hōnen, Yamazaki Ansai, Ogyū Sorai, Itō Jinsai, Fukuzawa Yukichi and Kitamura Tōkoku. We noted the idea of egalitarianism espoused by Yukichi, and that of Hōnen, Jinsai and Tōkoku. We also briefly referred to the theories of Western thinkers, including Thomas Hobbes, John Locke, Jean-Jacques Rousseau, Karl Marx and John Rawls. The main discussion focused on the relationship between "respect for the strong" (Social Darwinism) and "sympathy for the weak" (egalitarianism) in a manner that problematised two points. The first is the fact that "respect for the strong" and "sympathy for the weak" often appear in the history of Japanese thought and literature simultaneously and contradictorily as both respect for endeavour (respect for the strong) and egalitarianism (sympathy with the weak). The second point problematised the close relationship between egalitarianism and nationalism.

In the history of Japanese thought, representative discussions concerning "respect for the strong", which we might label the modernistic valorisation of rationalism and endeavour, appear through the genealogy of Saichō, Myōe, Yamazaki Ansai, Ogyū Sorai and Fukuzawa Yukichi. Representative notions of "sympathy for the weak", on the other hand, were first apparent in the thought of Hōnen, partly heralded by Genshin, expanded upon by Itō Jinsai, though in an incomplete form, and – if only in a fictional world – further developed by Kitamura Tōkoku.

In this regard, we have distinguished between philosophical, religious and political language and fictional literary language. The former requires a monologic narrative which does not allow any inconsistency such as exists, for example, in simultaneous respect for both egalitarianism and endeavour. This is exemplified by the problems associated with Genshin's contradictory insistence on "sympathy for the weak" and "respect for hard work".

Conclusion 151

Itō Jinsai's contradiction between "absolute egalitarianism" and "approval of the current hierarchical social ranking" is also regarded as insoluble by means of philosophical language. This earlier monologic narrative of philosophical, religious and political language corresponds to contemporary notions of single individuality and identity. In contrast, fictional literary language is expressed by means of a polyphonic narrative which allows the coexistence of contradictory notions such as respect for both egalitarianism and endeavour. It thus corresponds to what we might regard as the multiple personality. For instance, we have seen the polyphonic narrative of the fictional language of *The Tale of Genji* unfolding "admiration for the strong, the beautiful, the young and the decent" while at the same time giving value to notions of "sympathy for the weak, the ugly, the old and the indecent". That is, fictional language has the capacity to evade a single mode of thinking and to express the coexistence of multiple and contradictory thoughts while nevertheless maintaining consistency throughout the whole work.

In the analysis of the *Engyō* text of *The Tale of the Heike* we noticed that the opposite of "sympathy for the weak" is not simply "respect for the strong". In this text we found both "deep sympathy and profound contempt for the weak" and "strong respect for and a stern grudge against the strong". We argued that, in general, as confirmed by the *Engyō* text, the stronger the contempt, the deeper the sympathy towards the object involved. Similarly, the deeper the respect, the sterner the grudge. If either element is eliminated, the other will also disappear. We noticed that this erasure of extremes occurred in the case of the *Kakuichi* text. Thus, it became apparent that the opposite of deep respect for the strong is not a stern grudge, while the opposite of strong sympathy with the weak is not profound contempt. These are, in fact, two sides of the same coin opposed to indifference. The process which saw the *Engyō* transformed into the *Kakuichi* text may well have followed a shift from both deep sympathy and profound contempt in society for women, humble men and the weak, and from both stern criticism of and high respect for strong authority. It is possible that these extreme positions were replaced by an attitude of calm and indifferent egalitarianism towards all social ranks.

Our discussion noted that the change from the *Engyō* text's juxtaposition of contradiction to the *Kakuichi* text's greater consistency as a literary entity parallels and is partially comparable to the change from Genshin's notions of antinomy to Hōnen's ideas of selection in religious commentary. However, while Hōnen adopts a position of sympathy with the weak and discards respect for the strong, the *Kakuichi* text removes both extremes. It is interesting to note that in philosophical and religious discourse Genshin's contradictory views are transformed into Hōnen's selection of one of two views. In literary fictional language, however, the *Engyō* text's coexistence of contradictory views is transfigured into the *Kakuichi* text's elimination of both extremes. We can see here, again, the difference between monologic and polyphonic narratives. In the former, coexistence of contradiction is regarded as an unacceptable inconsistency, and the solution is either sublation or selection of one of two

152 *Conclusion*

differing options. In the latter, on the other hand, the coexistence of contradiction is regarded as the sign of a fertile text, with the erasure of both extremes regarded as an acceptable style of literary narrative.

This understanding is also applicable to *The Eight Dog Chronicles*. In this work we traced the change from sacrifice, revenge, illicit love, erotic desire, discrimination and merciless fighting in the first part of the narrative, to an egalitarian fairness presented under the rubric of *jin* with an accompanying lack of eros and romance in the second half of the work. That is, the disappearance of strong love and discrimination in the guise of sacrifice, revenge, illicit love and anti-authoritarianism corresponds to the emergence of egalitarianism based on the concept of *jin*. This process is comparable with the *Heike monogatari* shift from the *Engyō* to *Kakuichi* texts.

In Kawabata Yasunari's work we again noted the close relationship between strong gender discrimination and deep romantic love. Kawabata's narratives displayed a pattern similar to that of the *Engyō*'s notion that the stronger the contempt, the deeper the sympathy towards an object, or *The Eight Dog Chronicles*' understanding that egalitarian indifferent fairness is located in a lack of deep love and strong discrimination. Kawabata's stories are organised around the notion that the more women are socially despised, discriminated against and abused, the more they are loved by the protagonist men and by readers who identify with these men. Kawabata's stories first describe the process by which strong and high-social-status male characters feel a superficial kindness for, show affection towards, or desire to assist, the socially weaker women from the lower classes who are discriminated against by society. However, deep in their psyches, the male characters discriminate against, abuse and bully these weaker women characters, thus injuring and humiliating them. Looking at the injured weak, however, the strong feel sympathy. The conflict in the minds of the strong between the desire to make the weak happy, on the one hand, and the desire to discriminate against, abuse and bully them, on the other, generates pity and sadness. Once an egalitarian relationship between the strong and the weak develops, the "beauty" of the kind of romantic love depicted by Kawabata disappears. In order to ensure that this beauty endures, it is necessary to endure the sadness of discrimination.

Finally, concerning the close relation between egalitarianism and nationalism, we have noted that, as early as the ninth century, Saichō insisted on egalitarianism for the purpose of protecting the nation. Furthermore, when we analysed the relation between the disappearance of sacrifice, revenge, illicit love and anti-authoritarian conflict, and the appearance of egalitarianism in *The Eight Dog Chronicles*, we identified a monopoly of violence by means of the egalitarian concept of *jin*. We also saw the subsequent danger of confined nationalistic egalitarianism which leads members of an egalitarian society to fight aggressively against other discriminative societies. This kind of nationalistic egalitarianism can also be found in Fukuzawa Yukichi's thought. There is little doubt that one of the purposes of Yukichi's insistence on

Conclusion 153

egalitarianism was to maintain social unity. When conflict with other societies is imminent, as it was in Yukichi's day, the call for an egalitarian society is often a survival strategy. Therefore, egalitarianism and help for the weak in one society can be used to cement nationalistic bonds between members of that society in order to compete with outside interests. Yukichi's insistence well coincides with this formula. Saichō's, Bakin's and Yukichi's writings lead us to confirm that, as in the European case shown in the thought of Hobbes, Locke and Rousseau, the appearance of egalitarianism and that of the idea of nation-state are almost coterminous. If respect for the strong creates the context needed for an individual power struggle, the concept of egalitarianism supports warfare at the level of the nation-state. Thus, both respect for the strong and sympathy with the weak can create the conditions necessary for a power struggle – the former within the group and the latter between groups. In other words, both precepts confirm the idea that "might is right".

Concerning this point, as a means to sever the close relationship between egalitarianism and nationalism, we have here argued that, as suggested in the writing of Hōnen, Jinsai and Tōkoku in Japan and of Marx and Rawls in the West, it is necessary to reject the reification and appropriation of the idea of egalitarianism, as well as that of freedom, for the purpose of competition and conflict. This necessity remains even if the conflict is for evolution and progress. Once we reject egalitarianism based on competition, we can consider egalitarianism as cooperation and collaboration in the manner of Hōnen, Jinsai and Tōkoku in Japan and of Marx and Rawls in the West. In this case, the point is not how can we unite to defeat others, but how can we unite for mutual aid. Unlike competition and conflict where one party must inevitably triumph, cooperation values the contribution of all equally. Equality based on cooperation rather than competition might be thought of as an ideal rather than a state of nature.

The above argument identifies at least two varieties of "equality". First is the equality of people in a nation-state, which was born of the overthrow of the unequal aristocratic and feudal class society of the past, and which eventually serves to preserve the nation-state by means of fighting against other like states. This is equality for the sake of the development of nation-state – the nation-state grants equality to its members, who in turn must fight on its behalf. The second variety is a humanistic form of equality based on a sort of agnosticism that assumes that we cannot measure the whole value of any human being. This is equality not as a meritocratic tool for fighting others, but as a way to emancipate all from discrimination of any kind. As I have mentioned many times, the first variety of egalitarianism appears in the thought of Saichō and Yukichi, and also in the latter half of *The Eight Dog Chronicles* in Japan, and in the writing of Hobbes and Locke in Europe. The second form appears in Japan in the thought of Hōnen, Jinsai, and Tōkoku, and of Marx and Rawls in the West. This second form, however, does not appear in the literary works discussed in the preceding chapters.

154 *Conclusion*

We can further assert that the idea of egalitarianism should not be confined to the realm of the nation-state and/or religious group, but should be expanded to the whole world. As discussed in the section on Fukuzawa Yukichi and *The Eight Dog Chronicles*, if the ideology of egalitarianism covers all societies in the world, then the aspect of egalitarianism which supports a nationalistic power struggle between nation-states and religious groups must disappear. Thus, if a global perspective prevails, egalitarianism will come to represent an absence of conflict and fair respect for human nature. But, as we have also noticed in the discussion on *The Eight Dog Chronicles* and Fukuzawa Yukichi, should this egalitarian Utopia develop, it will bring with it the danger of being confined indefinitely within a stagnant society in which a single value pervades. Should that occur, there is no doubt that it would be the storyteller who would create an innovative narrative presenting a new beauty and associated set of values in a fantasy society of indifferent egalitarianism.

Notes

1. Introduction

1. See also McGuigan (1999): ch. 6.
2. See Anderson (2006): 4–7, 11–12, 46; Gellner (1983): 138; Hobsbawm and Ranger (eds) (1983): 13–14; and Smith (1986): 10–11.

2. The strong and the weak in Japanese religious, philosophical and political writings

1. The teachings of Pure Land Buddhism are said to have been introduced to Japan in the late sixth and early seventh centuries, with the priest Ennin (794–864) later importing the nembutsu zammai (nembutsu samadhi) from China. See Inoue (2001): 3, 86–7. See also Sueki (1990): 134–5; (1993): 240–1.
2. The English translation is from Senchakushū English Translation Project (trans.) (1998): 189. See also Inagaki (2000): 243. Concerning Pure Land teachings, see Suzuki Daisetsu (1973): 6–7; Marra (1988b): 295–6; Shigematsu (1996): 267–312; and Hirokawa Takatoshi (1998): 20.
3. See also Hirokawa Takatoshi (1998): 20.
4. *The Kakaishō* writes: "The bishop of Yokawa is Genshin. He escaped from the world and lived in Yokawa, calling himself the bishop of Yokawa. The mother and sister of the bishop of Yokawa (in *The Tale of Genji*) also resemble Genshin's mother and sister" (Tamagami (ed.) 1968: 593; Tamagami 1968: 340–2). Shirato Waka points out that the connecting link between *Ōjōyōshū* and *The Tale of Genji* is the view that human beings lead a sinful existence (Shirato 1987: 675). Concerning the relation between Pure Land teaching and *The Tale of Genji*, see Misumi (1996).
5. I have considered Kitamura Tōkoku's thought elsewhere. See Murakami Fuminobu (1991); (1996), ch. 1.
6. The primary source materials concerning the controversy between Saichō and Tokuitsu are compiled in Saichō (1975), vols 2 and 3. For secondary sources, see Shioiri (1937): 318–66; Tokiwa (1944): 25–7, 313–83; Sonoda (1974): 486–502; Tamura Kōyū (1977): 7–32, esp. 21–30; (1979): 13–18; (1988): 158–89; (1992); Tamura Kōyū (ed.) (1986): 145–242; Takahashi Tomio (1990); Sueki (1993): 226–9; Hakamaya (1998): 27–30, 179–81. For English-language studies of the controversy between Saichō and Tokuitsu, see Groner (1984): 91–106; (1989): 61.
7. See Saichō's *Commentary on the Protection of the Nation* (*Shugo kokkai shō*) in Saichō (1975), 2: 631–81. Also, Saichō's *Elegant Words Concerning the "Lotus Sutra"* (*Hokke shūku*) in Saichō (1975), 3: 52–3, 68–71. An abridged and modern Japanese translated version of *Elegant Words Concerning the "Lotus Sutra"* is available in Fukunaga (ed.) (1977): 186–7, 201–2. See also Tokiwa (1944): 313–88; Tamura Kōyū (1977): 21–2; (1988): 186–7; Groner (1984): 98, 101.

156   *Notes*

8. Saichō's *Mirror Illuminating the Provisional and the Real* (*Shō gonjitsu ron*), in Saichō (1975), 2: 5–8, and *A Treatise on Distinguishing the Real from the Provisional* (*Ketsu gonjitsu ron*) in Saichō (1975), 2: 689. Saichō's *Elegant Words Concerning the "Lotus Sutra"* (*Hokke shūku*) also well demonstrates his egalitarian position in this controversy (Saichō 1975, 3: 3–280; Fukunaga (ed.) 1977: 171–250).

9. Concerning the Doctrinal Debate of the Ōwa Era, see Onkaku (1972): 1–4. English translation is in Groner (2002), app. 5: 331–5. See also Hirabayashi (1987): 69–82; McMullin (1989): 119–41; Rhodes (1992): 25–30; Groner (2002), ch. 6: 94–117.

10. *Determining the Essentials of the One Vehicle* (*Ichijō yōketsu*) is collected in Takakusu and Watanabe (eds) (1931), 74: 327–72; Genshin (1971), 2: 1–212; Iwano Shin'yū (ed.) (1979), 18: 243–366. Concerning the secondary sources of *Determining the Essentials of the One Vehicle*, see Tokiwa (1944): 413–32; Yagi (1962); Kawasaki (1972): 41–2; Tajima Tokuon (1979), 18: 239–40; Tamura Kōyū (1982): 323–33; Shimaji (1986); Ōkubo (1990): esp. 60–1, 68–70, 144–6. For English-language studies of *Determining the Essentials of the One Vehicle*, see Rhodes (1992).

11. See Tokiwa (1944): 413; Yagi (1962): 357, 407, 409, 490; Tamura Kōyū (1982): 331; Shimaji (1986): 394; Ōkubo (1990): 46.

12. Concerning Genshin and *Essentials of Rebirth [into the Pure Land of Amida Buddha]* (*Ōjōyōshū*), see Genshin (1971); (1994): this is the edition cited hereafter in the format: *Essentials of Rebirth* (Iwanami bunko), volume, page; Ishida Mizumaro (ed.) (1970); Kawasaki Tsuneyuki (ed.) (1972); Hanayama Shōyū (trans.) (1972); Ōjōyōshū kenkyū kai (ed.) (1987); Hayami (1988). A bibliography of studies on Genshin and *Essentials of Rebirth* is available in Ōjōyōshū kenkyū kai (ed.) (1987): 707–34. For English-language studies on Genshin and his work, see Genshin (1930): 16–97; Andrews (1973); (1989): 20–32; Marra (1988a): 25–54; Rhodes (1992).

13. Michele Marra discusses the fact that Genshin, in the Tendai tradition, recognised the superiority of the contemplative nembutsu throughout the *Essentials of Rebirth*. However, he also points out that, since Genshin addressed an audience living in the Final Age (*mappō*), he felt obliged to borrow the Pure Land idea of different practices suitable to the different capacities of the people. Those without any capability, notes Marra, were unable to understand or meditate on the Dharma-body (*hosshin*) of the Buddha. They therefore had no option but to follow easier practices. To this end, they were able to achieve the extinction of a large amount of bad karma merely by replacing the complicated Buddha-mark contemplation and other types of contemplative nembutsu with the simple invocation of Amida's name. See Marra (1988a): 46–7.

14. Concerning Genshin's *A Register of Deaths of Twenty-five Members of the Nembutsu-Samādhi Society Who Gathered at the Shuryōgon'in Temple and Prayed for Rebirth in Paradise* (*Shuryōgon'in nijūgo zammai kechien kakochō*), see Genshin (1971), 2: 679; Kawasaki Tsuneyuki (ed.) (1972): 375–6.

15. See Tsuji (1944–55), 2: 145–56; Ienaga (1997): 173–210; Ishimoda (1957): 239, 260–2, 466–7; Inoue (1971).

16. For a summary of studies of this nature, see Sueki (1998): 29–32; Satō Hiroo (1987): 73–7.

17. A summary of the arguments concerning Kuroda's theory of Esoteric Buddhism can be found in Sueki (1998), "Part I" and "Concluding Chapter". Introducing Kuroda's theory, James C. Dobbins argues that New Kamakura Buddhism was peripheral throughout medieval times and Old Heian Buddhism was the true representative of the religious culture of the era (Dobbins 1998: 27).

18. Hōnen, *Senchaku hongan nembutsu shū* (Tokyo: Iwanami bunko 1997). This is the edition cited for the Japanese version, hereafter in the format: *Senchakushū*

Notes 157

(Iwanami bunko, page). English translation is Senchakushū English Translation Project (trans.) (1998). This is the edition cited for the English translation, hereafter in the format: *Senchakushū* (Kuroda Institute, page).

19. See also Ishii (1959): 3–4.
20. See also Hirokawa Takatoshi (1998): 37, 48; Tanabe (1983): 145, 161, 170–1, 173; (1992): 85, 91, 94–5. Inoue Mitsusada also mentions that the major difference between the Tendai Pure Land school and Kamakura Buddhism is, first, while the former insists on the importance of the *kansō* contemplative nembutsu, the latter argues that only the *shōmyō* invocational nembutsu can lead people to the Pure Land. Second, while the former emphasises that ascetic practices and good deeds are necessary for rebirth in the Pure Land, the latter insists that all people, including evil persons, can achieve rebirth. See Inoue (2001): 433–4.
21. See Myōe (1971): 44–105, 317–90. See also Tanabe (1983), ch. 3: Controversy with Hōnen: 144–238. In this thesis Tanabe notes that the difference between Hōnen and Myōe is that "Myōe's simple method is self-practice based on the aspiration for enlightenment and does not exclude other practices, though they are not always necessary" (p. 221). In his book *Myōe the Dreamkeeper: Fantasy and Knowledge in Early Kamakura Buddhism* (1992), Tanabe slightly changes the wording, which goes: "Myōe's simple method of self-assertion based on the aspiration for enlightenment did not exclude other practices, though they were not always necessary" (p. 116). Concerning the comparison between Hōnen and Myōe, Machida Sōhō writes that, while Hōnen insists on absolute egalitarianism before death, Myōe focuses on the type of self-endeavour which helps people attain enlightenment. See Machida (1998): 7–9, 41, 162–8.
22. Also see Suzuki Daisetsu (1973): 8.
23. Hōnen pays attention to Genshin's *Essentials of Rebirth* because, compared with other Tendai doctrine, this work gives greater value to the *shōmyō* invocational nembutsu. However, since Genshin's *Essentials of Rebirth* does not teach that the invocational nembutsu alone can bring people to the Pure Land, Hōnen seeks this position in Zendō's teaching (Inoue 2001: 307–10).
24. See Ishida Ichirō (1960): 140; Yoshikawa (1975): 14. See also Itō Jinsai (1966): 86–8; Iwasaki (1997), 1: 180.
25. See also Itō Jinsai (1966): 73, 80–95.
26. When citing passages from Mencius, I amend it as necessary.
27. In translating Itō Jinsai's *Gomō jigi* into English, I referred to John Allen Tucker's translation (Tucker 1998) and amended this as necessary. See also Yoshikawa (1975): 21.

   Jinsai added the following to this phrase: "The difference consists in the relative ease or difficulty they encounter in trying to follow it in practice." Exactly what is being referred to here is unclear both in the Iwanami *Nihon shisō taikei* text (Hōei 2–nen kanpon) and the Chikuma *Nihon no shisō* text (Hayashi-bon). Although Tucker considers that Jinsai is talking about the difference between the sagely way of Confucius and the teaching of Buddhism and Daoism, which is dealt with in the next paragraph, I regard this sentence as dealing with the difference between kings, nobles, great men, worthies and wise men, on the one hand, and commoners, ignorant and unworthy people, on the other. For these groups are the topic of this paragraph. Thus, the sentence should read: "The difference between the kings, nobles, great men, worthies and wise men, on the one hand, and the commoners, ignorant and unworthy people, on the other, consists in the relative ease or difficulty they encounter in trying to follow the Way in practice." This sentence therefore seems to indicate Jinsai's tendency to emphasise endeavour (admiration for the strong). Ultimately, Jinsai appears to argue that, in order to achieve the Way, commoners, ignorant and unworthy people must work harder

158 *Notes*

than kings, nobles, great men, worthies and wise men. But, first, he does not emphasise the distinction between easy and difficult practices. Second, if we compare Jinsai's understanding with the interpretations given by Ansai and Sorai, which I shall introduce soon, we see that Jinsai's insistence on egalitarianism (sympathy with the weak) remains much stronger than his recognition of any orientation towards the strong. In addition, as we shall soon note, Jinsai's downgrading of endeavour is apparent in his assertion that the Way is easy to attain.

28. Concerning the meanings of *kokoro* and *kihin*, see Nishi et al. (eds) (1980): 23–6.

29. See Nishida Taichirō, "Explanatory Notes" (Kaisetsu) in Yoshikawa, Maruyama, Nishida and Tsuji (eds) (1973): 662–3. See also Najita (1998): ix–x.

30. However, a clear distinction between normal and abnormal men can be seen in Jinsai's writings. For instance, in *A Child's Inquiries* (*Dōjimon*), Jinsai interprets the Mencius passage: "whoever is devoid of the heart of compassion is not human, whoever is devoid of the heart of shame is not human, whoever is devoid of the heart of courtesy and modesty is not human, and whoever is devoid of the heart of right and wrong is not human" (Mencius 1970, 2A (6): 82–3). Although most scholars interpret the passage to mean that all men possess compassion, shame, courtesy and righteousness, Jinsai says that, just as there are people who are born without ears, eyes, mouth, or nose, so in similar fashion there are those who lack the feelings of compassion, shame, modesty and the sense of right and wrong. It is in this sense, Jinsai continues, that Mencius says that those without these four human feelings are not human. Since such mentally or spiritually disabled persons are extremely rare, constituting only one or two individuals among millions, for Jinsai, the nature of all men is generally said to possess compassion, shame, courtesy and righteousness. Concerning this point, the following saying from the *Analects* of Confucius, book XVII, is also significant: "Men are close to one another by nature. They diverge as a result of repeated practice. . . . It is only the most intelligent and the most stupid who are not susceptible to change." In his *Ancient Meanings of the Analects* (*Rongo kogi*), Jinsai makes no criticism of this passage (Kaizuka (ed.) 1983: 385). Concerning Jinsai's interpretation of the Mencius passage in *A Child's Inquiries* (*Dōjimon*), Yoshikawa Kōjirō assumes that Jinsai is proud of the original nature of his interpretation (Yoshikawa 1975: 20 (English), 29 (Japanese)). Koyasu Nobukuni criticises Yoshikawa by saying that Jinsai does not demonstrate undue pride in his own ideas. Koyasu says that, although it is true that Jinsai mentions persons who do not have human feelings, he presents them as exceptional cases. For Koyasu, Jinsai's point is that such exceptions should not hinder the general rule that all men are wholly compassionate, shameful, courteous and righteous (Koyasu 2004: 287).

31. See also Ishida Ichirō (1960): 141–2. Concerning the concept of *jin*, see also Confucius (1979): 12: 2; 15: 24, and Mencius (1970): 2A: 6. Also see Chan Wingtsit's introduction to Wang (1963): xxxix–xli.

32. See also Koyasu (1982): 118–22, 130–1.

33. See Shinoda (2004): 225. Harimoto Shin'ichi also mentions that, while Bakin is critical of Ogyū Sorai, he highly acclaims Jinsai. See Harimoto (2004): 58, 61.

34. The essay was originally published in *Selected Works of Fukuzawa Yukichi* (*Fukuzawa Yukichi senshū*), vol. 4 (Tokyo: Iwanami, 1952). Concerning Maruyama's assessment of Yukichi, see Ida (2001): 33–51.

35. See Yasukawa (1989): 16–37; (2000): 40–8, 119–33, 201–40; (2002); (2003): 226–33.

36. Oguma Eiji's book for school students and the general public very lucidly summarises this aspect of Yukichi's thought. See Oguma (2006).

37. See Fukuzawa (1969): 16–20; (1970): 37, 171, 195; (1980): 71–6; (1981a): 50, 219, 251; (1981c): 272–4.

Notes 159

38. The original version was published in Ienaga's *The Modern Spirit and Its Limit* (*Kindai seishin to sono genkai*) in 1950 by Kadokawa.
39. Following Clastres' study, Deleuze and Guattari trace the process whereby the war machine was appropriated by the state. See Deleuze and Guattari (1988): 418.
40. The system of "nation-state" is said to appear in the nineteenth century. See Smith (1986): 11.
41. See also Jones (2002): 163.
42. Concerning the concept of equality, Thomas Hobbes in his *Leviathan* considers that differences between individuals are not as considerable as the similarities. For, as to body strength, even the weakest is able to kill the strongest, either by secret machination or through confederacy with others (Hobbes 1996: 82). In contrast to Hobbes, who pays particular attention to the equality of human physical and mental strength, John Locke in his *Two Treatises of Government* emphasises equality in terms of jurisdiction while arguing for physical, intellectual and hereditary differences (Locke 1967: 322). Jean-Jacques Rousseau's *Discourse on the Origin of Inequality* also differentiates between "natural or physical inequality" and "moral or political inequality" (Rousseau 1992, 3: 18). The game-rule governing the nation comprised of juristically and politically equal individuals is "the greatest happiness principle" as presented in Jeremy Bentham's *An Introduction to the Principles of Morals and Legislation* (Bentham 1996: 12).
43. Hobbes writes: "*NATURE* hath made men so equal, in the faculties of the body, and mind" (Hobbes 1996: 82; my italics). Locke also says that all men are *naturally* in a state of equality (Locke 1967: 287; my italics). Rousseau writes that *man was/is born free*, and *all are born equal and free* (Rousseau 1994, 4: 131–2; my italics). As I have mentioned, this kind of understanding is also expressed in the American Declaration of Independence adopted on 4 July 1776. This document states: "We hold these truths to be self-evident – that all men *are created* equal; that they *are endowed by their Creator* with certain unalienable rights; that among these are life, liberty, and the pursuit of happiness" (United States of America, Continental Congress, *Constitution* 1798: 29; my italics). Also the first article of the "Declaration of the Rights of Man and of the Citizen of France" adopted on 26 August 1789 says: "All men *are born and remain equal* in their rights" (Bell 1992: 261; my italics).
44. In this sense, as J. W. Gough points out, in the end Locke's "state of nature" does not differ markedly from Hobbes's. See Gough (1957): 138. See also Nozick (1974): 10, and Kukathas and Pettit (1990): ch. 5.
45. See also Kayano (2005): 9–16.
46. See also Kaldor (2003): 115–16. She writes:

> the key characteristic of the modern state, which came into being somewhere between the fifteenth and eighteenth centuries, was its control of violence within a given territory. . . . Domestically, the modern state provided security for its citizens both through coercion and surveillance and through the extension of the rule of law. Internationally, the state defended its territory through war-making. . . . Bounded civil society depended on the existence of an "other" even if there were different categories of "other" – "civilized" Europeans and "less civilized" outsiders. The end of war as a unilateral option for state politics presupposes an acceptance of human equality; it eliminates the justification for the preservation of statist politics and the distinction between the inside and outside.

47. Compared to Hobbes and Locke, Rousseau takes a different position on the matter of the social contract. In place of Hobbes's "war of every man against

160 *Notes*

every man", as the given state of nature, Rousseau suggests pity. In his *Discourse on the Origin of Inequality* (1754), Rousseau writes that pity is "a disposition that is appropriate to beings as weak and subject to as many ills as we are; a virtue all the more universal and useful to man because it precedes in him the use of all reflection; and so Natural that even Beasts sometimes give perceptible signs of it" (Rousseau 1992: 36). In his *Social Contract* (1762), Rousseau also states that the essence of the social compact is that "*Each of us puts his person and all his power in common under the supreme direction of the general will; and in a body we receive each member as an indivisible part of the whole*" (Rousseau 1994, 4: 139; Rousseau's italics). By using terms like "pity", "supreme direction of the general will" or "indivisible part of the whole", Rousseau focuses on the common traits shared by individuals rather than the differences which invite conflict. As J. W. Gough concludes, the ultimate significance of Rousseau in the history of political thought is as a precursor of a collectivist attitude to the individual's place in society rather than as a vindicator of individual liberty (Gough 1957: 173). It is this collective attitude that also links Marx's communism to Hōnen's cooperative and collaborative situation.

48. In order to solve the problem of stagnation and economic destruction, Rawls presents his famous two conditions under which social and economic inequalities are permitted: first, they must be attached to offices and positions open to all under conditions of fair equality of opportunity; and, second, they must be to the greatest benefit of the least advantaged members of society (Rawls 1973: 302; 1993: 291).

49. See also Murakami Fuminobu (1996): 7.

50. Concerning Tōkoku's criticism of Yukichi, see Kitamura Tōkoku (1950–5), 2: 119, 172–3.

51. Aizan's utilitarian literary view is found in his "On Rai Jō" ("Rai Jō o ronzu)", in Yamaji (1983–5), 2: 286–96.

52. See especially Kitamura Tōkoku, "What Does It Mean 'To Benefit Mankind'?" ("Jinsei ni aiwataru towa nanno ii zo") (February 1893), in Kitamura Tōkoku (1950–5), 2: 113–25; "Personal View of Meiji Literature" ("Meiji bungaku kanken") (April–May 1893), in Kitamura Tōkoku (1950–5), 2: 146–78; "On the Inner Life" ("Naibu seimei ron") (May 1893), in Kitamura Tōkoku (1950–5), 2: 238–49. Concerning Tōkoku's ideal world, see Harootunian (1974): 129–30.

53. Concerning Tōkoku's romanticism, see Yamanouchi (1978): 20–33; and Keene (1984), 1: 186–201.

54. As we shall see in Chapter 5, Mencius (372?–289? BC) urges "love between father and son, duty between ruler and subject, distinction between husband and wife, precedence of the old over the young, and faith between friends" (Mencius 1970, 3A: 4: 102). One of the reasons why Mencius urges "distinction between husband and wife" is perhaps related to the fact that the bond uniting husbands and wives or lovers is regarded as resulting from carnal and vulgar sexual desire.

3. Ugly ladies in *The Tale of Genji*

1. In this regard, there are two valuable compilations of *Genji* studies in Japan: Mitani and Higashihara (eds) (1991); and Matsui and Ueta (eds) (1998–9). Both collections include explanatory notes written by the editors and have provided valuable guidance for this trend in *Genji* scholarship.

2. See, for instance, Mitani (1980): 212. For the English references, see Okada (1991): 342, n. 2; Shirane (1987): 59–62, 99–100; Field (1987): 87; Gatten (1981a): 42–98; (1981b).

Notes 161

3. Abe divides the first eleven chapters into two groups. The first group includes the chapters of "Lavender" ("Wakamurasaki"), "An Autumn Excursion" ("Momiji no ga"), "The Festival of the Cherry Blossoms" ("Hana no en"), "Heartvine" ("Aoi"), "The Sacred Tree" ("Sakaki"), "The Orange Blossoms" ("Hanachirusato") and "Suma". The second encompasses "The Broom Tree" ("Hahakigi"), "The Shell of the Locust" ("Utsusemi"), "Evening Faces" ("Yūgao") and "The Safflower" ("Suetsumuhana"). See Abe Akio (1969–1982): 32–52. Takeda Munetoshi divides the first thirty-three chapters into two groups. See Takeda (1950a–b). For more on the order of the writing the early chapters of *Genji*, see also Kazamaki (1951).

Takahashi Kazuo asserts that the "Suetsumuhana" chapter was written after the "An Autumn Excursion" chapter. Furthermore he supposes that "The Wormwood Patch" and "The Gatehouse" might have been written after "The Wind in the Pines", or even after "The Morning Glory". See Takahashi Kazuo (1966): 56–95. Aileen Gatten supposes that "The Broom Tree", "The Shell of the Locust", "Evening Faces", "The Safflower", "The Wormwood Patch" and "The Gatehouse" were written after "Channel Buoys". See Gatten (1981b): 5–46.

For the original Japanese text, I referred to Murasaki (1993–7), abbreviated here to volume and page. English translations of character names, chapter titles and translations of the passages from *Genji* have generally been made with reference to Edward Seidensticker's translation, *The Tale of Genji*. Hereafter it is abbreviated: S page. On occasions I also refer to Royall Tyler's translation, *The Tale of Genji*. Hereafter it is abbreviated: T volume page.

4. In his later book, Abe Akio further developed his supposition and summarised the outline of the Wakamurasaki group as a story of Genji's splendid life, while the outline of the Hahakigi group, which originates in the "rainy night critique" (*amayo no shina sadame*) in "The Broom Tree" ("Hahakigi") chapter, is given as Genji's relations with women of the middle class. See Abe Akio (1959): 939–1009.

5. Hinata Kazumasa's recent study adopts this view as the basic structure of the story of Hikaru Genji. See Hinata (2004): 32–3.

6. Concerning the ambition to rise in the world harboured by both the Kiritsubo lady and her mother, see Masuda Shigeo (1992): 16. See also Yoshikai (2003): 33–60.

7. Murai Toshihiko (1968): 12–23; (1969–82), 4: 73–86; Murofushi (1980): 154–71; Masuda Shigeo (1980a): 172–84; Hinata (1998), 1: 66–70; Suzuki Hideo (2003): 245–7.

8. Concerning women who aspire to promote their families by serving at court, see Hinata (1998), 1: 65.

9. The following is the original Japanese text.

> いまは、たゞ品にも寄らじ、かたちをばさらにも言はじ、いとくちおしくねぢ
> けがましきおぼえだになくは、たゞひとへにものまめやかに静かなる心のお<u>も</u>
> <u>むきならむ</u>よるべをぞつゐの頼み所には思ひをくべかりける。<u>あまりゆへよし</u>
> 心ばせうち添へたらむをばよろこびに思ひ、すこしをくれたる方あらむをもあ
> ながちに求め加へじ。<u>うしろやすくのどけき</u>所だに強くは、うはべのなさけは
> をのづからもてつけつべきわざをや。

(I 41; my underlining)

10. Hayasaka (1971): 33–4; Suzuki Kazuo (1994): 1–17; Hinata (1998), 1: 54–7; (2004): 36–7.

11. I call her Gen-no-naishi instead of Naishi or Gen-no-naishi-no-suke.

162 *Notes*

12. According to *Mingō nisso*, Sanjō-Nishi Saneki comments that "these people" refers to Murasaki and Suetsumuhana (Nihon tosho sentā (ed.) 1978, 1: 371). However, Hagiwara Hiromichi argues that, since this is the ending of the four chapters which deal with Utsusemi, Nokiba-no-ogi, Yūgao and Suetsumuhana, the expression "these people" means Utsusemi, Nokiba-no-ogi and Suetsumuhana (Yūgao is no longer alive) (Hagiwara 1978, 4: 436). Since then, following Hagiwara, commentators usually interpret "these people" as Suetsumuhana, Utsusemi and Nokiba-no-ogi. See, for instance, Murasaki Shikibu (1957–68), 1: 268; (1970–6), 1: 380; (1993–7), 1: 235; (1994–8), 1: 307.

13. Takehara Hiroshi argues the importance of the sentence "I wonder what happened to all these people in the end" (I 235; T I: 131), which appears at the close of the "Suetsumuhana" chapter, as follows: "The author of this story does not plan to end the Suetsumuhana story with her disgraceful figure being mocked by Genji. The narrator's comment at the end of the 'Suetsumuhana' chapter 'I wonder what happened to all these people in the end' is proof of this." See Takehara (1996): 263.

14. Suetsumuhana's lack of talent for playing musical instruments and composing poems is well contrasted with Lady Murasaki's talent for these activities.

15. Regarding Genji's ridicule, while Lady Murasaki joins the ridicule at the end of the "Safflower" chapter, Tamakazura here sympathises with Suetsumuhana. As we shall see later, this well shows the different ideologies of these two women.

16. Citing this passage, Takehara Hiroshi argues that we should refrain from criticising Suetsumuhana's poem, since the comments of Genji differ from those of the old women serving Suetsumuhana, and it is unclear which is the author's own evaluation. See Takehara (1996): 261.

17. Concerning Suetsumuhana's old-fashioned character, see Imanishi (1980).

18. Concerning Suetsumuhana's wish to live in the past, see Hirokawa Katsumi (1980), 4: 39–47.

19. Seidensticker translates "*ohodoka*" into "a lack of forwardness and impertinence", "serenity" and "repose" (S 119–20), Tyler into "to behave with dignity and to do nothing eccentric" and "quiet composure" (T I: 120).

20. For the relationship between Suetsumuhana and Murasaki Shikibu, see Fujiwara (1993): 103–19. Also see Akahane (1995): 53–72.

21. Concerning this narrative perspective, see Abe Akio (1954): 138–40.

22. Fujii Sadakazu highlights Suetsumuhana's father's influence, her old-fashioned character, her fortune, and her ridiculous outlook and conduct as unchangeable aspects of Suetsumuhana. See Fujii (1974): 68–70.

23. Concerning the Gen-no-naishi story, see also Ikeda Kikan (1951), 1: 136; Abe Akio (1969–82): 41; Takahashi Kazuo (1966): 89–95; Ikeda Tsutomu (1974): 172–93.

24. Concerning the polyphonic narrative in *The Tale of Genji*, see Murakami Fuminobu (1998); (2009).

25. I translated the original into English referring to Seidensticker's and Tyler's translations, in order that the translated text might reflect the original syntax as faithfully as possible. The original Japanese text reads as follows:

年いたう老たる内侍のすけ、人もやむごとなく、心ばせあり、あてにおぼえ高くはありながら、いみじうあだめいたる心ざまにて、そなたにはをもからぬあるを、かうさだ過ぐるまで、などさしも乱るらむと、いぶかしくおぼえ給ければ、戯れ事言ひふれて心みたまふに、似げなくも思はざりける。

(I 258)

Notes 163

26. In this case, I referred mainly to Seidensticker's translation and amended it so as to be as faithful as possible to the original syntax. The following is the original Japanese text:

かはぼりのえならずゑかきたるをさし隠して見かへりたるまみ、いたう見延べたれど、目皮らいたく黒み落ち入りて、いみじうはつれそゝけたり。

似つかはしからぬ扇のさまかなと見給て、わが持たまへるにさしかへて見給へば、赤き紙の、うつるばかり色深きに、木高き森のかたを塗り隠したり。片つ方に、手はいとさだ過ぎたれど、よしなからず、「森の下草老ひぬれば」など書きすさびたるを、ことしもあれ、うたての心ばへやと、笑まれながら、...

(I: 259)

27. The following is the original Japanese text.

この君も人よりはいとことなるを、かのつれなき人の御慰めにと思ひつれど、見まほしきは限りありけるをとや、うたての好みや。

(I: 260)

28. Concerning the relation between *The Tale of Genji* and *Tales of Ise* (*Ise monogatari*), see Ishikawa Tōru (1996): 358–84, and Akiyama (1964): 58–71.
29. The original wording is " 世の常のあだ事の引きつくろひ飾れる" (II: 177).
30. Originally published in *Nihon bungaku*, January 1958.
31. Originally published in *Kokugo to kokubungaku*, 36 (4), April 1959.
32. Hereafter, the page numbers of citation from *The Lotus Sutra* indicate this version.
33. The multiple personality disorder (MPD) might be related to fictional language. See Burr (1995): 125–39; Harré (1998): 147–79.

4. Women, humble men and insulted people in *The Tale of the Heike*

1. Some general introductions and introductions of *Heike* textual criticism are available in English. For instance, in the 1960s, Kenneth Dean Butler published three articles: Kenneth Dean Butler (1966a); (1966b); (1969). See also Hasegawa Tadashi (1967).
   From the 1970s to the 1990s three books on the history of Japanese literature which introduce *The Tale of the Heike* appeared: Katō (1979): 258–62; Konishi (1991): 334–49; Keene (1993): 629–42. Kitagawa Hiroshi and Bruce T. Tsuchida's preface to their English translation (Kitagawa and Tsuchida 1975) and Helen Craig McCullough's essay "The 'Heike' as Literature", appended to her English translation (McCullough 1988) are also useful introductions. In addition to the above, readers are referred to Varley (1994): 78–115, and his chapter contribution "Warriors as Courtiers: The Taira in *Heike monogatari*", in Heinrich (ed.) (1997): 53–70.
   David T. Bialock's more recent study of the *Heike* also needs to be consulted. See David T. Bialock, "Nation and Epic: *The Tale of the Heike* as Modern Classic", in Shirane and Suzuki (eds) (2000): 151–78. More recently, two books on the topic of *The Tale of the Heike* appeared. See Oyler (2006) and Bialock (2007). Elizabeth Oyler's and David Bialock's works refer to Michael Watson's doctoral thesis, "A Narrative Study of the Kakuichi-bon *Heike monogatari*" (Queen's College, University of Oxford, 2003). I have tried unsuccessfully to access this work.

164 *Notes*

2. Concerning the *Shibu kassenjō* text, see Kenneth Dean Butler (1966a); (1966b); (1969).
3. There are various possible pronunciations of the name of the era (1308–11) in which part of the text was hand-copied, and after which the title of the text is named – *Enkyō*, *Engyō* and *Enkei*. The *Engyō* text is now stored in the Daitōkyū kinen bunko library and, according to its colophons, was originally copied in 1309–20 and copied again in 1419–20.
4. See Kitahara and Ogawa (eds) (1990): 1–3; Bialock (2007): xiii.
5. See Saeki Shin'ichi's explanatory notes collected in Saeki and Koakimoto (eds) (1999): 271–85. Concerning the *Engyō* text, see Mizuhara (1971); (1979); Mizuhara (ed.) (1992–7). See also Kobayashi Yoshikazu (1986); (2000); Takehisa (1986); (1996); Saeki (1996b).
6. The colophon of the *Kakuichi* text says that the text was dictated by *biwa hōshi* Kakuichi in 1371. Of the six extant versions of the *Kakuichi* text, three omit the story of Giō and that of Kozaishō, although the others include these narratives. Concerning the *Engyō* and *Kakuichi* texts, see Bialock (1999).
7. Concerning the *Kakuichi* text's emotional sympathy with the weak, Ubukata Takashige points out that the *Kakuichi* focuses on the defeated, rather than on those who defeat (Ubukata 1984: 145–62). Matsuo Ashie also mentions that the *Kakuichi* text often openly expresses its sympathy with people who are overcome by tragic circumstances (Matsuo 1985: 18; 1996: 334–50). See also Hyōdō (2000).
8. For the literary controversy regarding the concept of impermanence, see Sekiguchi (1996): 338–66; (1998): 3–24; Mizuhara (1970): 1–37. Concerning Hōnen's Buddhist teaching, see Murakami Manabu (1998); Imanari (1970): 204–37.
9. Concerning the fictionalisation of *Heike*, see Uwayokote (1985).
10. Concerning the meaning of *monogatari*, see Fujii (1990). Concerning the placatory nature of the *Heike*, see Plutschow (1990): 220–8; (1997): 71–80. Also refer to Takagi Makoto's argument concerning Hyōdō's power analysis in Takagi (2001): 133–9. See also Saeki (1996a).
11. See Mizuhara (1970): 9; (1971): 102–116, 320–34; (1995): 103–10; Mizuhara (ed.) (1992–7), 4: 7–24. Some parts of Mizuhara (1979) also draw our attention to the viewpoint of the weak. Examples include the viewpoints of Koremori (94), women (405) and poor priests (407–29). Concerning Imanari Genshō's study of the weak in the *Heike*, see Imanari (1971).
12. Concerning women in the *Heike*, see Tanaka Takako (1998); Yokoi (1994).
13. In most cases, I have supplied three versions of the *Heike* for references: (1) the original Japanese texts cited from Kitahara and Ogawa (eds) (1990) for the *Engyō* text (roman numerals indicate volumes and arabic numerals pages); (2) Kajihara and Yamashita (eds) (1991–3) for the *Kakuichi* text (roman numerals indicate volumes and arabic numerals pages); and (3) Helen Craig McCullough's English translation (McCullough, page). Unless otherwise mentioned, the English translation of the *Engyō* text is mine.
14. Shigemori's rebirth in the Pure Land is also narrated in the *Engyō* text by Dharma Seal Jōken (*Engyō* I: 302).
15. Concerning "to maintain or stay in correct thoughts" (*rinjū shōnen ni jūsu*) as a sign of rebirth in the Pure Land, see the entry "*rinjū*" in Nakamura, Fukunaga, Tamura and Konno (eds) (1989). Hōnen mentions in his letter to Shōnyobō that if a person chants the Buddha's name many times, and if as a result the Buddha comes to lead that person to paradise, we can say that this is an example of "to maintain or stay in correct thoughts (*rinjū shōnen ni jūsu*)". See Ōhashi Shunnō (ed.) (1971): 199. See also Kasahara (1975): 150.

Notes 165

16. The text says: "Upon hearing her poem, one night [Emperor Go-Toba] called her [to his bedroom]. But, soon she was given leave whereupon she left the palace and reached Seisuiji Temple. Here, she took the name Shinnyo and became a nun" (*Engyō* II: 125).
17. Concerning this part, see Saeki (1992–7), 3: 140–56.
18. Makino Kazuo here regards *Taihei kōki* (*Later Record of Great Peace*) not as the mistaken title of the Chinese book *Taihei kōki* (*Wide Record of Great Peace*), but as a book edited by a Japanese editor. See Makino (1993), 15: 90–3.
19. Concerning this memorial writing, see Takehisa (1996): 112–14.
20. This sort of women's participation in war can also be seen in the passage in which a message comes to Tohi no Jirō Sanehira from his wife (*Engyō* I: 523). Following this passage, the story that Tohi no Yatarō Tōhira attempted to betray his father and his master for the sake of his wife's family is narrated (*Engyō* I: 523–4). This story also suggests a woman's influence on the battlefield.
21. The meaning of the phrase "*otto ni myōtai awaseba*" is ambiguous. *Myōtai* is a Buddhist term which indicates the name (*myō*) and body (*tai*), but it does not fit well in this context. Probably it means that "if we agree with husbands both in body and soul". However, the expression clearly recalls the synonym *meutai* (a beautiful mysterious body), although this word has a different character notation. Using this second term, the phrase means "if we unite our beautiful and mysterious bodies with our husbands".

5. Sacrifice and revenge, love and war, and a world without violence in *The Eight Dog Chronicles*

1. See Konishi (1992), 5: 218–42; Kyokutei Bakin (1995–).
2. Concerning the study of *The Eight Dog Chronicles* and Bakin written in English, see Keene (1955): 423–8; (1976): 426–8; Zolbrod (1965); (1966a); (1967a); (1967b); (1985); Katō (1983): 53–6; Shirane (ed.) (2002): 885–909.
3. Concerning the definition of modernism and postmodernism, see Chapter 1 and also Murakami Fuminobu (2002): 127–41; (2005): 1–11.
4. Kyokutei Bakin, *The Eight Dog Chronicles* (*Nansō Satomi hakkenden*), ed. Koike Tōgorō (Tokyo: Iwanami bunko, 1990), is the edition cited. Roman numerals indicate volumes and arabic numerals pages.
5. For example, as we have seen in Chapter 2, Mencius urges "love between father and son, duty between ruler and subject, distinction between husband and wife, precedence of the old over the young, and faith between friends". See Mencius (1970), 3A: 4: 102.
6. For example, *Greater Learning for Women* (*Onna daigaku*), a book of unknown authorship written on the basis of chapter 5 of Kaibara Ekiken's *Precepts of the Popular Morals for Japanese Children* (*Wazoku dōji kun*), first published in the early eighteenth century and repeatedly reprinted throughout the Tokugawa period, says:

> It is the chief duty of a girl living in the parental house to practise filial piety towards her father and mother. But after marriage her duty is to honour her father-in-law and mother-in-law, to honour them beyond her father and mother, to love and reverence them with all ardour, and to tend them with the practice of every filial piety.

> (Kaibara 1979: 37)

7. René Girard defines the role of sacrifice as to stem a rising tide of indiscriminate violence and to redirect it into proper channels. The scapegoat, argues Girard, is

166 *Notes*

killed in order to discharge the people's desire for indiscriminate violence, and thereby saves society from the violent forces which threaten it. See Girard (1977): 11.

Imamura Hitoshi has drawn on Girard's ideas in his analysis of violence and the role of sacrifice in the Japanese context. He argues that, in order to avoid a vicious circle of reciprocal violence, two antagonistic parties in one society select a third party as a scapegoat. By directing the desire for violence towards the third party, the two antagonistic parties overcome the crisis of violence. See Imamura Hitoshi (1982): 234–8; (1992).

Akasaka Norio, referring to René Girard and Imamura Hitoshi, theorises the bullying problematised in the 1980s and 1990s in schools in Japan as an example of scapegoating. Akasaka suggests that school bullying is a form of discharging the desire for violence which was suppressed in the overly democratic and egalitarian educational system of the 1970s and 1980s. See Akasaka (1995): 61–3.

8. For a discussion on revenge, refer to Hirade (1990).
9. Wang Yang-ming also considers filial piety and brotherly love to be the starting-point of the self's identification with all things. Father–son or fraternal relations are for Wang a gateway to the experience of an all-inclusive commonality. See Wang (1963): 55–6, 118–19, 272.
10. Since Confucian society is patriarchal, the central self must be a male.
11. See Kimura Ki (1982): 84; Yanagida (1987): 125; Tanizawa (1971): 4; Ochi (1984): 255.
12. Concerning the impact of Shōyō's *The Essence of the Novel* in later years, see Kornicki (1982): 25–42.
13. Bakin writes in his own commentary at the beginning of *The Eight Dog Chronicles*, vol. 9, ch. 33: "Though the novel and the romance are not very useful, their value lies in their 'encouraging virtue and chastising vice' " (IX 6).
14. Concerning the general assessment of Tokugawa fiction, including Bakin's fiction, in modern Japan, see Kornicki (1982).
15. Takayama Chogyū, "The Novel in the Meiji Period" ("Meiji no shōsetsu"), in Takayama (1914), 2: 408–9. Original version was published in 1897. See also Kimura Ki (1982): 80; Tanizawa (1971): 242.
16. *Sharebon* stories are mostly about the licensed quarter. See Miner, Odagiri and Morrell (1985): 297.
17. *Kibyōshi* is a kind of popular story for adults. See Miner, Odagiri and Morrell (1985): 283.
18. *Yomihon* are books with didactic ends of a Buddhist or Confucian kind. See Miner, Odagiri and Morrell (1985): 304. See also Zolbrod (1966b).
19. See also Kornicki (1982): 27.
20. Also see introductory chapter (pp. 1–18) written by Racheal Hutchinson and Mark Williams for Hutchinson and Williams (eds) (2007).
21. Tsuda Sōkichi's *A Study of Our People's Mind as Mirrored in Literature* (*Bungaku ni arawaretaru waga kokumin shisō no kenkyū*) was published in 1916–21. The book was later revised under the new title of *A Study of the People's Mind as Mirrored in Literature* (*Bungaku ni arawaretaru kokumin shisō no kenkyū*) in 1951–65. The quotation is from Tsuda (1964): 257. The English abridged version is Tsuda (1970): 86.
22. Matsuda Osamu, "The Androgynous at the End of the Tokugawa Period: An Attempt to Discuss Bakin" ("Bakumatsu no andorogyunusu tachi – Bakin ron no kokoromi"), in Matsuda (1975): 208; (2002), 3: 211.
23. While Hamada Keisuke reveals an attitude which rejects interpreting *The Eight Dog Chronicles* as an expression of Confucian authoritarianism (Hamada 1993: 360), Maeda Ai (Yoshimi) commends Bakin for skilfully narrating the evil side of the anti-heroes in this narrative (Maeda 1989).

Notes 167

24. *The Tale of Tsuneyo Which Encourages Virtue* is compiled in Kyokutei Bakin (1995–), vol. 4.
25. Ishikawa Hidemi, Leon Zolbrod and Takada Mamoru divide *The Eight Dog Chronicles* into three parts: the establishment of the Satomi family or the story of Fusehime (chs 1–14), an account of the activities of the eight heroes until their assembly under the Satomi banner (chs 15–131), and the struggles of the Satomi family against the combined forces of the shogun's deputies (chs 131–81). See Zolbrod (1983); Ishikawa Hidemi (1991a); (1991b); (1993); Takada (2005). However, as I shall later discuss, like many other Japanese scholars I prefer to place the second and first parts given above together as a single section.
26. See Yoshikawa and Shimizu (eds) (1971): 38, 71; Tucker (1998): 115, 177; Yoshikawa, Maruyama, Nishida and Tsuji (eds) (1973): 53; Najita (1998): 48.
27. Shinoda Jun'ichi argues that the concept of *jin* in *The Eight Dog Chronicles* is deeply influenced by that of Jinsai. See Shinoda (2004): 225.
28. Wang Yang-ming criticises Mo Tzu's (500?–420? BC) doctrine of universal love and argues that it makes no distinction in human relations. He further notes that, according to such a doctrine, one's own father, sons, elder and younger brothers have no greater significance than passers-by. See Wang (1963): 56–7; Confucius (1979), 1: 2; Mencius (1970), 3B: 9. For Mo Tzu's doctrine, see Mo Tzu (1929), chs 14–16: 78–97; (1963): 39–49.
29. Concerning this point, see Murakami Fuminobu (2005): 91–2.
30. See also Kayano (2005): 9–16.

6. Dancing girl, geisha, mistress and wife in Kawabata Yasunari's stories

1. In the marketing material attached to the book cover of Imamura Junko (1988).
2. Concerning the feminine characteristics in *The Dancing Girl of Izu*, see Komashaku (1989): 9.
3. In most cases I have supplied two versions of Kawabata Yasunari's stories: (1) original Japanese versions cited from *The Complete Work of Kawabata Yasunari* (*Kawabata Yasunari zenshū*) (1980–4), which is abbreviated as J: volume page; and (2) English translations of the selected texts. The latter are *The Dancing Girl of Izu*, trans. Martin J. Holman, in Kawabata (1997); *Snow Country*, trans. Edward Seidensticker (Kawabata 1957; *Thousand Cranes*, trans. Edward Seidensticker (Kawabata 1967); and *The Sound of the Mountain*, trans. Edward Seidensticker (Kawabata 1971). English versions are abbreviated as E: page. I sometimes amend the English translations by referring to the original Japanese.
4. As I shall explain later, this not only demonstrates Kaoru's innocent childishness, but also satisfies male voyeuristic desire.
5. For further discussion on Yoko's insanity and the concept of sacrifice and punishment, see Tajima Yōko (1989): 26–30.
6. For the discrimination depicted in *The Dancing Girl of Izu*, see Tamura Mitsumasa (1992): 565–6, and Morimoto (1990): 6–7.
7. See Hayashi (1984): 46–9; Hasegawa Izumi (1991): 259–60, 270–1. See also Starrs (1998): 43.
8. See also Hara (1999): 80; Morimoto (1990): 8–10.
9. Wayne C. Booth writes: "I have called a narrator *reliable* when he speaks for or acts in accordance with the norms of the work (which is to say, the implied author's norms), *unreliable* when he does not" (Booth's italics). See Booth (1983): 158–9.
10. See http://www16.ocn.ne.jp/~pacohama/sensosekinin/renkoutoukai.html retrieved on 24 April 2009. See also Takeuchi (1991): 25; and Chōsenjin kyōsei renkō shinsō chōsadan (ed.) (1997): 344.

168 Notes

The fact that the old woman and her three grandchildren do not talk to the student at all supports the supposition that they might be Korean.

11. Kawabata writes that during his trip as a student to Izu, the journey upon which the story is based, he realised that members of Kaoru's family were suffering from a similar dropsy-like disease which saw the body become distended and swollen. However, after much consideration, he did not include this in the story. See Kawabata Yasunari (1980–4), 33: 81.

12. See also Hara (1999): 80; Morimoto (1990): 8–10.

13. I have supplied two versions of Nagai Kafū's *Geisha in Rivalry* (*Udekurabe*). (1) The original Japanese version cited from *The Complete Work of Nagai Kafū* (*Nagai Kafū zenshū*, vol. 12) (Tokyo: Iwanami, 1992), which is abbreviated as J: page; and (2) the English translation *Geisha in Rivalry*, trans. Kurt Meissner. The English version is abbreviated as E: page. I sometimes amend the English translation by referring to the original Japanese.

14. Concerning the term "waste of effort", see Kawasaki Toshihiko (1973): 191–3.

15. For a discussion of the ugly and unpleasant women in Kawabata's stories, see Kobayashi Hiroko (1992).

16. Many of the romantic scenes in *The Tale of Genji* include seductive conversations between male characters on a veranda and female characters sequestered in a room separated by shutters or curtains.

17. In this story, sympathy for the mistress, Kinu, is skilfully obscured by her strong-hearted and independent character.

18. Fusako, the daughter of Shingo and Yasuko, is also described as an ugly woman. But her tender character is clearly implied. When Shingo scolds Yasuko for opening Fusako's purse, Fusako feels that she must do something to relieve the tension (J: XII 265; E: 25). She also seems to try to conceal her husband's bad treatment which forced her to return to her parents' house on New Year's Eve by claiming that she left her husband's house voluntarily (J: XII 344–5; E: 98). There are suggestions that she sent money to her husband (J: XII 439; E: 181–2). Though Fusako's perspective is not fully developed in the story, nevertheless we can say that her tenderness is not completely neglected.

Bibliography

Abe Akio (1954) "Hikaru Genji's Appearance" ("Hikaru Genji no yōshi"), *Bulletin of the University of Tokyo, Faculty of Arts and Sciences, Department of Humanities* (*Tokyo daigaku, kyōyō gakubu, jinbun kagakuka kiyō*), 4 (1): 99–165.

Abe Akio (1959) *An Introduction to the Study of "The Tale of Genji"* (*Genji monogatari kenkyū josetsu*) (Tokyo: University of Tokyo Press).

Abe Akio (1969–82) "The Order of Writing *The Tale of Genji*: On the Chapters Surrounding the 'Lavender' Chapter" ("*Genji monogatari* shippitsu no junjo: 'Wakamurasaki' no maki zengo no shojō ni tsuite"), *Kokugo to kokubungaku* (Tokyo: University of Tokyo), August–September 1939. Cited from Nihon bungaku kenkyū shiryō kankōkai (ed.) (1969–82), 3: 32–52.

Abe Yoshitomi (1979) "The Position and the Role of Ōmi-no-kimi" ("Ōmi-no-kimi no ichi to yakuwari"), *Chūko bungaku*, 24: 11–20.

Abelove, Henry, Barale, Michèle Aina and Haplerin, David M. (eds) (1993) *Lesbian and Gay Studies Reader* (New York/London: Routledge).

Akahane Shuku (1995) *Women in "The Tale of Genji"* (*Genji monogatari no onna tachi*) (Tokyo: Kanrin shobō).

Akasaka Norio (1986) "The Tale of the Heike and Kingship" ("Heike monogatari to ōken"), *Kokubungaku: Kaishaku to kyōzai no kenkyū*, June: 74–9.

Akasaka Norio (1995) *The Phenomenology of Exclusion* (*Haijo no genshōgaku*) (Tokyo: Chikuma bunko).

Akiyama Ken (1964) *The World of "The Tale of Genji"* (*Genji monogatari no sekai*) (Tokyo: University of Tokyo Press).

Akiyama Ken (ed.) (1980) *A Lecture Series on the World of "The Tale of Genji"* (*Kōza Genji monogatari no sekai*), 9 vols (Tokyo: Yūhikaku).

Anderson, Benedict (2006) *Imagined Communities: Reflections on the Origin and Spread of Nationalism*, revised edn (London/New York: Verso).

Andrews, Allan A. (1973) *The Teachings Essential for Rebirth: A Study of Genshin's Ōjōyōshū* (Tokyo: Sophia University).

Andrews, Allan A. (1989) "Genshin's 'Essentials of Pure Land Rebirth' and the Transmission of Pure Land Buddhism to Japan. Part I. The First and Second Phases of Transmission of Pure Land Buddhism to Japan: The Nara Period and the Early Heian Period", *The Pacific World*, new series, 5: 20–32.

Aquinas, Thomas (1911) *The Summa Theologica of St Thomas Aquinas*, pt I, trans. Fathers of the English Dominican Province (London: R. & T. Washbourne).

Araya Keizaburō kyōju koki kinen ronbunshū kankō iinkai (ed.) (1992) *Interlaced Language* (*Kōsaku suru gengo*) (Tokyo: Meichofukyūkai).

170 Bibliography

Arendt, Hannah (2004) *The Origins of Totalitarianism* (New York: Schocken Books).

Association for Japanese–Chinese Comparative Literature Studies (Wakan hikaku bungakukai) (ed.) (1993) *A Japanese–Chinese Comparative Literature Series* (*Wakan hikaku bungaku sōsho*) (Tokyo: Kyūko shoin).

Bargen, Doris G. (1997) *Genji, a Woman's Weapon: Spirit Possession in the "Tale of Genji"* (Honolulu: University of Hawaii Press).

Bataille, Georges (1986) *Erotism: Death & Sensuality*, trans. Mary Dalwood (San Francisco, Calif.: City Lights).

Bauman, Zygmunt (1989) *Modernity and the Holocaust* (Cambridge: Polity Press).

Beck, Ulrich, Giddens, Anthony and Lash, Scott (1994) *Reflexive Modernization: Politics, Tradition, and Aesthetics in the Modern Social Order* (Cambridge: Polity Press).

Bell, John (1992) *French Constitutional Law* (Oxford: Clarendon Press).

Benjamin, Walter (1996) "Critique of Violence", in Marcus Bullock and Michael W. Jennings (eds), *Walter Benjamin: Selected Writings*, vol. 1, *1913–1926* (Cambridge, Mass./London: The Belknap Press of Harvard University Press).

Bentham, Jeremy (1996) *An Introduction to the Principles of Morals and Legislation*, ed. J. H. Burns and H. L. A. Hart, with a new introduction by F. Rosen and an interpretive essay by H. L. A. Hart (Oxford: Clarendon Press).

Bialock, David T. (1999) "Heike monogatari", in Steven D. Carter (ed.), *Dictionary of Literary Biography*, vol. 203, *Medieval Japanese Writers* (Detroit, Mich./ Washington, DC/London: The Gale Group), pp. 73–84.

Bialock, David T. (2000) "Nation and Epic: *The Tale of the Heike* as Modern Classic", in Shirane and Suzuki (eds) (2000): 151–78.

Bialock, David T. (2007) *Eccentric Spaces, Hidden Histories: Narrative, Ritual, and Royal Authority from "The Chronicles of Japan" to "The Tale of the Heike"* (Stanford, Calif.: Stanford University Press).

Blacker, Carmen (1964) *The Japanese Enlightenment* (London/New York: Cambridge University Press).

Boehm, Christopher (1999) *Hierarchy in the Forest: The Evolution of Egalitarian Behavior* (Cambridge, Mass./London: Harvard University Press).

Booth, Wayne C. (1983) *The Rhetoric of Fiction*, 2nd edn (Chicago, Ill.: University of Chicago Press).

Bowring, Richard (1982) *Murasaki Shikibu: Her Diary and Poetic Memoirs* (Princeton, NJ: Princeton University Press).

Burr, Vivien (1995) *An Introduction to Social Constructionism* (London: Routledge).

Butler, Judith (1990) *Gender Trouble: Feminism and the Subversion of Identity* (New York/London: Routledge).

Butler, Kenneth Dean (1966a) "The *Heike Monogatari* and Theories of Oral Epic Literature", *Bulletin of the Faculty of Humanities, Seikei University*, 2: 37–54.

Butler, Kenneth Dean (1966b) "The Textual Evolution of the *Heike Monogatari*", *Harvard Journal of Asiatic Studies*, 26: 5–51.

Butler, Kenneth Dean (1969) "The *Heike Monogatari* and the Japanese Warrior Ethic", *Harvard Journal of Asiatic Studies*, 29: 93–108.

Chō Munju (Jo Mun Jo) (2001) "The Creation of Kenreimon'in's Character in *The Tale of the Heike*: With Special Emphasis on the *Engyō* Text" ("*Heike monogatari* no Kenreimon'in zōkei – *Engyō-bon* o chūshin ni –"), *Studies in Japanese Literature* (*Nihon bungaku kenkyū*) (Japanese Literature Society of Baiko Jogakuin College (Baikō jogakuin daigaku, Nihon bungaku kai)), 36: 12–21.

Bibliography   171

Chōsenjin kyōsei renkō shinsō chōsadan (ed.) (1997) *A Record of the Investigation into the Forced Immigration of Korean People: Chūbu and Tōkai Regions* (*Chōsenjin kyōsei renkō chōsa no kiroku – Chūbu/Tōkai hen*) (Tokyo: Kashiwa shobō).

Cixous, Hélène (1980) "The Laugh of the Medusa", in Marks and Courtivron (eds) (1980): 245–64.

Clastres, Pierre (1994) *Archeology of Violence*, trans. Jeanine Herman (New York: Semiotext(e)).

Confucius (1979) *Analects*, trans. D. C. Lau (London/New York/Ringwood, NJ/Toronto/Auckland: Penguin).

Deleuze, Gilles and Guattari, Félix (1984) *Anti-Oedipus*, trans. Robert Hurley, Mark Seem, and Helen R. Lane (London: Athlone Press).

Deleuze, Gilles and Guattari, Félix (1988) *A Thousand Plateaus*, trans. Brian Massumi (London: Athlone Press).

Dobbins, James C. (1998) "Envisioning Kamakura Buddhism", in Payne (ed.) (1998): 24–42.

Dore, Ronald P. (1984) *Education in Tokugawa Japan* (London: Athlone Press).

Duke, Benjamin C. (ed.) (1989) *Ten Great Educators of Modern Japan: A Japanese Perspective* (Tokyo: University of Tokyo Press).

Eastern Buddhism Society (ed.) (1973) *Collected Writings on Shin Buddhism* (Kyoto: Shinshū Ōtaniha).

Egusa Mitsuko and Urushida Kazuyo (eds) (1992) *Readings by Women of Modern Japanese Literature: An Attempt at Feminist Critique* (*Onna ga yomu nihon kindai bungaku: Feminizumu hihyō no kokoromi*) (Tokyo: Shin'yōsha).

Field, Norma (1987) *The Splendor of Longing in the "Tale of Genji"* (Princeton, NJ: Princeton University Press).

Foard, James, Solomon, Michael and Payne, Richard K. (eds) (1996) *The Pure Land Tradition: History and Development*, Berkeley Buddhist Studies Series (Berkeley, Calif.: The Regents of the University of California).

Foucault, Michel (1978–86) *The History of Sexuality*, 3 vols (London/New York/Ringwood, NJ/Toronto/Auckland: Penguin).

Freud, Sigmund (1964) "The 'Uncanny'", in *The Standard Edition of the Complete Psychological Works of Sigmund Freud*, vol. XVII, pp. 217–52, trans. under the general editorship of James Strachey, in collaboration with Anna Freud, assisted by Alix Strachey and Alan Tyson (London: Hogarth Press).

Fujii Sadakazu (1974) "Yomogiu", *Kokubungaku: Kaishaku to kyōzai no kenkyū* (Tokyo: Gakutōsha), September: 68–70.

Fujii Sadakazu (1980) "The Method of the Safflower Chapter" ("Suetsumuhana maki no hōhō"), in Akiyama (ed.) (1980), 2: 132–48.

Fujii Sadakazu (1990) *The Origin and Present State of "The Tale of Genji"* (*Genji monogatari no shigen to genzai*) (Tokyo: Sunagoya shobō). The original version was published by San'ichi shobō (Tokyo) in 1972.

Fujimura Kiyoshi (1971) *The Structure of "The Tale of Genji"*, vol. 2 (*Genji monogatari no kōzō*: Dai 2) (Kyoto: Akao shōbundō).

Fujiwara Katsumi (1993) "*The Tale of Genji* and *Collected Works of Bai Juyi* (*Genji monogatari* to *Hakushi monjū*)", in Association for Japanese–Chinese Comparative Literature Studies (Wakan hikaku bungakukai) (ed.) (1993), 12: 103–19.

Fukunaga Mitsuji (ed.) (1977) *Saichō and Kūkai* (*Great Books of Japan* (*Nihon no meicho*), vol. 3) (Tokyo: Chūōkōronsha).

172 Bibliography

Fukuzawa Yukichi (1951–2) *Selected Works of Fukuzawa Yukichi* (*Fukuzawa Yukichi senshū*), 8 vols (Tokyo: Iwanami).

Fukuzawa Yukichi (1969) *An Encouragement of Learning*, trans. David A. Dilworth and Umeyo Hirano (Tokyo: Sophia University).

Fukuzawa Yukichi (1970) *Fukuzawa Yukichi's "An Outline of a Theory of Civilization"*, trans. David A. Dilworth and G. Cameron Hurst (Tokyo: Sophia University).

Fukuzawa Yukichi (1980) *An Encouragement of Learning* (*Gakumon no susume*), in Fukuzawa Yukichi (1980–1), vol. 3.

Fukuzawa Yukichi (1980–1) *Selected Works of Fukuzawa Yukichi* (*Fukuzawa Yukichi senshū*), 14 vols (Tokyo: Iwanami).

Fukuzawa Yukichi (1981a) *An Outline of a Theory of Civilization* (*Bunmeiron no gairyaku*), in Fukuzawa Yukichi (1980–1), vol. 4.

Fukuzawa Yukichi (1981b) *On the Nation's Right for the Common People's Understanding* (*Tsūzoku kokken ron*), in Fukuzawa Yukichi (1980–1), vol. 7.

Fukuzawa Yukichi (1981c) *Old Yukichi's Hundred-Odd Stories* (*Fukuō hyaku-yo wa*), in Fukuzawa Yukichi (1980–1), vol. 11.

Gatten, Aileen (1981a) "The Secluded Forest: Textual Problems in the *Tale of Genji*", dissertation submitted to the University of Michigan in 1977 (Ann Arbor, Mich.: UMI Dissertation Services).

Gatten, Aileen (1981b) "The Order of the Early Chapters in the *Genji monogatari*", *Harvard Journal of Asiatic Studies*, 41 (1): 5–46.

Gatten, Aileen (1986) "Weird Ladies: Narrative Strategy in the *Genji monogatari*", *The Journal of the Association of Teachers of Japanese*, 20 (1): 29–48.

Gellner, Ernest (1983) *Nations and Nationalism* (Ithaca, NY: Cornell University Press).

Genji monogatari tankyūkai (ed.) (1980) *Research into "The Tale of Genji"* (*Genji monogatari no tankyū*), vol. 5 (Tokyo: Kazama shobō).

Genshin (1930) "Genshin's Ojo Yoshu: Collected Essays on Birth Into Paradise", trans. A. K. Reischauer, *Transactions of the Asiatic Society of Japan*, 2nd series, 7: 16–97.

Genshin (1971) *A Complete Work of Eshin* (*Eshin sōzu zenshū*), ed. Eizan gakuin (Kyoto: Shibun kaku), vol. 2.

Genshin (1994) *Ōjōyōshū*, annotated by Ishida Mizumaro, 2 vols (Tokyo: Iwanami bunko).

Giddens, Anthony (1990) *The Consequences of Modernity* (Stanford, Calif.: Stanford University Press).

Giddens, Anthony (1991) *Modernity and Self-Identity: Self and Society in the Late Modern Age* (Stanford, Calif.: Stanford University Press).

Girard, René (1977) *Violence and the Sacred*, trans. Patrick Gregory (Baltimore, Md: Johns Hopkins University Press). The original French text was published in 1972.

Gough, J. W. (1957) *The Social Contract: A Critical Study of Its Development*, 2nd edn (Oxford: Clarendon Press).

Groner, Paul (1984) *Saicho: The Establishment of the Japanese Tendai School*, Berkeley Buddhist Studies Series (Seoul: Po Chin Chai).

Groner, Paul (1989) "The *Lotus Sutra* and Saichō's Interpretation of The Realization of Buddhahood with This Very Body", in Tanabe and Tanabe (eds) (1989): 53–74.

Groner, Paul (2002) *Ryōgen and Mount Hiei: Japanese Tendai in the Tenth Century* (Honolulu: University of Hawaii Press).

Bibliography 173

Hagiwara Hiromichi (1978) "Genji monogatari *hyōshaku*", in Nihon tosho sentā (1978), vol. 4.

Hakamaya Noriaki (1998) *Hōnen and Myōe* (*Hōnen to Myōe*) (Tokyo: Daizō shuppan).

Hall, John Whitney (ed.) (1991) *The Cambridge History of Japan*, vol. 4, *Early Modern Japan* (Cambridge/New York/Port Chester/Melbourne/Sydney: Cambridge University Press).

Halperin, David M. (1995) *Saint Foucault: Towards a Gay Hagiography* (New York/Oxford: Oxford University Press).

Hamada Keisuke (1993) *The Tokugawa Novel: Personal Views on Its Activity and Style* (*Kinsei shōsetsu: Eii to yōshiki ni kansuru shiken*) (Kyoto: Kyoto University Press).

Hanayama Shōyū (trans.) (1972) *Ōjōyōshū* (Tokyo: Tokuma shoten).

Hara Zen (1999) *Kawabata Yasunari, His Perspective* (*Kawabata Yasunari, sono enkinhō*) (Tokyo: Taishūkan).

Harimoto Shin'ichi (2004) "Bakin's Standpoint" ("Bakin no tachiba"), *Bungaku* (Iwanami), May–June: 53–70.

Harootunian, Harry D. (1974) "Between Politics and Culture", in Silberman and Harootunian (eds) (1974): 110–55.

Harré, Rom (1998) *The Singular Self: An Introduction to the Psychology of Personhood* (London/Thousand Oaks, Calif./New Delhi: Sage).

Hasegawa Izumi (1991) *Studies on Kawabata Yasunari* (*Kawabata Yasunari ronkō*), in *Selected Works of Hasegawa Izumi* (*Hasegawa Izumi chosaku sen*), vol. 5 (Tokyo: Meiji shoin).

Hasegawa Tadashi (1967) "The Early Stage of the *Heike monogatari*", *Monumenta Nipponica*, 22 (1–2): 65–81.

Hatori Tetsuya (1993) *The Development of the Writer, Kawabata* (*Sakka Kawabata no tenkai*) (Tokyo: Kyōiku shuppan sentā).

Hattori Kōzō (1983) "Woman's Rebirth in Paradise in the *Kakuichi* Text of *The Tale of the Heike*" ("*Kakuichi-bon 'Heike monogatari*' ni okeru nyonin ōjō"), *Kokugo kokubungaku* (The Association for Japanese Language (*Kokugo gakkai*), Fukui University), 23: 28–38.

Hayami Tasuku (1988) *Genshin* (*A Personal Life Series* (*Jinbutsu sōsho*)) (Tokyo: Yoshikawa kōbunkan).

Hayasaka Reigo (1971) "Hahakigi, Utsusemi, Yūgao", in Yamagishi and Oka (eds) (1971), 3: 27–46.

Hayashi Takeshi (1984) *Previous Studies on Kawabata Yasunari's Work* (*Kawabata Yasunari kenkyūshi*) (Tokyo: Kyōiku shuppan sentā).

Hegel, G. W. Friedrich (1900) *The Philosophy of History*, trans. J. Sibree (New York: Colonial Press).

Heinrich, Amy Vladeck (ed.) (1997) *Currents in Japanese Culture: Translations and Transformations* (New York: Columbia University Press).

Hinata Kazumasa (1998) "The Theme of the Three 'Broom Tree' Chapters" ("'Hahakigi' sanjō no shudai"), in Masuda, Suzuki and Ii (eds) (1998), 1: 47–87.

Hinata Kazumasa (2004) *The World of "The Tale of Genji"* (*Genji monogatari no sekai*) (Tokyo: Iwanami).

Hirabayashi Moritoku (1987) *Ryōgen* (*A Personal Life Series* (*Jinbutsu sōsho*)) (Tokyo: Yoshikawa kōbunkan).

Hirade Kōjirō (1990) *Revenge* (*Katakiuchi*) (Tokyo: Chūkō bunko).

Hirayama Yō (2004) *The Truth of Fukuzawa Yukichi* (*Fukuzawa Yukichi no shinjitsu*) (Tokyo: Bunshun shinsho).

174   Bibliography

Hirokawa Katsumi (1980) "A Lady in a Garden in Disrepair" ("Haien no himegimi"), in Akiyama (ed.) (1980), 4: 39–47.

Hirokawa Takatoshi (1998) "Introduction", in Senchakushū English Translation Project (trans.) (1998): 1–55.

Hobbes, Thomas (1996) *Leviathan*, ed. J. C. A. Gaskin (Oxford/New York: Oxford University Press).

Hobsbawm, Eric and Ranger, Terence (eds) (1983) *The Invention of Tradition* (Cambridge/New York/Melbourne/Madrid/Cape Town: Cambridge University Press).

Hōnen (1999) *Senchaku hongan nembutsu shū* (Tokyo: Iwanami bunko). English translation is Senchakushū English Translation Project (trans.) (1998).

Hutchinson, Racheal and Williams, Mark (eds) (2007) *Representing the Other in Modern Japanese Literature: A Critical Approach* (London/New York: Routledge).

Hyōdō Hiromi (1985) *Introduction to Katarimono* (*Katarimono josetsu*) (Tokyo: Yūseidō).

Hyōdō Hiromi (1989) *Kingship and Monogatari* (*Ōken to monogatari*) (Tokyo: Seikyūsha).

Hyōdō Hiromi (2000) *The History and Performing Arts of "The Tale of the Heike"* (*Heike monogatari no rekishi to geinō*) (Tokyo: Yoshikawa kōbunkan).

Ichiko Teiji (ed.) (1970) *A Survey of Various Views: "The Tale of the Heike"* (*Shosetsu ichiran: Heike monogatari*) (Tokyo: Meiji shoin).

Ida Shin'ya (2001) *History and Text: From Saikaku to Yukichi* (*Rekishi to tekusuto – Saikaku kara Yukichi made*) (Tokyo: Kōbōsha).

Ienaga Saburō (1997) "A History of Thought on the Establishment of Shinran's Religion" ("Shinran no shūkyō no seiritsu ni kansuru shisōshi kenkyū"), cited from Ienaga Saburō (1997–9), 2: 173–210. Original text published in 1947, and later collected in *A Study of the History of Medieval Buddhist Thought* (*Chūsei bukkyō shisōshi kenkyū*) (Kyoto: Hōzōkan, 1955).

Ienaga Saburō (1997–9) *Collected Works of Ienaga Saburō* (*Ienaga Saburō shū*), 16 vols (Tokyo: Iwanami).

Ienaga Saburō (1998) "Fukuzawa Yukichi's Class Consciousness" ("Fukuzawa Yukichi no kaikyū ishiki"), in Ienaga Saburō (1997–9), 4: 191–212.

Ienaga Saburō et al. (eds) (1966) *A Collection of Tokugawa Thinkers' Writings* (*Kinsei shisōka bunshū*) (Nihon koten bungaku taikei, vol. 97) (Tokyo: Iwanami).

Ikeda Kikan (1951) *New Lecture of "The Tale of Genji"* (*Shinkō Genji monogatari*) (Tokyo: Shibundō).

Ikeda Tsutomu (1974) *Essays on "The Tale of Genji"* (*Genji monogatari shiron*) (Tokyo: Furukawa shobō).

Imai Takuji et al. (eds) (1991) *People Who Weave Narratives: A "The Tale of Genji" Lecture Series* (*Monogatari o orinasu hitobito: Genji monogatari kōza*) (Tokyo: Benseisha).

Imai Takuji et al. (eds) (1992) *The Story of the Shining Prince: "The Tale of Genji" Lecture Series* (*Hikaru kimi no monogatari: Genji monogatari kōza*), vol. 3 (Tokyo: Benseisha).

Imamura Hitoshi (1982) *The Ontology of Violence* (*Bōryoku no ontorogī*) (Tokyo: Keisō shobō).

Imamura Hitoshi (1992) *The Structure of Exclusion* (*Haijo no kōzō*) (Tokyo: Chikuma gakugei bunko).

Imamura Junko (1988) *A Study of Kawabata Yasunari* (*Kawabata Yasunari kenkyū*) (Tokyo: Shinbisha).

Bibliography 175

Imanari Genshō (Motoaki) (1970) "*The Tale of the Heike* and Buddhism" ("*Heike monogatari* to bukkyō"), in Ichiko (ed.) (1970): 204–37.

Imanari Genshō (Motoaki) (1971) *A Study of the Dissemination and Transmission of "The Tale of the Heike"* (*Heike monogatari ruden kō*) (Tokyo: Kazama shobō).

Imanari Genshō (Motoaki) (ed.) (1996) *The Idea of Buddhist Literature* (*Bukkyō bungaku no kōsō*) (Tokyo: Shintensha).

Imanishi Yūichirō (1980) "An Old-Fashioned Person: Safflower" ("Kodai no hito: Suetsumuhana"), in Akiyama (ed.) (1980), 4: 48–60.

Inagaki Hisao (2000) *The Three Pure Land Sutras: A Study and Translation from Chinese*, in collaboration with Harold Stewart (Kyoto: Nagata bunshodo).

Inoue Mitsusada (1971) *The Ancient Japanese State and Buddhism* (*Nihon kodai no kokka to bukkyō*) (Tokyo: Iwanami).

Inoue Mitsusada (2001) *A Study of the History of Japanese Pure Land Teaching's Establishment: A Newly-Revised Version* (*Shintei: Nihon jōdokyō seiritsushi no kenkyū*) (Tokyo: Yamakawa shuppan).

Ishibashi Gishū et al. (eds) (1998) *The Context of Buddhist Literature* (*Bukkyō bungaku to sono shūhen*) (Osaka: Izumi shoin).

Ishida Ichirō (1960) *Itō Jinsai* (*A Personal Life Series* (*Jinbutsu sōsho*)) (Tokyo: Yoshikawa kōbunkan).

Ishida Mizumaro (1970) "The Significance of *Ōjōyōshū* in the History of Thought" ("'Ōjōyōshū' no shisōshi teki igi"), in Ishida Mizumaro (ed.) (1970): 427–95.

Ishida Mizumaro (1987) *Buddhism and Literature* (*Bukkyō to bungaku*) (*A Study of Japanese Buddhist Thought* (*Nihon bukkyō shisō kenkyū*), vol. 5) (Kyoto: Hōzōkan).

Ishida Mizumaro (ed.) (1970) *Genshin* (*Nihon shisō taikei*, vol. 6) (Tokyo: Iwanami).

Ishii Kyōdō (1959) *A Lecture on The Collection of Passages Concerning the Nembutsu of the Selected Original Vow* (*Senchaku shū zenkō*) (Kyoto: Heirakuji shoten).

Ishikawa Hidemi (1991a) "A Story in Kyoto" ("Miyako no monogatari"), *Wayō National Literature Study* (*Wayō kokubun kenkyū*), 26: 25–37.

Ishikawa Hidemi (1991b) "An Inversion of the Ending Plot" ("Dan'en kōsō no tenkai"), *Wayō Women's College Research Bulletin, Arts Section* (*Wayō Joshi daigaku kiyō, bunkei hen*), 31: 23–44.

Ishikawa Hidemi (1993) "The Light Source of the Order in the Eight States of Kantō – The Notes for the *Eight Dog Chronicles*" ("Kan-hasshū chitsujo no kōgen – *Nansō Satomi Hakkenden* nōto"), *Edo Literature* (*Edo bungaku*) (Pelican sha), 11: 29–45.

Ishikawa Tōru (1996) *A History of the Novel in the Ancient Period: Enlarged and Reprinted Version* (*Kodai shōsetsu shi kō: Zōho fukkoku ban*) (Tokyo: Parutosu sha).

Ishimoda Shō (1957) *The Formation of the Medieval World* (*Chūseiteki sekai no keisei*) (Tokyo: University of Tokyo Press).

Itō Jinsai (1966) *A Child's Inquiries* (*Dōjimon*), in Ienaga et al. (eds) (1966): 25–291.

Itō Jinsai (1970) *Itō Jinsai shū* (*Nihon no shisō*, vol. 11), ed. Kimura Eiichi (Tokyo: Chikuma shobō).

Iwano Shin'yū (ed.) (1979) *Kokuyaku issaikyō; Wakan senjutsu bu; Shoshū bu* (Tokyo: Daitō shuppansha), vol. 18.

Iwasaki Chikatsugu (1997) *An Introduction to the History of Edo Thought* (*Nihon kinsei shisōshi josetsu*) (Tokyo: Shin nihon shuppansha), 2 vols.

Iwashita Mitsuo (1967) *On "The Tale of Genji"* (*Genji monogatari ron*) (Ina, Nagano: Sakisha).

176 Bibliography

Jones, Tudor (2002) *Modern Political Thinkers and Ideas* (London/New York: Routledge).

Kaibara Ekiken (1979) *The Way of Contentment and Women and Wisdom of Japan [Greater Learning for Women]*, trans. Ken Hoshino and Shingoro Takaishi (Washington, DC: University Publications of America). Original text published in 1913.

Kaizuka Shigeki (ed.) (1983) *Itō Jinsai* (*Great Books of Japan* (*Nihon no meicho*), vol. 13) (Tokyo: Chūōkōronsha).

Kajihara Masaaki (ed.) (1998) *A Series of Studies of Literature of Warfare* (*Gunki bungaku kenkyū sōsho*), vol. 6 (Tokyo: Kyūko shoin).

Kajihara Masaaki and Yamashita Hiroaki (eds) (1991–3) *The Tale of the Heike, Iwanami New Compendium of Classical Literature* (*Iwanami Shin nihon koten bungaku taikei, Heike monogatari*), 2 vols (Tokyo: Iwanami).

Kaldor, Mary (2003) *Global Civil Society: An Answer to War* (Cambridge: Polity Press).

Kamata Shigeo and Tanaka Hisao (eds) (1971) *Kamakura Old Buddhism* (*Kamakura kyū bukkyō*) (*Nihon shisō taikei*, vol. 15) (Tokyo: Iwanami).

Kasahara Kazuo (1975) *The Genealogy of Women's Rebirth in Paradise in Japan* (*Nyonin ōjō shisō no keifu*) (Tokyo: Yoshikawa kōbunkan).

Katō Shuichi (1979) *A History of Japanese Literature* (Tokyo: Kodansha).

Katō Shūichi (1983) *A History of Japanese Literature*, vol. 3, trans. Don Sanderson (Tenterden: Paul Norbury). Original Japanese text published in 1980 by Chikuma shobō (Tokyo).

Katsuhara Haruki (1999) "Agony and Sadness in *Snow Country*" ("*Yukiguni*, sono kutsū to hiai"), in Tamura Mitsumasa, Baba and Hara (eds) (1999): 9–34.

Kauffman, Linda S. (ed.) (1993) *American Feminist Thought at Century's End: A Reader* (Cambridge, Mass./Oxford: Blackwell).

Kawabata Kaori, Komori Yōichi, Nakayama Masahiko, Ashida Takaaki and Hara Shirō (panellists); Toeda Hirokazu and Nakamura Akira (coordinators) (2000) "Symposium: On the Expression of Kawabata Yasunari's *Snow Country*" ("Shinpojiumu: Kawabata Yasunari *Yukiguni* no hyōgen o megutte"), *Studies in Stylistics* (*Buntairon kenkyū*) (Tokyo: Japan Society of Stylistics (Nihon buntairon gakkai)), 46: 82–129.

Kawabata Yasunari (1957) *Snow Country*, trans. Edward Seidensticker (Rutland, Vt/Tokyo: Charles E. Tuttle).

Kawabata Yasunari (1967) *Thousand Cranes*, trans. Edward Seidensticker (Rutland, Vt/Tokyo: Charles E. Tuttle).

Kawabata Yasunari (1971) *The Sound of the Mountain*, trans. Edward Seidensticker (Rutland, Vt/Tokyo: Charles E. Tuttle).

Kawabata Yasunari (1980–4) *The Complete Work of Kawabata Yasunari* (*Kawabata Yasunari zenshū*), 37 vols (Tokyo: Shinchōsha).

Kawabata Yasunari (1997) *The Dancing Girl of Izu and Other Stories*, trans. Martin J. Holman (Washington, DC: Counterpoint).

Kawasaki Toshihiko (1973) "Kawabata Yasunari *Snow Country*" ("Kawabata Yasunari 'Yukiguni'"), in Nihon bungaku kenkyū shiryō kankōkai (ed.) (1973): 185–97.

Kawasaki Tsuneyuki (1972) "The Life and Thought of Genshin" ("Genshin no shōgai to shisō"), in Kawasaki Tsuneyuki (ed.) (1972): 5–48.

Kawasaki Tsuneyuki (ed.) (1972) *Genshin* (*Great Books of Japan* (*Nihon no meicho*), vol. 4) (Tokyo: Chūōkōronsha).

Bibliography 177

Kayano Toshihito (2005) *What Is the State?* (*Kokka to wa nani ka*) (Tokyo: Ibunsha).

Kazamaki Keijirō (1951) "An Essay on the Formation of *The Tale of Genji*" ("*Genji monogatari* no seiritsu ni kansuru shiron"), *Kokugo kokubun* (Kyoto: Kyoto University), 20 (4): 1–18.

Keene Donald (1955) *Anthology of Japanese Literature* (London: Allen & Unwin).

Keene, Donald (trans.) (1961) *Major Plays of Chikamatsu* (New York: Columbia University Press).

Keene, Donald (1976) *World within Walls: Japanese Literature of the Pre-Modern Era* (Rutland, Vt/Tokyo: Charles E. Tuttle).

Keene, Donald (1984) *Dawn to the West: Japanese Literature of the Modern Era*, 2 vols (New York: Holt, Rinehart & Winston).

Keene, Donald (1993) *Seeds in the Heart: Japanese Literature from Earliest Times to the Late Sixteenth Century* (New York: Henry Holt).

Kimura Hiroshi and Mio Hiroko (eds) (1988) *New Horizon of Culture and Civilisation: Series of Studies of International Relations* (*Bunka, bunmei no atarashiki chihei – Kokusai kankei gaku sōsho*) (Tokyo: Hokuju shuppan).

Kimura Ki (1982) *A Survey of Meiji Literature* (*Meiji bungaku tenbō*) (Tokyo: Kōbunsha).

Kinmonth, Earl H. (1978) "Fukuzawa Reconsidered: *Gakumon no Susume* and Its Audience", *Journal of Asian Studies*, 37 (4): 677–96.

Kinoshita Naoe (1972) "Fukuzawa Yukichi and Kitamura Tōkoku" ("Fukuzawa Yukichi to Kitamura Tōkoku"), in Nihon bungaku kenkyū shiryō kankōkai (ed.) (1972): 283–5.

Kitagawa Hiroshi and Tsuchida, Bruce T. (trans.) (1975) *The Tale of the Heike* (Tokyo: University of Tokyo Press).

Kitahara Yasuo and Ogawa Eiichi (eds) (1990) *The Engyō Text of The Tale of the Heike: Main Text* (*Engyō-bon Heike monogatari: Honmon hen*), 2 vols (Tokyo: Bensei shuppan).

Kitamura Tōkoku (1950–5) *A Complete Work of Tōkoku* (*Tōkoku zenshū*), ed. Katsumoto Seiichirō, 3 vols (Tokyo: Iwanami).

Kobayashi Hiroko (1992) "Kawabata Yasunari's Longing for 'Quasi-Motherhood'" ("Kawabata Yasunari no 'giji bosei' shibo"), *Shin nihon bungaku*, 47 (1): 28–37.

Kobayashi Hiroko (1999) "On *The Sound of the Mountain*: Shingo's Misconception and the Narrator's Insensibility" ("*Yama no oto* – Shingo no sakkaku to katarite no henken"), in Tamura Mitsumasa, Baba and Hara (eds) (1999): 203–27.

Kobayashi Yoshikazu (1986) *The Generative Process of "The Tale of the Heike"* (*Heike monogatari seisei ron*) (Tokyo: Miyai shoten).

Kobayashi Yoshikazu (1991) "Changes of War Narration" ("Ikusa gatari no hen'yō"), in Mizuhara (ed.) (1991): 64–78.

Kobayashi Yoshikazu (2000) *Producing "The Tale of the Heike"* (*Heike monogatari no seiritsu*) (Osaka: Izumi shoin).

Koizumi Shinzō (1951) "Kaidai" ("Bibliographical Notes"), in Fukuzawa (1951–2), vol. 1.

Komashaku Kimi (1989) "*The Dancing Girl of Izu*: The Structure of Contact" ("*Izu no odoriko* – Fureai no kōzō –"), *Espace des femmes* (*Josei kūkan*), 6: 3–12.

Konishi Jin'ichi (1991) *A History of Japanese Literature*, vol. 3 (Princeton, NJ: Princeton University Press).

Konishi Jin'ichi (1992) *A History of Japanese Literature* (*Nihon bungei shi*), vol. 5 (Tokyo: Kodansha) (Japanese version).

178 Bibliography

Kornicki, Peter F. (1981) "The Survival of Tokugawa Fiction in the Meiji Period", *Harvard Journal of Asiatic Studies*, 41 (2): 461–82.

Kornicki, Peter F. (1982) *The Reform of Fiction in Meiji Japan* (London: Ithaca Press).

Koyano Atsushi (1990) *Fantastic Ideas in "The Eight Dog Chronicles" (Hakkenden kisō)* (Tokyo: Fukutake).

Koyasu Nobukuni (1982) *Itō Jinsai* (Tokyo: University of Tokyo Press).

Koyasu Nobukuni (2004) *The World of Itō Jinsai (Itō Jinsai no sekai)* (Tokyo: Perikan sha).

Kukathas, Chandran and Pettit, Phillip (1990) *Rawls: A Theory of Justice and Its Critics* (Cambridge: Polity Press).

Kuroda Toshio (1975) *The Development of the Kenmitsu System in the Medieval Period (Chūsei ni okeru kenmitsu taisei no hatten)* (Tokyo: Iwanami). Later collected in his *Collected Works of Kuroda Toshio (Kuroda Toshio chosakushū)*, vol. 2 (Kyoto: Hōzōkan, 1994). The partial English translation was published in 1996 in *Japanese Journal of Religious Studies*, 23 (3–4): 233–69, 353–86, trans. James C. Dobbins and Fabio Rambelli, entitled "The Development of the Kenmitsu System as Japan's Medieval Orthodoxy" and "The Discourse on the 'Land of Kami' (Shinkoku) in Medieval Japan: National Consciousness and International Awareness".

Kyokutei Bakin (1990) *The Eight Dog Chronicles (Nansō Satomi hakkenden)*, ed. Koike Tōgorō (Tokyo: Iwanami bunko).

Kyokutei Bakin (1995–) *A Collection of Bakin's Middle-Length Yomihon (Bakin chūhen yomihon shūsei)*, vols 1– (Tokyo: Kyūko shoin).

Lee Sun-Young (I Son'yon) (1994) "The Creation of Women's Figures in *The Tale of the Heike* and 'Shame': With Special Emphasis on Giō" ("*Heike monogatari* no nyonin zōkei to 'haji' – Giō o chūshin ni –"), *Tsukuba University Heike Section Collected Papers (Tsukuba daigaku Heike bukai ronshū)*, 4: 15–28.

Lee Sun-Young (I Son'yon) (2002) "Kogō Story" ("Kogō monogatari"), *Tsukuba University Heike Section Collected Papers (Tsukuba daigaku Heike bukai ronshū)*, 9: 37–48.

Locke, John (1967) *Two Treatises of Government* (London/New York: Cambridge University Press).

McCullough, Helen Craig (trans.) (1968) *Tales of Ise* (Stanford, Calif.: Stanford University Press).

McCullough, Helen Craig (trans.) (1988) *The Tale of the Heike* (Stanford, Calif.: Stanford University Press).

Macfarlane, Alan (2002) *The Making of the Modern World: Visions from the West and East* (Basingstoke/New York: Palgrave Macmillan).

McGreal, Ian P. (ed.) (1996) *Great Literature of the Eastern World* (New York: HarperCollins).

McGuigan, Jim (1999) *Modernity and Postmodern Culture* (Buckingham/Philadelphia, Pa: Open University Press).

Machida Sōhō (1998) *Hōnen versus Myōe (Hōnen tai Myōe)* (Tokyo: Kōdansha).

McMullin, Neil (1989) "The *Lotus Sutra* and Politics in the Mid-Heian Period", in Tanabe and Tanabe (ed.) (1989): 119–41.

Maeda Ai (Yoshimi) (1989) "The World of *The Eight Dog Chronicles*" ("*Hakkenden* no sekai"), in *Collected Works of Maeda Ai (Yoshimi) (Maeda Ai chosakushū)* (Tokyo: Chikuma), 1: 66–91. Original article was published in *Literature (Bungaku)* (December 1969).

Bibliography 179

Makibayashi Kōji (2000) *A Study of Kitamura Tōkoku* (*Kitamura Tōkoku kenkyū*) (*Collected Works of Makibayashi Kōji* (*Makibayashi Kōji chosaku shū*), vol. 1) (Osaka: Izumi shoin).

Makibayashi Kōji (2001) *The Development of Early Meiji Literature* (*Meiji shoki bungaku no tenkai*) (*Collected Works of Makibayashi Kōji* (*Makibayashi Kōji chosaku shū*), vol. 2) (Osaka: Izumi shoin).

Makino Kazuo (1993) "The War Tale and the Circumstances of 'Learning' in the Temple: Taking the *Engyō* Text of *The Tale of the Heike* and Others as Examples" ("Gunki monogatari to jiin no 'gakumon' shūhen – Engyō-bon '*Heike monogatari*' nado o rei ni –"), in Association for Japanese–Chinese Comparative Literature Studies (Wakan hikaku bungakukai) (ed.) (1993), 15: 81–105.

Marks, Elaine and Courtivron, Isabelle de (eds) (1980) *New French Feminism: An Anthology* (New York: Schocken Books).

Marra, Michele (1988a) "The Development of Mappō Thought in Japan (I)", *Japanese Journal of Religious Studies*, 15 (1): 25–54.

Marra, Michele (1988b) "The Development of Mappō Thought in Japan (II)", *Japanese Journal of Religious Studies*, 15 (4): 287–305.

Maruyama Masao (2001) *Philosophy of Fukuzawa Yukichi, and Other Six Essays* (*Fukuzawa Yukichi no tetsugaku, ta roku hen*), ed. Matsuzawa Hiroaki (Tokyo: Iwanami bunko).

Marx, Karl (1976) *Capital*, 3 vols (London/New York/Victoria/Toronto/Auckland: Penguin).

Marx, Karl (1989) *Critique of the Gotha Programme*, in Karl Marx and Frederick Engels, *Collected Works*, vol. 24 (London: Lawrence & Wishart).

Masuda Katsumi (1954) "Minor Characters in *The Tale of Genji*" ("*Genji monogatari* no hayaku tachi"), *Bungaku* (Tokyo: Iwanami), 22 (2): 15–21.

Masuda Shigeo (1980a) "A Woman of Determined Position: Utsusemi" ("Shina sadamareru hito, Utsusemi"), in Akiyama (ed.) (1980), 1: 172–84.

Masuda Shigeo (1980b) "Utsusemi and Yūgao: The One Who Knows Well How to Deal with One's Circumstances Best and the One Who Does Not" ("Utsusemi to Yūgao – Shosei no kashikosa to tsutanasa"), in Genji monogatari tankyūkai (ed.) (1980): 1–22.

Masuda Shigeo (1992) "The Emperor Kiritsubo's Court" ("Kiritsubotei no kōkyū"), in Imai Takuji et al. (eds) (1992): 9–20.

Masuda Shigeo, Suzuki Hideo and Ii Haruki (eds) (1998) *A Collection of Studies of "The Tale of Genji"* (*Genji monogatari kenkyū shūsei*) (Tokyo: Kazama shobō).

Matsuda Osamu (1975) *Utopia in the Dark* (*Yami no yūtopia*) (Tokyo: Shinchōsha).

Matsuda Osamu (2002) *Collection of Matsuda Osamu's Writings* (*Matsuda Osamu chosakushū*) (Tokyo: Yūbun shoin).

Matsui Kenji and Ueta Yasuyo (eds) (1998–9) *"The Tale of Genji": Collection of Research Papers on Japanese Literature* (*Genji monogatari: Nihon bungaku kenkyū ronbun shūsei*), 2 vols (Tokyo: Wakakusa shobō).

Matsumoto Shirō (1990) "A Personal View on the *Lotus Sutra* and Japanese Culture" ("*Hokekyō* to nihon bunka ni kansuru shiken"), *Journal of Buddhist Studies* (*Komazawa daigaku bukkyō gakubu ronshū*), 21: 216–35.

Matsuo Ashie (1985) *Studies of "The Tale of the Heike"* (*Heike monogatari ronkyū*) (Tokyo: Meiji shoin).

Matsuo Ashie (1996) *Studies of Tale of Warfare* (*Gunki monogatari ronkyū*) (Tokyo: Wakakusa shobō).

180   Bibliography

Matsuo Ashie (1998) "From Two Versions of *The Tale of the Heike*" ("Futatsu no *Heike monogatari* kara"), in Kajihara (ed.) (1998): 74–93.

Mencius (1970) *Mencius*, trans. D. C. Lau (London/New York/Ringwood, NJ/Toronto/Auckland: Penguin).

Miller, Stephen D. (1996) "*The Tale of the Heike*", in McGreal (ed.) (1996): 313–17.

Miner, Earl, Odagiri Hiroko and Morrell, Robert E. (1985) *The Princeton Companion to Classical Japanese Literature* (Princeton, NJ: Princeton University Press).

Misumi Yōichi (1996) "*The Tale of Genji*" and *Tendai Jōdo Teaching* (*Genji monogatari to Tendai jōdo kyō*) (Tokyo: Wakakusa shobō).

Mitani Kuniaki (1980) "The Story of Gen-no-naishi-no-suke" ("Gen-no-naishi-no-suke no monogatari"), in Akiyama (ed.) (1980), 2: 212–32.

Mitani Kuniaki and Higashihara Nobuaki (eds) (1991) "*The Tale of Genji*": *Narrative and Expression* (*Genji monogatari: Katari to hyōgen*) (*Nihon bungaku kenkyū shiryō shinshū*, vol. 5) (Tokyo: Yūseidō).

Mito Takamichi, Ho Chi Ming and Miyazoe-Wong Yuko (2008) *Japanese Studies in the Asia-Pacific Region* (Hong Kong: Society of Japanese Language Education (Hong Kong)).

Miyazoe-Wong Yuko (ed.) (2003) *Japanese Language Education and Japanese Studies in Asia-Pacific: Current Trends and Future Directions* (Hong Kong: Society of Japanese Language Education (Hong Kong) and Himawari Publishing Company).

Mizuhara Hajime (1970) "The Theme and Structure of *The Tale of the Heike*" ("*Heike monogatari* no shudai to kōsei"), in Ichiko (ed.) (1970): 1–37.

Mizuhara Hajime (1971) *The Formation of "The Tale of the Heike"* (*Heike monogatari no keisei*) (Tokyo: Katō chūdōkan).

Mizuhara Hajime (1979) *A Study of the Engyō Text of "The Tale of the Heike"* (*Engyō-bon Heike monogatari ronkō*) (Tokyo: Katō chūdōkan).

Mizuhara Hajime (1995) *Searching for Representations in Old Medieval Literature* (*Chūsei kobungaku zō no tankyū*) (Tokyo: Shintensha).

Mizuhara Hajime (ed.) (1991) *The Old Strata of Oral Tradition* (*Denshō no kosō*) (Tokyo: Ōfūsha).

Mizuhara Hajime (ed.) (1992–7) *An Investigation of the Engyō Text of "The Tale of the Heike"* (*Engyō-bon Heike monogatari kōshō*), 4 vols (Tokyo: Shintensha).

Mizuhara Hajime (ed.) (1994) "*The Tale of the Heike*": *Setsuwa and Narrative* (*Heike monogatari: Setsuwa to katari*), in "*The Tale of the Heike*" for Readers (*Anata ga yomu Heike monogatari*), vol. 2 (Tokyo: Yūseidō).

Mizuhara Hajime (ed.) (1996) *The Catchment Area of Classical Literature* (*Kobungaku no ryūiki*) (Tokyo: Shintensha).

Mo Tzu (1929) *The Ethical and Political Works of Motse*, trans. Yi-Pao Mei (London: Arthur Probsthain).

Mo Tzu (1963) *Mo Tzu: Basic Writings*, trans. Burton Watson (New York/London: Columbia University Press).

Mori Ichirō (1965) "The Relationship between the Method of Character Creation and the Theme in *The Tale of Genji*" ("*Genji monogatari* ni okeru jinbutsu zōkei no hōhō to shudai to no renkan"), *Kokugo kokubun* (Kyoto: Kyoto University) (April): 1–17.

Morimoto Osamu (1990) *The Wandering Orphan* (*Koji hyōhaku*) (Ōmiya: Rindōsha).

Mulvey, Laura (1999) "Visual Pleasure and Narrative Cinema", in Sue Thornham (ed.), *Feminist Film Theory: A Reader* (Edinburgh: Edinburgh University Press), pp. 58–69.

Murai Shōsuke (1995) "Ninth Century Changes to Notions of Kingdom and Subjects of the King" ("Ōdo ōmin shisō to kyūseiki no tenkan"), *Shisō* (Tokyo: Iwanami), 847: 23–45.

Murai Toshihiko (1968) "The Inductive Character of the Three Broom Tree Chapters (Part 1)" ("Hahakigi sanjō kashō ron (jō)"), *Bungei to hihyō* (Tokyo: Bungei to hihyō dōjin), 2 (9): 12–23. This article also later appeared in Nihon bungaku kenkyū shiryō kankōkai (ed.) (1969–1982), 4: 73–86.

Murakami Fuminobu (1991) "Tōkoku-Aizan Ronsō", *The American Asian Review*, 9 (4): 76–92.

Murakami Fuminobu (1996) *Ideology and Narrative in Modern Japanese Literature* (Assen: Van Gorcum).

Murakami Fuminobu (1998) "Using Epistemic Modal Suffixes and Sensation/Emotion Adjectives to Determine Narrative Distance in *The Tale of Genji*", *The Journal of the Association of Teachers of Japanese* (Boulder, Colo.: University of Colorado), 32 (2): 1–26.

Murakami Fuminobu (2002) "Murakami Haruki's postmodern world", *Japan Forum*, 14 (1): 127–41.

Murakami Fuminobu (2005) *Postmodern, Feminist and Postcolonial Currents in Contemporary Japanese Culture: A Reading of Murakami Haruki, Yoshimoto Banana, Yoshimoto Takaaki and Karatani Kōjin* (London/New York: Routledge).

Murakami Fuminobu (2009) "Person, Honorifics and Tense in *The Tale of Genji*", in Richard Stanley-Baker, Jeremy Tambling and Murakami Fuminobu (eds), *Reading "The Tale of Genji"* (Folkeston: Global Oriental).

Murakami Manabu (1998) "Revision of 'Hōnen's Buddhist Teaching': With Special Emphasis on the Watanabe Study" ("'Hōnen-gi' kaiko – Watanabe-shi no ronkō o chūshin ni shite –"), in Ishibashi et al. (eds) (1998): 245–61.

Murasaki Shikibu (1957–68) *The Tale of Genji, Iwanami Compendium of Classical Japanese Literature* (*Iwanami nihon koten bungaku taikei, Genji monogatari*), ed. Yamagishi Tokuhei (Tokyo: Iwanami).

Murasaki Shikibu (1970–6) *The Tale of Genji, Shōgakukan Compendium of Classical Japanese Literature* (*Shōgakukan nihon koten bungaku zenshū, Genji monogatari*), ed. Abe Akio et al. (Tokyo: Shōgakukan).

Murasaki Shikibu (1981) *The Tale of Genji*, trans. Edward Seidensticker (Harmondsworth/New York/Ringwood, NJ/Ontario/Auckland: Penguin).

Murasaki Shikibu (1993–7) *The Tale of Genji, Iwanami New Compendium of Classical Literature* (*Iwanami shin nihon koten bungaku taikei, Genji monogatari*), ed. Yanai Shigeshi et al. (Tokyo: Iwanami).

Murasaki Shikibu (1994–8) *The Tale of Genji, The New Shōgakukan Compendium of Classical Japanese Literature* (*Shinpen Shōgakukan nihon koten bungaku zenshū, Genji monogatari*), ed. Abe Akio et al. (Tokyo: Shōgakukan).

Murasaki Shikibu (2001) *The Tale of Genji*, trans. Royall Tyler (New York/London/Ringwood, NJ/Toronto/Auckland: Viking).

Murofushi Shinsuke (1980) "Method in the Story of Utsusemi" ("Utsusemi monogatari no hōhō"), in Akiyama (ed.) (1980), 1: 154–71.

Myōe (1971) *Zaijarin*, in Kamata and Tanaka (eds) (1971): 43–105, 317–90. An abridged modern Japanese translated version of *Zaijarin* is in Tsukamoto (ed.) and Satō (trans.) (1971): 387–454.

Nagai Kafū (1963) *Geisha in Rivalry*, trans. Kurt Meissner with the collaboration of Ralph Friedrich (Tokyo/Rutland, Vt/Singapore: Charles E. Tuttle).

182 Bibliography

Nagai Kafū (1965) "A Strange Tale from East of the River", trans. Edward Seidensticker, in Seidensticker (1965): 278–328.

Nagai Kafū (1992) *The Complete Work of Nagai Kafū* (*Nagai Kafū zenshū*) (Tokyo: Iwanami).

Najita, Tetsuo (1987) *Visions of Virtue in Tokugawa Japan: The Kaitokudō Merchant Academy of Osaka* (Chicago. Ill./London: University of Chicago Press).

Najita, Tetsuo (1998) *Tokugawa Political Writings* (Cambridge/New York: Cambridge University Press).

Nakamura Hajime, Fukunaga Mitsuji, Tamura Yoshirō and Konno Tōru (eds) (1989) *Iwanami Dictionary of Buddhism* (*Iwanami Bukkyō Jiten*) (Tokyo: Iwanami).

Nakamura Hajime, Hayashima Kyōshō and Kino Kazuyoshi (eds) (1963–4) *The Three Pure Land Sutras* (*Jōdo sanbu kyō*), 2 vols (Tokyo: Iwanami bunko).

Nakayama Masahiko (1984) "Literature as Salvation" ("Kyūsai to shite no bungaku"), *Gendai bungaku* (Yokohama: Gendai bungaku henshū iinkai) (June): 32–64.

Nihon bungaku kenkyū shiryō kankōkai (ed.) (1969–82) *The Tale of Genji I–IV* (*Genji monogatari I–IV*) (Nihon bungaku kenkyū shiryō sōsho) (Tokyo: Yūseidō).

Nihon bungaku kenkyū shiryō kankōkai (ed.) (1972) *Kitamura Tōkoku* (Nihon bungaku kenkyū shiryō sōsho) (Tokyo: Yūseidō).

Nihon bungaku kenkyū shiryō kankōkai (ed.) (1973) *Kawabata Yasunari* (Nihon bungaku kenkyū shiryō sōsho) (Tokyo: Yūseidō).

Nihon tosho sentā (ed.) (1978) *Genji monogatari kochūshaku taisei* (Tokyo: Nihon tosho sentā).

Nishi Junzō et al. (eds) (1980) *The Yamazaki Ansai School* (*Yamazaki Ansai gakuha*) (Nihon shisō taikei, vol. 31) (Tokyo: Iwanami).

Nomura Seiichi (1969) *The Creation of "The Tale of Genji"* (*Genji monogatari no sōzō*) (Tokyo: Ōfūsha).

Nozick, Robert (1974) *Anarchy, State, and Utopia* (Oxford: Blackwell).

Ochi Haruo (1984) *A Study of the Formational Period of Modern Literature* (*Kindai bungaku seiritsuki no kenkyū*) (Tokyo: Iwanami).

Ōchō monogatari kenkyū kai (ed.) (1996) *Research Lecture Series: A View of "The Tale of Genji"*, vol. 3, *Hikaru Genji and Ladies* (*Kenkyū kōza: Genji monogatari no shikai, 3: Hikaru Genji to onnagimi tachi*) (Tokyo: Shinten sha).

Odagiri Hideo (1974) *A Survey of Japanese Tokugawa Literature* (*Nihon kinsei bungaku no tenbō*), in *Selected Works of Odagiri Hideo* (*Odagiri Hideo chosakushū*), vol. 5 (Tokyo: Hōsei daigaku shuppankyoku). Originally published in 1967 by Ochanomizu shobō.

Ogino Anna (1991) "The Dancing Girl in the Snow Country" ("Yukiguni no odoriko"), *Kaien* (Tokyo: Fukutake shoten) (March): 108–25.

Oguma Eiji (2006) *A Nation Called Japan* (*Nihon to iu kuni*) (Tokyo: Rironsha).

Ōhashi Shunnō (ed.) (1971) *Hōnen/Ippen* (*Nihon shisō taikei*, vol. 10) (Tokyo: Iwanami).

Ōjōyōshū kenkyū kai (ed.) (1987) *Studies on the "Ōjōyōshū"* (*Ōjōyōshū kenkyū*) (Kyoto: Nagata bunshōdō).

Okada, Richard H. (1991) *Figures of Resistance: Language, Poetry and Narrating in "The Tale of Genji" and Other Mid-Heian Texts* (Durham, NC/London: Duke University Press).

Ōkubo Ryōjun (1990) *Determining the Essentials of the One Vehicle* (*Ichijō yōketsu*) (A Course of Buddhist Scriptures (Butten kōza), vol. 33) (Tokyo: Daizō shuppan).

Bibliography 183

Onkaku (1972) "A Record of the Doctrinal Debate of the Ōwa Era" ("Ōwa shūron ki"), in Suzuki gakujutsu dan (ed.) (1972): 1–4.

Ooms, Herman (1998) *Tokugawa Ideology: Early Constructs, 1570–1680* (Ann Arbor, Mich.: Center for Japanese Studies, The University of Michigan).

Orikuchi Shinobu (1985) "Literature in the Yamato Period" ("Yamato jidai no bungaku"), in *The Complete Work of Orikuchi Shinobu* (*Orikuchi Shinobu zenshū*), vol. 8 (Tokyo: Chūōkōronsha).

Ōsumi Kazuo (1968) "Value System Changes in the Late Ancient Era" ("Kodai makki ni okeru kachikan no hendō"), *Bulletin of the Faculty of Arts, Hokkaido University* (*Hokkaido daigaku bungakubu kiyō*), 16 (1): 55–94.

Ōtsu Yūichi (2005) *Ideology of Tales of Warfare and Kingship* (*Gunki to ōken no ideogogī*) (Tokyo: Kanrin shobō).

Oyler, Elizabeth (2006) *Swords, Oaths, and Prophetic Visions: Authoring Warrior Rule in Medieval Japan* (Honolulu: University of Hawaii Press).

Payne, Richard K. (ed.) (1998) *Re-visioning "Kamakura" Buddhism* (Honolulu: University of Hawaii Press).

Plutschow, Herbert (1990) *Chaos and Cosmos: Ritual in Early and Medieval Japanese Literature* (Leiden/New York/Copenhagen/Cologne: E. J. Brill).

Plutschow, Herbert (1997) "The Placatory Nature of *The Tale of the Heike*: Additional Documents and Thoughts", in Heinrich (ed.) (1997): 71–80.

Rawls, John (1973) *A Theory of Justice* (Oxford: Oxford University Press).

Rawls, John (1993) *Political Liberalism* (New York: Columbia University Press).

Reiter, Rayna R. (ed.) (1975) *Toward an Anthropology of Women* (New York/London: Monthly Review Press).

Rhodes, Robert Franklin (1992) "Genshin and the *Ichijō yōketsu*: A Treatise on Universal Buddhahood in Heian Japan", PhD thesis presented to the Department of East Asia Languages and Civilizations, Harvard University (Ann Arbor, Mich.: UMI Dissertation Services).

Rodd, Laurel Rasplica with Henkenius, Mary Catherine (trans.) (1984) *Kokinshū: A Collection of Poems Ancient and Modern* (Princeton, NJ: Princeton University Press).

Rousseau, Jean-Jacques (1992) *Discourse on the Origin of Inequality*, in *The Collected Writings of Rousseau*, vol. 3, ed. Roger D. Masters and Christopher Kelly, trans. Judith R. Bush, Roger D. Masters, Christopher Kelly and Terence Marshall (Hanover, NH: University Press of New England).

Rousseau, Jean-Jacques (1994) *Social Contract*, in *The Collected Writings of Rousseau*, vol. 4, ed. Roger D. Masters and Christopher Kelly, trans. Judith R. Bush, Roger D. Masters and Christopher Kelly (Hanover, NH: University Press of New England).

Rubin, Gayle (1975) "The Traffic in Women: Notes on the 'Political Economy' of Sex", in Reiter (ed.) (1975): 157–210.

Rubin, Gayle (1984) "Thinking Sex: Notes for a Radical Theory of the Politics of Sexuality", in Vance (ed.) (1984): 267–319. This paper was later reprinted in Kauffman (ed.) (1993): 3–64, and in Abelove, Barale and Haplerin (eds) (1993): 3–44.

Saegusa Kazuko (1991) *The Trap of the Love Story* (*Ren'ai shōsetsu no kansei*) (Tokyo: Seidosha).

Saeki Shin'ich (1992–7) "The 'Incest' Story and *Hōbutsushū*" ("Chikushōdō gatari to '*Hōbutsushū*'"), in Mizuhara (ed.) (1992–7), 3: 140–56.

184   Bibliography

Saeki Shin'ichi (1996a) "Nyoin's Three Narratives" ("Nyoin no mittsu no katari"), in Mizuhara Hajime (ed.) (1996): 108–31.

Saeki Shin'ichi (1996b) *Visiting the Origin of "The Tale of the Heike"* (*Heike monogatari sogen*) (Tokyo: Wakakusa shobō).

Saeki Shin'ichi and Koakimoto Dan (eds) (1999), "The Tale of the Heike/Record of Great Peace" ("Heike monogatari/Taiheiki"), in *A Collection of Papers of Japanese Literature Studies* (*Nihon bungaku kenkyū ronbun shūsei*), vol. 14 (Tokyo: Wakakusa shobō).

Saichō (1974) *Saichō* (*Nihon shisō taikei*, vol. 4), ed. Andō Toshio and Sonoda Kōyū (Tokyo: Iwanami).

Saichō (1975) *The Complete Work of Saichō* (*Dengyō daishi zenshū*). 1 vol (Tokyo: Sekai seiten kankō kyōkai and Nihon bussho kankō kai).

Sakata Chizuko (1992) "*The Sound of the Mountain*: A Symphony of Discrepancy" ("*Yama no oto* – Zure no kōkyō"), in Egusa and Urushida (eds) (1992): 181–206.

Sarra, Edith (1999) *Fictions of Femininity: Literary Inventions of Gender in Japanese Court Women's Memoirs* (Stanford, Calif.: Stanford University Press).

Satō Hiroo (1987) *The Nation and Buddhism in the Medieval Japan* (*Nihon chūsei no kokka to bukkyō*) (Tokyo: Yoshikawa kōbunkan).

Satō Miyuki (1988) "Memoranda for *The Eight Dog Chronicles*" ("*Nansō Satomi hakkenden oboegaki*"), in Kimura and Mio (eds) (1988), 3: 90–107.

Sedgwick, Eve Kosofsky (1991) *Epistemology of the Closet* (Hemel Hempstead: Harvester Wheatsheaf).

Seidensticker, Edward (1965) *Kafū the Scribbler* (Stanford, Calif.: Stanford University Press).

Sekiguchi Tadao (1996) "Memoranda for the Introductory Chapter of *The Tale of the Heike*: With Special Emphasis on the Notion of Impermanence Therein" ("*Heike monogatari joshō oboegaki* – Shu to shite sono mujōkan o megutte –"), in Imanari (ed.) (1996): 338–66.

Sekiguchi Tadao (1998) "*The Tale of the Heike* in the History of Japanese Literary Criticism" ("Nihon bungaku hihyōshi no naka no *Heike monogatari*"), in Yamashita (ed.) (1998): 3–24.

Senchakushū English Translation Project (trans.) (1998) *Hōnen's Senchakushū: Passages on the Selection of the Nembutsu in the Original Vow (Senchaku hongan nembutsu shū)* (Honolulu/Tokyo: University of Hawaii Press/Sōgō Bukkyō Kenkyūjo, Taishō University, A Kuroda Institute Book).

Shibundō (ed.) (1986) *How to Read "The Tale of Genji": A Special Issue of National Literature: Interpretation and Appreciation* (*Genji monogatari o dō yomuka: Kokubungaku kaishaku to kanshō bessatsu*) (Tokyo: Shibundō).

Shigematsu Akihisa (1996) "An Overview of Early Japanese Pure Land", trans. Michael Solomon, in Foard, Solomon and Payne (eds) (1996): 267–312.

Shimaji Taitō (Daitō) (1986) *A History of Tendai Teaching* (*Tendai kyōgaku shi*) (Tokyo: Ryūbunkan).

Shinoda Jun'ichi (2004) *Bakin's Big Dream: The World of the "Eight Dog Chronicles"* (*Bakin no taimu: Satomi hakkenn den no sekai*) (Tokyo: Iwanami).

Shioiri Ryōchū (1937) *Dengyō daishi* (Tokyo: Dengyō daishi hōsan kai and Nihon hyōron sha).

Shioiri Ryōchū (1986) "The Debate with Tokuitsu" ("Tokuitsu to no ronsō"), in Tamura Kōyū (ed.) (1986): 170–92.

Shirane, Haruo (1987) *The Bridge of Dreams* (Stanford, Calif.: Stanford University Press).

Bibliography 185

Shirane, Haruo (ed.) (2002) *Early Modern Japanese Literature: An Anthology, 1600–1900* (New York: Columbia University Press).

Shirane, Haruo and Suzuki, Tomi (eds) (2000) *Inventing the Classics: Modernity, National Identity, and Japanese Literature* (Stanford, Calif.: Stanford University Press).

Shirato Waka (1987) "The *Ōjōyōshū* and Japanese Literature: Focusing on Heian Literature", in Ōjōyōshū kenkyū kai (ed.) (1987): 669–706.

Silberman, Bernard S. and Harootunian, Harry D. (eds) (1974) *Japan in Crisis* (Princeton, NJ: Princeton University Press).

Smith, Anthony D. (1986) *The Ethnic Origins of Nations* (Oxford/New York: Blackwell).

Snyder, Stephen (2000) *Fictions of Desire: Narrative Form in the Novels of Nagai Kafū* (Honolulu: University of Hawaii Press).

Sonoda Kōyū (1974) "Saichō and His Thought" ("Saichō to sono shisō"), in Saichō (1974): 439–515.

Starrs, Roy (1998) *Soundings in Time: The Fictive Art of Kawabata Yasunari* (Folkestone: Japan Library).

Sueki Fumihiko (1990) "Pure Land Buddhism in the Heian Period", *Tōhō* (*The East*) (Tokyo: The Eastern Institute), 6: 134–42.

Sueki Fumihiko (1993) *A Study of the History of Japanese Buddhist Thought* (*Nihon bukkyō shisōshi ronkō*) (Tokyo: Daizō shuppan).

Sueki Fumihiko (1998) *A Theory of the Formation of Kamakura Buddhism* (*Kamakura bukkyō keisei ron*) (Kyoto: Hōzōkan).

Sugiura Minpei (1976) "Literature of Edo" ("Edo no bungaku"), in Iwanami (ed.), *Iwanami Lectures in Literature* (*Iwanami kōza bungaku*), vol. 6 (Tokyo: Iwanami), pp. 304–22.

Sugiyama Yasuhiko (1953) "The Laugh in the Ōchō Period" ("Ōchōki no warai"), *Bungaku* (Tokyo: Iwanami), 21 (8): 31–8.

Suzuki Daisetsu (1973) "The Development of the Pure Land Doctrine", in Eastern Buddhism Society (ed.) (1973): 3–31.

Suzuki gakujutsu dan (ed.) (1972) *Dai nihon bukkyō zensho*, vol. 61 (Tokyo: Suzuki gakujutsu dan).

Suzuki Hideo (2003) *"The Tale of Genji" as Fiction* (*Genji monogatari kyokō ron*) (Tokyo: University of Tokyo Press).

Suzuki Kazuo (1994) "On the 'Rainy Night Critique'" ("'Amayo no shina sadame' ron"), *Jūmonji gakuen joshi tanki daigaku kenkyū kiyō*, 25: 1–17.

Tabata Chieko (1991) "Gen-no-naishi-no-suke", in Imai Takuji et al. (eds) (1991), 2: 131–8.

Tabata Yasuko (1987) *Woman in Medieval Japan* (*Nihon chūsei no josei*) (Tokyo: Yoshikawa kōbunkan).

Taira Masayuki (1992) *Society and Buddhism in Medieval Japan* (*Nihon chūsei no shakai to bukkyō*) (Tokyo: Hanawa shobō).

Tajima Tokuon (1979) "A Bibliographical Introduction to *Determining the Essentials of the One Vehicle*" ("*Ichijō yōketsu* kaidai"), in Iwano (ed.) (1979), 18: 239–40.

Tajima Yōko (1989) "Discrimination against Women and the Nobel Prize" ("Josei sabetsu to Nōberu shō"), *Espace des femmes* (*Josei kūkan*), 6: 13–30.

Tajima Yōko (1992) "A Reading of *Snow Country* from Komako's Point of View" ("Komako no shiten kara yomu Yukiguni"), in Egusa and Urushida (eds) (1992):

186 Bibliography

149–79. The English version is "A Reading of *Snow Country* from Komako's Point of View", in *US–Japan Women's Journal*, English Supplement, 4 (January 1993): 26–48.

Takada Mamoru (2005) *A Complete Version of the World of "Eight Dog Chronicles"* (*Kanpon Hakkenden no sekai*) (Tokyo: Chikuma gakugei bunko).

Takagi Makoto (2001) *"The Tale of the Heike": Narrative Imagining* (*Heike monogatari: Sōzōsuru katari*) (Tokyo: Shinwasha).

Takahashi Kazuo (1966) *The Theme and Structure of "The Tale of Genji"* (*Genji monogatari no shudai to kōsō*) (Tokyo: Ōfūsha).

Takahashi Rita, Miyazoe-Wong Yuko, Yamaguchi Toshiyuki and Leung, Maggie (eds) (2005) *Global Networking in Japanese Studies and Japanese Language Education*, 2 vols (Hong Kong: Society of Japanese Language Education (Hong Kong), Division of Language Studies, City University of Hong Kong and Himawari Publishing Company).

Takahashi Tomio (1990) *Tokuitsu and Saichō* (*Tokuitsu to Saichō*) (Tokyo: Chūkō shinsho).

Takakusu Junjirō and Watanabe Kaikyoku (eds) (1931) *Taisho Edition of the Tripitaka* (*Taishō shinshū daizōkyō*), vol. 74 (Tokyo: The Taisho Issai-kyo Kanko Kwai).

Takayama Chogyū (1914) *Complete Work of Chogyū* (*Chogyū zenshū*), 6 vols (Tokyo: Hakubunkan).

Takeda Munetoshi (1950a/1950b) "The Earliest Form of *The Tale of Genji*, (1) and (2)" ("*Genji monogatari* no saisho no keitai, (jō) and (ge)"), *Bungaku* (Tokyo: Iwanami), 18 (6): 69–80; 18 (7): 71–80. The articles were later collected in Takeda's *A Study of "The Tale of Genji"* (*Genji monogatari no kenkyū*) (Tokyo: Iwanami, 1954), Nihon bungaku kenkyū shiryō kankōkai (ed.) (1969–82), 1: 251–71, and Shibundō (ed.) (1986): 113–34.

Takehara Hiroshi (1996) "On Safflower" ("Suetsumuhana ron"), in Ōchō monogatari kenkyū kai (ed.) (1996): 257–73.

Takehisa Tsuyoshi (1986) *A Study of Production Process of "The Tale of the Heike"* (*Heike monogatari seiritsu katei kō*) (Tokyo: Ōfūsha).

Takehisa Tsuyoshi (1996) *Overview of "The Tale of the Heike"* (*Heike monogatari no zentaizō*) (Osaka: Izumi shoin).

Takeuchi Yasuto (1991) "Mines in the Izu Region and the Forced Immigration of Korean People" ("Izu kōzan to Chōsenjin kyōsei renkō"), *Shizuoka Prefecture Modern History Studies* (*Shizuoka-ken kindaishi kenkyū*), 17: 15–49.

Tamagami Takuya (1968) *Annotation of "The Tale of Genji"* (*Genji monogatari hyōshaku*), vol. 12 (Tokyo: Kadokawa).

Tamagami Takuya (ed.) (1968) *Shimeishō/Kakaishō* (Tokyo: Kadokawa).

Tamura Kōyū (1977) "The Backbone of Japanese Buddhism: Saichō" ("Nihon bukkyō no sekiryō: Saichō"), in Fukunaga (ed.) (1977): 7–32.

Tamura Kōyū (1979) *Saichō Dictionary* (*Saichō jiten*) (Tokyo: Tōkyōdō shuppan).

Tamura Kōyū (1982) "On Genshin's *Determining the Essentials of the One Vehicle*: Through a Comparison with the Debate between Saichō and Tokuitsu" ("Genshin *Ichijō yōketsu* ni tsuite – Saichō Tokuitsu ronsō to no hikaku o tōshite –"), in Tamura Yoshirō hakase kanreki kinen kai (ed.) (1982): 323–33.

Tamura Kōyū (1988) *Saichō* (*A Personal Life Series* (*Jinbutsu sōsho*)) (Tokyo: Yoshikawa kōbunkan).

Tamura Kōyū (1992) *A Study of Saichō's Teaching* (*Saichō kyōgaku no kenkyū*) (Tokyo: Shunjūsha).

Tamura Kōyū (ed.) (1986) *A Collection of Writings on Tokuitsu* (*Tokuitsu ronsō*) (Tokyo: Kokusho kankōkai).

Tamura Mitsumasa (1992) "An Essay on *The Dancing Girl of Izu*: The Catharsis of Fiction" ("*Izu no odoriko* shiron – Kyokō no katarushisu"), in Araya Keizaburō kyōju koki kinen ronbunshū kankō iinkai (ed.) (1992): 551–70.

Tamura Mitsumasa, Baba Shigeyuki and Hara Zen (eds) (1999) *Kawabata Yasunari's World* (*Kawabata Yasunari no sekai*), vol. 2, *Its Development* (*Sono hatten*) (Tokyo: Bensei shuppan).

Tamura Yoshirō hakase kanreki kinen kai (ed.) (1982) *Studies of Buddhology: A Collection of Papers Commemorating Dr Tamura Yoshirō's 60th Birthday* (*Bukkyō kyōri no kenkyū: Tamura Yoshirō hakase kanreki kinen ronbunshū*) (Tokyo: Shunjūsha).

Tanabe, George Joji Jr (1983) "Myōe Shōnin (1173–1232): Tradition and Reform in Early Kamakura Buddhism", PhD thesis presented to the Graduate School of Arts and Sciences, Columbia University (Ann Arbor, Mich.: UMI Dissertation Services).

Tanabe, George Joji Jr (1992) *Myōe the Dreamkeeper: Fantasy and Knowledge in Early Kamakura Buddhism* (Cambridge, Mass: Council on East Asian Studies, Harvard University).

Tanabe, George Joji Jr and Tanabe, Willa Jane (eds) (1989) *The Lotus Sutra in Japanese Culture* (Honolulu: University of Hawaii Press).

Tanaka Hiroshi (1993) *Modern Japan and Liberalism* (*Kindai nihon to jiyūshugi*) (Tokyo: Iwanami).

Tanaka Hiroshi (2000) *The Genealogy of Japanese Liberalism* (*Nihon riberarizumu no keifu*) (Tokyo: Asahi shinbunsha).

Tanaka Takako (1998) "*The Tale of the Heike* Viewed from the Perspective of the History of Woman" ("Joseishi no shiten kara mita *Heike monogatari*"), in Yamashita (ed.) (1998): 89–106.

Tanizawa Eiichi (1971) *Literary Criticism in the Meiji Period* (*Meijiki no bungei hyōron*) (Tokyo: Yagi shoten).

Tokiwa Daijō (1944) *A Study of Buddha-Dhātu* (*Busshō no kenkyū*) (Tokyo: Meiji shoin).

Tomikura Tokujirō (1966) *A Complete Annotation of "The Tale of the Heike"* (*Heike monogatari zenchūshaku*) (Tokyo: Kadokawa).

Tsubouchi Shōyō (1977) *Selected Works of Shōyō* (*Shōyō senshū*), 17 vols (Tokyo: Daiichi shobō).

Tsuda Sōkichi (1964) *Complete Work of Tsuda Sōkichi* (*Tsuda Sōkichi zenshū*), vol. 6 (Tokyo: Iwanami).

Tsuda Sōkichi (1970) *An Inquiry into the Japanese Mind as Mirrored in Literature*, trans. Matsuda Fukumatsu (Tokyo: Japan Society for the Promotion of Science).

Tsuji Zennosuke (1944–55) *A History of Japanese Buddhism* (*Nihon bukkyō shi*), 10 vols (Tokyo: Iwanami).

Tsukamoto Zenryū (ed.) and Satō Seijun (trans.) (1971) *Hōnen* (*Great Books of Japan* (*Nihon no meicho*), vol. 5) (Tokyo: Chūōkōronsha).

Tsukudo Reikan (1976) "Memoranda for *The Tale of the Heike*" ("*Heike monogatari* ni tsuite no oboegaki"), in *A Collection of Tsukudo Reikan's Work* (*Tsukudo Reikan chosaku shū*) (Tokyo: Serika shobō), 1: 271–99.

Tsuruta Kin'ya (1985) "From Illusion to Reality: Misinterpretation and Discovery in *The Sound of the Mountain*" ("Maboroshi kara utsutsu e – *Yama no oto* no sakkaku

188   Bibliography

to hakken"), in Tsuruta Kin'ya and Hirakawa Sukehiro (eds) *A Study of Kawabata Yasunari's "The Sound of the Mountain"* (*Kawabata Yasunari "Yama no oto" kenkyū*) (Tokyo: Meiji shoin), pp. 16–50.

Tucker, John Allen (1998) *Itō Jinsai's Gomō Jigi and the Philosophical Definition of Early Modern Japan* (Leiden/Boston, Mass./Cologne: E. J. Brill).

Ubukata Takashige (1984) *The Basic Stratum and Structure of "The Tale of the Heike"* (*Heike monogatari no kisō to kōzō*) (Tokyo: Kindai bungeisha).

Ubukata Takashige (1996) "A Short Essay on the Prologue of *The Tale of the Heike*" ("*Heike monogatari* purorōgu-bu shōkō"), in Mizuhara (ed.) (1996): 132–49.

Ueda Wataru (1991) "The Structure of *The Dancing Girl of Izu* and the Duality of 'I'" ("*Izu no odoriko* no kōzō to <watashi> no nijūsei"), *Kokugakuin zasshi*, 92 (1): 482–95.

Uemura Shinchō (1986) "Saichō Seen in the Tendai–Hossō Theological Debate" ("Tendai to Hossō no kyōgaku ronsō yori mita Dengyō daishi"), in Tamura Kōyū (ed.) (1986): 193–215.

United States of America, Continental Congress (1798) *Constitution* (Newark, NJ: Printed by Pennington & Dodge).

Uwayokote Masataka (1985) *Fiction and Reality in "The Tale of the Heike"* (*Heike monogatari no kyokō to shinjitsu*), 2 vols (Tokyo: Hanawa shinsho).

Vance, Carole S. (ed.) (1984) *Pleasure and Danger: Exploring Female Sexuality* (Boston, Mass./London/Melbourne/Henley: Routledge).

Varley, Paul (1994) *Warriors of Japan as Portrayed in Tales of War* (Honolulu: University of Hawaii Press).

Varley, Paul (1997) "Warriors as Courtiers: The Taira in *Heike monogatari*", in Heinrich (ed.) (1997): 53–70.

Walker, Janet A. (1979) *The Japanese Novel of the Meiji Period and the Ideal of Individualism* (Princeton, NJ: Princeton University Press).

Wang Yang-ming (1963) *Instructions for Practical Living and Other Neo-Confucian Writings by Wang Yang-ming*, trans. Chan Wing-tsit (New York/London: Columbia University Press).

Watson, Burton (trans.) (1993) *The Lotus Sutra* (New York: Columbia University Press).

Weber, Max (2004) "Politics as a Vocation", in his *The Vocation Lectures*, ed. and with an introduction by David Owen and Tracy B. Strong, trans. Rodney Livingstone (Indianapolis, Ind.: Hackett).

Williams, Mark A. (1999) *Endō Shūsaku: A Literature of Reconciliation* (London/ New York: Routledge).

Wittig, Monique (1992) *The Straight Mind and Other Essays* (New York/London/ Toronto/Sydney/Tokyo/Singapore: Harvester Wheatsheaf).

Yagi Kōe (1962) *A Fundamental Study of Eshin Buddhology* (*Eshin kyōgaku no kisoteki kenkyū*) (Kyoto: Nagata bunshōdō).

Yamagishi Tokuhei and Oka Kazuo (eds) (1971) *The "Tale of Genji" Lecture Series* (*Genji monogatari kōza*), vol. 3 (Tokyo: Yūseidō).

Yamaguchi Masao (1979) *Anthropological Thought* (*Shinpen jinruigakuteki shikō*), new edn (Tokyo: Chikuma shobō).

Yamaji Aizan (1983–5) *A Collection of Yamaji Aizan's Writings* (*Yamaji Aizan shū*) (*Min'yūsha shisō bungaku sōsho*, vols 2 and 3), ed. Oka Toshirō (Tokyo: San'ichi shobō).

Yamanouchi Hisaaki (1978) *The Search for Authenticity in Modern Japanese Literature* (Cambridge: Cambridge University Press).

Bibliography 189

Yamashita Hiroaki (ed.) (1998) *"The Tale of the Heike": Criticism and Cultural History* (*Heike monogatari: Hihyō to bunkashi*), A Series of Studies of Literature of Warfare (Gunki bungaku kenkyū sōsho), vol. 7 (Tokyo: Kyūko shoin).

Yamazaki Ansai (1936) *A Complete Work of Yamazaki Ansai* (*Yamazaki Ansai zenshū*), ed. Nihon koten gakkai (Nagoya: Matsumoto shoten).

Yanagida Izumi (1987) *A Study of "The Essence of the Novel"* (*Shōsetsu shinzui kenkyū*), in Nakamura Kan (Introductory Notes), *A Series of Modern Writers Studies* (*Kindai sakka kenkyū sōsho*), vol. 55 (Tokyo: Nihon tosho centre).

Yasukawa Junosuke (1989) "Fukuzawa Yukichi [1834–1901]", in Duke (ed.) (1989): 16–37.

Yasukawa Junosuke (2000) *Fukuzawa Yukichi's Understanding of Asia* (*Fukuzawa Yukichi no Ajia ninshiki*) (Tokyo: Kōbunken).

Yasukawa Junosuke (2002) *The Structure of the Thought of Modern Japanese Education: Enlarged Version* (*Zoho-ban: Nihon kindai kyōiku no shisō kōzō*) (Tokyo: Shinhyōron).

Yasukawa Junosuke (2003) *Fukuzawa Yukichi and Maruyama Masao* (*Fukuzawa Yukichi to Maruyama Masao*) (Tokyo: Kōbunken).

Yoda, Tomiko (2004) *Gender and National Literature: Heian Texts in the Constructions of Japanese Modernity* (Durham, NC: Duke University Press).

Yokoi Takashi (1994) "On Women's Sad Tales" ("Nyonin aiwa kō"), in Mizuhara (ed.) (1994): 107–28.

Yoshikai Naoto (2003) *A New Study of "The Tale of Genji"* (*Genji monogatari no shin kōsatsu*) (Tokyo: Ōfū).

Yoshikawa Kōjirō (1975) *Jinsai, Sorai, Norinaga* (Tokyo: Iwanami).

Yoshikawa Kōjirō, Maruyama Masao, Nishida Taichirō and Tsuji Tatsuya (eds) (1973) *Ogyū Sorai* (*Nihon shisō taikei*, vol. 36) (Tokyo: Iwanami).

Yoshikawa Kōjirō and Shimizu Shigeru (eds) (1971) *Itō Jinsai/Itō Tōgai* (*Iwanami shisō taikei*, vol. 33) (Tokyo: Iwanami).

Zolbrod, Leon M. (1965) "The Vendetta of Mr Fleacatcher Managorō, The Fifth", *Monumenta Nipponica*, 20 (1–2): 121–34.

Zolbrod, Leon M. (1966a) "Takizawa Bakin, 1767–1848", *Monumenta Nipponica*, 21 (1–2): 1–46.

Zolbrod, Leon M. (1966b) "Yomihon: The Appearance of the Historical Novel in Late Eighteenth Century and Early Nineteenth Century Japan", *The Journal of Asian Studies*, 25 (3): 485–98.

Zolbrod, Leon M. (1967a) "Tigers, Boars and Severed Heads: Parallel Series of Episodes in *Eight 'Dogs'* and *Men of the Marshes*", *Chung Chi Journal*, 7 (1): 30–9.

Zolbrod, Leon M. (1967b) *Takizawa Bakin* (New York: Twayne).

Zolbrod, Leon M. (1983) "Nansō Satomi hakkenden", in *Kodansha Encyclopedia of Japan* (Tokyo: Kodansha).

Zolbrod, Leon M. (1985) "Takizawa Bakin: Major Edo Author (1767–1848)", PhD thesis submitted to Columbia University in 1963 (Ann Arbor, Mich.: UMI Dissertations Service).

Index

A Child's Inquiries 26–7
Abe Akio 44–5, 49–50, 58
Abe Yoshitomi 64
abortion 146
absolute egalitarianism 151
admiration for the strong 4, 19, 45, 56, 65, 68–70, 91, 151, 157
afterlife 42
agnosticism 118, 153
ai 27
Akasaka Norio 71
Akiyama Ken 62–4
alter ego 128
Amaterasu circle 2
American Declaration of Independence 6
Amida 8–10, 12, 17–21, 24, 42, 74–5, 81
ancient truthfulness 24
Anderson, Benedict 6
Aquinas, Thomas 6
Arendt, Hannah 36
aristocratic nationalism 13
asceticism 11, 14, 23–4
Asia–Pacific War 92, 104
ātman 18–19

Bargen, Doris G. 44
Bashō 92
Bataille, Georges 120
battle equality 30–43
    see also war
Bauman, Zygmunt 1
beauty 120–1, 126–8, 152
Beck, Ulrich 1–2
belligerence 118
benevolence 28
Benjamin, Walter 116
Bentham, Jeremy 5, 36
binarism 2–3, 5, 44, 93, 120

blushing 120–4, 128–9
Booth, Wayne C. 132
Buddha 8–10
Buddhahood 8–16, 19, 22, 42
building stupas 17–18
bullying 140–1, 152
Bunmei ron no gairyaku 30
burlesque 66
Bushidō 92

cannibalism 101
Capital 20
castration 117
chi 27, 95
Chikamatsu Monzaemon 92, 106–7, 109
Christianity 8–10, 39–41, 106
Chronicles of Japan 54
chū 95
Cixous, Hélène 96
class distinction 28–30, 35, 42
class-based society 23–30
collaboration 105
compassion 27
    see also jin
Complete Work of Fukuzawa 31–2
concept of *Jin* 23–30
Confucian aspect of *Eight Dog Chronicles* 92–102
Confucianism 4, 9, 21–3, 29–30, 41, 92, 103–4, 107, 115
contempt 83, 85, 87, 90–1, 115, 130, 151
contrast between weak and strong 69–72
Critique of the Gotha Programme 38
cultivation with reverence 22

"Dame of Staff" 57–63
Dancing Girl of Izu 119–49
    discrimination against femininity 129–35

Index 191

dancing girls 119–49
Datsua ron 30
decency 88–91
Deleuze, Gilles 1
Derrida, Jacques 72
despotism 34–6
destructive subjugation 2
Dharmākara *see* Amida
didacticism 105, 120
diligence 15
Discourse on the Origin of Inequality 36
discrimination against femininity
    129–41
Divine Comedy 14
"Doctrinal Debate of the Ōwa Era" 13
Dōjimon 26–7
Dōshō 10
Drake, Chris 92

egalitarianism 5–6, 12, 21–30, 34–9,
    103–4
  individual endeavour 26–8
  inherent ability 24–6
  Jinsai's class distinction 28–30
Eight Dog Chronicles 13, 92–118,
    120–1, 137–8, 141, 150–4
emancipation 10, 14, 18, 21, 30, 35
Encouragement of Learning 30–2, 103
Engyō text 69–91, 141, 151
  indecent text 88–92
  love between men and women 85–8
  polemics 81–5
  see also Tale of the Heike
enlightenment 8, 11, 14–21, 42, 74
Enlightenment, the 34, 103–4
enterprise 40–1
equality before God 30–43
erotic sexual desire 2, 23
eroticism 120
Eshin Sōzu *see* Genshin
Essence of the Novel 92, 104
Essentials of Rebirth 9–17, 68
exhibitionism 120

falsehood 16
family member love 85–8
feminist theory 2
femininity 53–4, 119–29
  created by male gaze 119–29
  discrimination against 129–41
feudalism 34–9, 105–7, 153
fiefdom 106
Field, Norma 44
filial piety 93–7, 101, 105, 113, 139

Five Women Who Loved Love 109
Foucault, Michel 2, 72
Freud, Sigmund 55
Fujii Sadakazu 53
Fujimura Kiyoshi 58
fukoku kyōhei 31
Fukuzawa Yukichi 13, 21–2, 30–43,
    103–4, 118, 141, 150–4
  concept of equality 30–9

Gakumon no susume 30, 103
Gauttari, Félix 1
Geisha in Rivalry 139–40
geishas 119–49
Gen-no-naishi 57–63
gender-free egalitarianism 120–1
generosity 116
genocidal warfare 35
Genpei war 29, 77
Genshin 9–19, 21, 29, 42, 68, 91,
    150–4
  see also Tale of Genji
gi 27, 95
Giddens, Anthony 1–2
Girard, Réne 71
Gomō jigi 24, 26–7

Hahakigi group 44–6, 48–9, 56, 58, 62,
    66–9
Hakamaya Noriaki 12, 18, 20–2, 24, 43
Hara Zen 130, 132, 134
Hasegawa Izumi 119, 130, 134
Hatori Tetsuya 134
Hattori Kōzō 78
Hegel, Georg Wilhelm Friedrich 1
Heian Pure Land teaching 16–17
Heike monogatari 70–1, 152
heterosexual love 85–8, 139
hidden discrimination against
    femininity 129–41
  Dancing Girl of Izu 129–35
  Snow Country 135–41
hierarchical society 21–2, 28–30,
    113–15, 151
Higuchi Ichiyō 121
Hirabayashi Taiko 121
Hirayama Yō 31–2
History of Japanese Literature 107
history of Japanese thought 150–4
Hobbes, Thomas 5, 36–9, 42, 116,
    150–4
Holocaust 1
Hōnen 9, 12, 15–23, 28, 37–40, 42–3,
    71, 76–7, 91, 118, 140–1, 150–4

192 *Index*

horizontality of human values 23
Hossō School 10–13
Hōzō 13
human psychology 45, 103
humble men 69–91
Hyōdo Hiromi 71

I-novels 106
Ida Shin'ya 31
ideas in *Tale of Genji* 44–5
Ienaga Saburō 33
Ihara Saikaku 109
Imanari Genshō 72–4
imperialism 104–5
impermanence 71
incest 84–5
indecency 88–92
independence 30, 40, 103
indifferent individualism 85–8, 154
individual endeavour 26–8, 34
inherent ability 24–6
insulted people 69–91
    associated issues 72–81
    indecent *Engyō* text 88–91
    introduction 69–72
    love between men and women 85–8
    polemical *Engyō* 81–5
*Introduction to the Principles of Morals
    and Legislation* 36
Ishida Mizumaro 15
Ishikawa Mikiaki 31–2
Ishizaka Minako 39, 41
Itō Jinsai 9–10, 23–30, 38–40, 42–3,
    140–1, 150–4
    class distinction 28–30
    concept of *Jin* 23–30
Iwanami Shoten 32
Iwashita Mitsuo 58

jealousy 50
jiga 106
jigyō 40–1
jin 23–30, 40, 42, 95, 112–18, 152
jiriki shugi 18
Jōdo Buddhism *see* Pure Land
    Buddhism
jūnen 9

Kabuki 125
Kakuichi text 69–91, 115, 141, 151
    decent text 88–91
    indifferent individualism 85–8
    moderation 81–5
    see also Tale of the Heike

Kamakura Pure Land teaching 9,
    16–17, 87, 96
Kansei Reform 104
karma 22, 82
Katō Shūichi 107
Katsuhara Haruki 119
Kawabata Yasunari 10, 119–49, 152
    discrimination against femininity:
        Dancing Girl of Izu 129–35
    discrimination against femininity:
        Snow Country 135–41
    femininity created by male gaze
        119–29
    ugly ladies: *Sound of the Mountain*
        141–9
    ugly ladies: *Thousand Cranes* 141–9
Keene, Donald 92–3
kei 27
kihin 25–6
Kimura Ki 103
Kinoshita Naoe 41
Kiritsubo 46–51, 67
Kitagawa Hiroshi 70
Kitamura Tōkoku 10, 39–43, 140–1,
    150–4
    concept of equality 39–43
kō 95
    see also filial piety
Kobayashi Hiroko 148
Kobayashi Yoshikazu 70
Kodama League 87
Koizumi Shinzō 32
kokoro 25–6
Komashaku Kimi 119
Komori Yōichi 119
Koyano Atsushi 115
Kuroda Toshio 17
Kyokutei Bakin 10, 30, 92–118, 120,
    137–8, 141, 153
    see also Eight Dog Chronicles

labour-power 20
ladies 44–68
    see also ugly ladies; women
Larger Sutra on Amitāyus 8
Lash, Scott 1–2
"law of the jungle" 36
Lee Sun-Young 79
Leviathan 36
Literary World 10
Locke, John 5, 36–9, 42, 116,
    150–4
Lotus Sutra 11, 64–5, 68
love 41–2, 45–8, 58, 85–8, 92–118

Love Suicides at Amijima 109
loyalty 95

McCullough, Helen Craig 69–75
Makibayashi Kōji 40
male gaze and femininity 88, 119–29
manipulation 144
marital love 85–8
Maruyama Masao 31, 43
Marx, Karl 20, 22–3, 38–9, 42–3, 140,
    150–4
Masuda Katsumi 63, 65
Masuda Shigeo 48
Matsuda Osamu 107
Matsumoto Shirō 12
Matsuo Ashie 70
Meiji period 8–10, 30, 41, 92–3, 103–6,
    118, 121
Mencius 23–7
"might is right" 34, 39–41, 153
mistresses 119–49
Misumi Yōichi 64–5
Mitani Kuniaki 58
Mizuhara Hajime 69–70, 72–4, 78, 90
mockery 52, 56–7, 61, 65–6
moderate *Kakuichi* 81–5
Modern Japan and Liberalism 31
modernism as ideology 1–7
modernist aspect of *Eight Dog
    Chronicles* 103–11
moral systems 97
Mori Ichirō 56
Morimoto Osamu 130, 134
Mount Fuji 117
mujō 71
Mulvey, Laura 120
Murai Shōsuke 13
Murasaki group *see* Wakamurasaki
    group
Murasaki Shikibu 45, 54, 58, 66–8
Muromachi period 87, 96
Myōe 18, 42, 150–4

Nagai Kafu 121, 139–40
Najita Tetsuo 23, 27
Nakayama Masahiko 119
narcissism 96, 130, 134
national consciousness 55
nembutsu 8–10, 12, 14–16, 19–21, 24, 28
ninjō 105–6
Nirvāna 8, 19
Nomura Seiichi 56, 63–4
non-violence 116
nostalgia 55

Odagiri Hideo 104
Oedipal triangle 2, 90
Ogino Anna 131
Ogyū Sorai 21–2, 25–8, 39, 42–3, 150–4
Ōjōyōshū 10–16
    see also Essentials of Rebirth
Okada, Richard H. 44, 49
Ōmi-no-kimi 63–8
*On the Nation's Right for the Common
    People's Understanding* 30
"One Hundred and Eight Lusts" 105–6
"one vehicle of unification" 12–13,
    19–21, 24
Ooms, Herman 93
open discrimination against femininity
    129–41
    Dancing Girl of Izu 129–35
    Snow Country 135–41
Opium War 33
Orikuchi Shinobu 71
Ōtsu Yūichi 13, 71–2, 84
"Our Lady of the Chronicles" 54
Outline of the Theory of Civilization 30,
    33, 103
Ōwa period 13

paradise 42, 73–4, 80
Parting from Asia 30
*Passages on the Selection of the
    Nembutsu in the Original Vow*
    16–23
paternalism 27, 29, 137
Paulownia 46–51, 68
"Peace and Bliss" 8
perspective of ugly ladies 141–9
    *see also Snow Country; Thousand
    Cranes*
perversion 117
philosophical writings 8–43
piety 93–7, 101, 105, 113
Plover on the Waves 129, 142
polemical *Engyō* 81–5
political turmoil 29
political writings 8–43
polyphonic narrative 67–70, 151–2
pornography 88–90
postmodernist aspect of *Eight Dog
    Chronicles* 111–18
Princess Safflower 51–7
propriety 27
Pure Land Buddhism 8–10, 12, 14,
    17–19, 21, 24, 28, 42, 71–84, 87, 90

queer theory 2

194   *Index*

"rainy night critique" 49–51
Rangaku 105
Rawls, John 38–9, 42–3, 140, 150–4
rebirth 15, 19, 77–84, 87
reciprocal violence 98
reflection 2
rei 27–9, 40, 95
religious writings 8–43
    egalitarianism in secluded class-based
        society 23–30
    equality in battle and before God
        30–43
    respecting the strong 10–16
    strong and weak in 8–10
    triumph of weak over strong 16–23
respecting the strong 8–16, 42
retribution 101
revenge 92–118
reverence 22, 27
    cultivation with 22
revolution 38, 116, 127
ridicule 56–7, 61
righteousness 27
Rousseau, Jean-Jacques 5, 36, 38,
    150–4
Rubin, Gayle 2
Ryōgen 13, 19–20, 42

sacrifice 39, 92–118
sadness 72–4, 77, 149, 152
Saegusa Kazuko 119, 138–9, 142
Saeki Shin'ichi 70
Saichō 6, 10–13, 19–21, 29–30, 34,
    37–9, 42, 55, 141, 150–4
Saikaku 92
Sakata Chizuko 146
salvation 28
Sambodhis 19
samurai 28, 96, 108, 117
San'ichi gonjitsu ronsō 11
Santō Kyōden 104
Sarra, Edith 44
Sata Ineko 121
Satō Miyuki 116
schizophrenic lines of escape 1
secluded class-based society 23–30
Second World War 12, 16, 105
Sekigahara 29
self-exile 58
self-respect 30, 106
selfishness 96, 106, 137, 144
Senchaku hongan nembutsu shū 16–23
seppuku 95
sexuality 51–7, 67

Shan-tao 17
shin 95
Shingon sect 16–17
Shinoda Jun'ichi 30, 117
Shinran 16, 43
Shioiri Ryōchū 12
Shirane, Haruo 44, 46, 51, 70–1
Shōsetsu shinzui 92
Shōwa government 104–5
Shugo kokkai shō 29–30
Sino-Japanese War 30–1, 104
Snow Country 119–49
    discrimination against femininity
        135–41
Snyder, Stephen 140
Social Contract 36
social Darwinism 3, 39–40, 150–4
Sound of the Mountain 119–49
    see also ugly ladies
stagnation 5, 39, 115, 154
Starrs, Roy 131–2
"state of nature" 36–8, 116
stupa building 17–18
subversion 30
Suetsumuhana 51–8, 62–3, 65–7
Sugiura Minpei 105
Sugiyama Yasuhiko 65
suicide 74, 85, 97, 113, 146
survival of the fittest 39–40
Suzuki Kazuo 50
sympathising with the weak 8–16,
    20, 42

Tabata Chieko 60
Tabata Yasuko 87, 96
Taira Masayuki 17–18, 22, 24, 43
Tajima Yōko 119
Takagi Makoto 72
Takayama Chogyū 104
Takeda Munetoshi 44–5
Tale of Genji 44–68, 92, 141, 144,
    150–4
    Gen-no-naishi 57–63
    Ōmi-no-kimi 63–8
    Princess Safflower 51–7
    two different views in 44–5
    weak, low, fragile characters 46–51
    see also Genshin; Hōnen
Tale of the Heike 69–92, 115–16, 141,
    150–4
    contrast between weak and strong
        69–72
Tale of Jōsanmi 62
Tales of Ise 60–3

Tamakazura group *see* Hahakigi group
T'an-luan 17
Tanaka Hiroshi 31
Tao-ch'o 17
tariki shugi 18
tea ceremony 126, 129–30, 133, 142–3
tei 95
Tendai School 10–17, 82–3
theory of violence 71
Thousand Cranes 119–49
  see also ugly ladies
"three treasures" 22
"to-be-looked-at-ness" 120
Tokugawa period 9–10, 23, 28–34,
  92–3, 96, 104–5, 117
Tokuitsu 11–13, 19, 25, 42, 150–4
Tomikura Tokujirō 80–1
torō 140
tragedy 93–4, 96–8
transcendental truth 23
triumph of weak over strong 16–23
Tsubouchi Shōyō 92, 103–6, 120
Tsuchida, Bruce T. 70
Tsuda Sōkichi 106–7
Tsukudo Reikan 71
Tsūzoku kokken ron 30
Two Treatises of Government 36

Ubukata Takashige 71
Ueda Wataru 130–4
ugly ladies 44–68, 141–9
  different views on weak and strong
  44–5
  Gen-no-naishi 57–63
  Ōmi-no-kimi 63–8
  perspective of 141–9
  Princess Safflower 51–7
  the weak, low and fragile 46–51
  see also ladies; women
ultra-nationalism 31
uncleanness 142, 145
unconditional egalitarianism 42–3
unfair egalitarianism 20
universal love 113–15

utilitarianism 33, 39–40
Utopia 154

"veil of ignorance" 38–9
vendettas 100
veneration 22
violence 36–7, 71, 92–118
voyeurism 119, 131, 133

Wakamurasaki group 44–5, 48–9, 56,
  58, 62–3, 66–7, 69
Walker, Janet 39–42
war 71–2, 92–118
  see also battle equality
waste of effort 140
Watanabe Kazan 105
Watson, Burton 70
"Way of the Ancient Kings" 21,
  25–9
weak, low, fragile characters 46–51
Weber, Max 37, 117
Williams, Mark 106
wisdom 27
wives 119–49
"woman is the messenger of a country's
  ruin" 86–7
women 69–91
  see also ladies; ugly ladies
world without violence 92–118
  Confucian aspect of *Eight Dog
  Chronicles* 92–102
  modernist aspect of *Eight Dog
  Chronicles* 103–11
  postmodernist aspect of *Eight Dog
  Chronicles* 111–18

Yamaguchi Masao 71
Yamaji Aizan 40–2
Yamazaki Ansai 23–6, 42, 150–4
Yasukawa Junosuke 31
Yoda, Tomiko 44
Yosano Akiko 121
Yoshihige no Yasutane 16
Yoshimoto Takaaki 43

eBooks – at www.eBookstore.tandf.co.uk

A library at your fingertips!

eBooks are electronic versions of printed books. You can store them on your PC/laptop or browse them online.

They have advantages for anyone needing rapid access to a wide variety of published, copyright information.

eBooks can help your research by enabling you to bookmark chapters, annotate text and use instant searches to find specific words or phrases. Several eBook files would fit on even a small laptop or PDA.

NEW: Save money by eSubscribing: cheap, online access to any eBook for as long as you need it.

Annual subscription packages

We now offer special low-cost bulk subscriptions to packages of eBooks in certain subject areas. These are available to libraries or to individuals.

For more information please contact webmaster.ebooks@tandf.co.uk

We're continually developing the eBook concept, so keep up to date by visiting the website.

www.eBookstore.tandf.co.uk